MILITARY LAW
IN A NUTSHELL®

FIFTH EDITION

L. LYNN HOGUE
Professor of Law Emeritus,
Georgia State University College of Law

Lieutenant Colonel, U.S. Army Reserve,
Judge Advocate General's Corps (Ret.)

WEST
ACADEMIC
PUBLISHING

444 Cedar Street, Suite 700
St. Paul, MN 55101
1-877-888-1330

Printed in the United States of America

ISBN: 978-1-64242-800-1

To my wife Carol and my daughter Lizzie for their loving support, inspiration, and encouragement

PREFACE

This fifth edition of *Military Law in a Nutshell* continues a series devoted to offering a concise, accurate, and authoritative source of information about military law and justice for those seeking to understand the workings of the military's distinctive legal system. It seeks to make the jurisprudence of the military, "a society apart from civilian society," comprehensible to civilians and useful to those familiar with the armed services. Its primary sources of this include the Constitution, federal statutes, executive orders, military regulations and decisions of courts, military and civilian, adjudicating military criminal law and service-related matters.

The primary audience for this Nutshell is law students taking a specialized course on military law and justice as well as JAG officers and other practicing lawyers seeking a succinct overview of military law, cadets at military academies and in college R.O.T.C. programs. It should also serve the needs of news media reporters and bloggers.

Members of the armed services should find it a useful source of information, particularly those faced with non-judicial punishment or more serious actions, although it is no substitute for professional legal advice on an individual matter. New to this edition is a section on overcoming "bad paper discharges" for those seeking veteran's status and benefits.

L. LYNN HOGUE
PROFESSOR OF LAW EMERITUS,
GEORGIA STATE UNIVERSITY
COLLEGE OF LAW

LIEUTENANT COLONEL, U.S. ARMY
RESERVE, JUDGE ADVOCATE
GENERAL'S CORPS (RET.)

February 2022

OUTLINE

TABLE OF CASES

References are to Pages

MILITARY LAW

IN A NUTSHELL®

FIFTH EDITION

CHAPTER 1

A BRIEF HISTORY OF AMERICAN MILITARY LAW

Even a brief survey of the history of military law will serve to acquaint one with the aspects that make the subject unique. Military law has evolved to govern a distinct society of warriors whose primary function is fighting or preparing to fight wars. War necessarily involves injuring, killing and destroying property, activities that are legally privileged under international and domestic law. An inherent tension in military law, apparent from its purpose, is the balance between a need for command and control of troops from whom is required immediate obedience and discipline on one hand, and the need to provide a fair and just system for punishing insubordination and criminality on the other.

A. EARLY ENGLISH MILITARY CODES AND COMMENTARY

Early military codes and regulations recognized the need for laws to regulate troops and promulgated rules to suppress killings and stealing within the ranks. typically prescribing heavy punishments. For example, the Ordinance of Richard I (A.D. 1190), intended to guide Crusaders setting off for the Holy Land, provided: "[w]hoever shall slay a man on shipboard, he shall be bound to the dead man and thrown into the sea. If he shall slay him on land he shall be bound to the dead man and buried in the earth."

The Articles of War of Richard II (1385) encompassed additional concerns such as the protection of churches and church property, clergy and religious noncombatants and women. These provisions restricted rape, pillage, and rioting. They also enhanced command and control (e.g., "that no man go out on an expedition by night or by day, unless with the knowledge and by the permission of the chieftain of the battail"; "every man . . . of our party, shall bear a large sign of the arms of St. George").

The "English Military Discipline" of James II (1686) provided for the conduct of Councels of War or Courts-Martial. A senior officer was designated as the President or presiding officer, responsible for interrogating the accused regarding allegations against him and hearing his defense. The sixty-four "Articles of War" of James II (1688) for the governance of the English army echoed concerns expressed in earlier codes and expanded protections of civilian property. For example, Article XXI provided that "No person shall extort Free quarter, or shall commit any Waste, or spoil or deface Walks of Trees, Parks, Warrens, Fishponds, Houses, or Gardens, tread down, or otherwise destroy Standing Corn in the Ear, or shall put their Horses into Meadows without Leave. . . ." Peculiarly military offenses such as failure to repair were codified ("[W]hoever shall fail at the Beating of a Drum, or sound of a Trumpet . . . to repair to his Coulours, with his Arms decently kept, and well fixed. . . ."). See also Code of Articles of King Gustavus Adolphus of Sweden (1621), Article No. 52 ("He that at the sound of Drumme or Trumpet repaires not to his Colours, shall be clapt in irons.").

The British Articles of War of 1765, the model for the 1775 American Articles of War, reflect a more mature administrative structure and include provisions similar to those in the modern day Uniform Code of Military Justice. For example, Section XIV (Of Duties in Quarters, in Garrison, or in the Field) included failure to repair (Art. IV), being drunk on duty (Art. V), sleeping on post (Art. VI), and misbehavior before the enemy (Art. XIII).

On the eve of the American Revolution, Sir William Blackstone's *Commentaries on the Laws of England* (1765–69) appeared, volumes generally judged to be among the most important legal treatises ever written in the English language. Blackstone's comments on the evolution and state of eighteenth-century British military law and national security law highlight issues that troubled the founding fathers, such as a prejudice against standing armies and a preference for a citizen-based army. For example, Blackstone quoted Montesquieu's reservations about standing armies, a threat of oppression by the executive power and a sorry history of their abuses, concluding that "[i]n the land of liberty it is extremely dangerous to make a distinct order of the profession of arms." Vol. I, 395–401. Blackstone says that an army "should wholly be composed of natural subjects; . . . enlisted for a short and limited time; the soldiers also should live intermixed with the people; no separate camp, no barracks, no inland fortresses should be allowed. And perhaps it might be still better if, by dismissing a stated number and enlisting others at every renewal of their term, a circulation could be kept up between the army and the people, and the citizen and the soldier be more intimately connected together." Vol. I, 401–02.

When America stood on the brink of revolution, it adopted a well-developed system of military law from the British. Military law in Britain began to take shape with the enactment of the first Mutiny Act of 1689. The events leading to its adoption are described by William Winthrop in his magisterial volume *Military Law and Precedents* (2d ed. 1896) as "the mutiny and desertion of a detachment of troops, mainly Scotch, which adhered to the cause of the Stuarts and, refusing to obey the order of William III. to proceed to Holland, march northward." Parliament seized this opportunity to provide for the punishment of officers or soldiers involved in mutiny, sedition or desertion by such punishment as a court-martial might adjudge, including death, a penalty previously unavailable during peacetime.

U.S. military law received much of its terminology, structure, procedure and substantive content from the British model. For example, during time of war, the Crown would issue orders or directives for the governance of the army through the royal prerogative. These were carried out with the aid of the High Constable and Earl Marshall who comprised a "King's Court of Chivalry" or "Court of the High Constable and Marshall of England." This latter court contracted to the more succinct title of "court-martial."

B. THE AMERICAN REVOLUTIONARY ERA

In addition to being the father of his country, George Washington was also the father of American military justice. As the prospect of hostilities with the British became increasingly apparent, Washington was appointed by the Continental Congress to chair a committee that would draft a set of rules and regulations for the Continental Army. The drafting committee's work was approved and America's first Articles of War were adopted on June 30, 1775.

British models served as the codes that governed both the American Army and Navy. The British Articles of War provided that "The Judge Advocate General, or some person deputed by him, shall prosecute in His Majesty's name." One of General Washington's first acts upon taking command of the Continental Army was to ask that William Tudor be commissioned as an officer and the first Judge Advocate. The 1775 Articles of War authorized general and regimental court-martial and punishments "by order of the commanding officer." The commander-in-chief or general had the power to pardon as well as to mitigate sentences imposed by a general court, and regimental commanders had similar authority with regard to regimental courts. Punishments were not prescribed but rather left to the discretion of the court.

After a year's experience with the 1775 Articles, General Washington, acting through Judge Advocate

Tudor, asked the Continental Congress to consider revising the Articles. The Congress appointed a committee comprised of John Adams, Thomas Jefferson, John Rutledge, James Wilson, and Robert R. Livingston to undertake the revision. The committee's handiwork closely followed the 1775 Articles modeled on the British Articles. Adams justified this approach and explained why the colonials followed in Britain's path: "There was extant one system of articles of war, which had carried two empires to the head of command, the Roman and the British, for the British Articles of War were only a literal translation of the Roman." Works of John Adams, 1850.

The 1776 revisions continued the practice of punishments within the court's discretion. The number of offenses for which the death penalty was authorized continued to expand although general court-martial sentences ordering executions were stayed until "after a report shall be made of the whole proceedings to Congress or to the General or Commander-in-Chief of the forces of the United States, and their or his direction be signified thereon." Appeals were permitted, but "if upon a second hearing, the appeal shall appear to be vexatious or groundless, the person so appealing shall be punished at the discretion of the . . . general court," a practice at odds with the modern notion of appellate justice. Tudor's office was renamed and he became the Judge Advocate General. He "or some person deputed by him [was to] prosecute in the name of the United States of America." The Judge

Advocate General personally presided over many early courts-martial.

Despite express provision in the U.S. Constitution (1787, effective 1789), for Congress to make rules for the governance of the land and naval forces (Art. I, § 8, cl. 14), as Winthrop points out, "Congress did not originally create the court-martial," but, rather, by statute merely continued the court-martial by [p]roviding that the Army should continue to be governed by the existing articles of war." The Fifth Amendment, which exempts military cases from its scope ("No person shall be held to answer for a capital or otherwise infamous crime, unless on a presentment or indictment of a Grand Jury, except in cases arising in the land or naval forces" etc.) has also been suggested as a source for the court-martial. Again, Winthrop dismisses this amendment as a source, finding it "rather a declaratory recognition and sanction of an existing military jurisdiction than an original provision initiating such a jurisdiction."

Strangely, little changed in military justice between the Revolutionary War and World War I; those who faced the Kaiser did so under a military justice system that had governed those who fought the Hessians. Military justice was immune to the improvements, both substantive and procedural, in the civilian justice system which could have served as models. Problems persisted because during wartime, the country was too preoccupied to address deficiencies in military justice, and during peacetime there was no felt need.

Two nineteenth-century U.S. Supreme Court cases well illustrate the tension between treating military law as an aspect of command or subjecting the military justice system to the rule of law.

Shortly after the midpoint of the nineteenth century, in *Dynes v. Hoover*, 61 U.S. 65 (1857), Congress' eighteenth-century system was subjected to scrutiny. Frank Dynes, a Navy seaman court-martialed for *desertion*, was found guilty of *attempting to desert* and sentenced to confinement for six months at hard labor. Dynes challenged his conviction on the ground that the offense for which he was convicted was not provided for in the Naval Articles and thus the court-martial lacked jurisdiction to try and punish him. The case defined several aspects of military law that would remain unchanged for decades to come. First, Justice Wayne's opinion for the Court acknowledged Congress' power to provide for the trial and punishment of military offenses, a power independent of and exercised apart from the judicial power conferred in Article III of the Constitution. As the Court said, "the two powers are entirely independent of each other." Second, Dynes' claim that he was convicted of a crime not defined in the law governing the Navy was disposed of by a Naval Article providing that "All crimes . . . not specified in the foregoing articles, shall be punished according to the laws and customs in such cases at sea." The article's vagueness was dismissed: "Notwithstanding the apparent indeterminateness of such a provision, it is not liable to abuse; for what those crimes are, and how they are to be punished, is well known by practical men in the navy and army, and by those who have studied the law of courts martial, and the offenses of which the different courts martial have cognizance." Third, so long as a court-martial is convened regularly, has proceeded legally, and imposed punishment allowed by law, "no appeal or jurisdiction of any kind has been given to the civil magistrate or civil courts." *Dynes* limited civilian supervision of military justice for almost a century until the adoption of the Uniform Code of Military Justice in 1950.

Although *Dynes* provided the dominant paradigm, a Supreme Court case decided thirty years later placed military justice more squarely in the mainstream of constitutional and legal authority, deemphasizing its role as merely an aspect of a commander's disciplinary authority. *Runkle v. United States*, 122 U.S. 543 (1887) involved a claim for compensation filed by Major Benjamin P. Runkle. Major Runkle had been court-martialed for allegedly embezzling money while serving as a disbursing officer with the Bureau of Refugees, Freedmen, and Abandoned Lands. Runkle was found guilty and sentenced to be cashiered, fined and imprisoned as the President of the United States might direct. The record of Runkle's court-martial was forwarded to the Secretary of War, who remitted the entire sentence except for the cashiering. In 1873, Runkle was ordered cashiered in General Order of the War Department No.7. Runkle then petitioned President Grant to revoke and annul his conviction and sentence because they had not been approved by the President of the United States "as required by law" in the sixty-fifth Article of War. President Grant referred Runkle's petition to the Judge Advocate General of the Army. Though he expressed doubt as to whether Runkle could "justly be held liable," Grant apparently took no further action. When President Rutherford B. Hayes subsequently reviewed Runkle's case, he concluded that the "conviction is not sustained by the evidence in the case, and the same, together with the sentence of the court thereon, are hereby disapproved; and it is directed that said order No. 7, so far as it relates to said Runkle, be revoked." Order of August 4, 1877.

The Supreme Court found the duty of presidential review and approval nondelegable. In delineating the statutory duties of the President under the Articles of War, Chief Justice Waite adopted the position taken by Attorney General Bates in an opinion provided to President Lincoln in 1864:

> Undoubtedly the president, in passing upon the sentence of a court-martial, and giving to it the approval without which it cannot be executed, acts judicially. The whole proceeding, from its inception, is judicial. The trial, finding, and sentence are the solemn acts of a court organized and conducted under the authority of and according to the prescribed forms of law. It sits to pass upon the most sacred questions of human rights that are ever placed on trial in a court of justice—rights which, in the very nature of things, can neither be exposed to danger, nor subjected to the uncontrolled will of any man, but which must be adjudged *according to law.*

> And the act of the officer who reviews the proceedings of the court, whether he be the commander of the fleet or the president, and without whose approval the sentence cannot be executed, is as much a part of this judgment, according to law, as is the trial or the sentence. When the president, then, performs this duty of approving the sentence of a court-martial dismissing an officer, his act has all the solemnity and significance of the judgment of a court of law.

In place of the *Dynes* Court's emphasis on the separateness of the military justice system, *Runkle* affirms the subordination of the military command to the rule of law.

C. THE ANSELL-CROWDER CONTROVERSY

The Ansell-Crowder Controversy, a dispute between Major General Enoch H. Crowder, the Judge Advocate General of the Army from 1911–1923 and his senior assistant, Brigadier General Samuel T. Ansell, played a significant role in the reform of military justice which had remained largely unchanged since the Civil War. General Crowder assumed responsibility for administration of the Selective Service System in World War I but delegated the day-to-day operations of the office to General Ansell.

The two had diametrically opposed views on review of court-martial proceedings. According to General Crowder:

> [T]he court-martial simply [is] the right hand of the commanding officer to aid him in the maintenance of discipline. It is his agent. He controls it. It is answerable not to the law but to him .... The court-martial is not a court at all; it is by an agency of military command governed and controlled by the will of the commander ....

Quoted in Major Terry W. Brown, "The Crowder-Ansell Dispute: The Emergence of General Samuel T. Ansell," 35 Mil. L. Rev. 1, 23 (1967). Conversely, General Ansell proposed a significant expansion of the powers of the Judge Advocate General to review the results of courts-martial. General Ansell believed that, under section 1199 of the Revised Statutes of 1878 ("Judge-Advocate-General shall receive, revise, and have recorded the proceedings of all courts-martial, courts of inquiry and military commissions"), the Judge Advocate General could modify or set aside the findings and sentence of a court-martial approved by a commander where jurisdiction was lacking or serious prejudicial error existed. The power to "revise," in Ansell's view, included the power "to reexamine for correction, to alter or amend."

Two extraordinary cases, both arising out of Texas in 1917, focused national attention on inadequacies of the system of military justice. The first involved a group of twelve or fifteen enlisted soldiers under arrest for a minor violation of the Articles of War of 1916 who refused to attend drill formation after being ordered to do so. The soldiers were correct as a matter of law; their refusal was based on an Army regulation that prohibited persons in arrest from attending drill. The soldiers were charged with mutiny, tried by general court-martial, convicted, given a dishonorable discharge, and sentenced to terms of imprisonment ranging from ten to twenty-five years. After the appointing authority reviewed and approved the cases and ordered the sentences executed, the cases were forwarded to the Office of the Judge Advocate General for disposition. Ansell and others in his office recognized the miscarriage of justice and directed that the findings be set aside. General Crowder objected, asserting that the Judge Advocate General lacked any authority to set aside findings after execution of sentence had been ordered by the appointing authority.

A second case further raised the profile of the dispute between Ansell and Crowder. After America's entry into World War I in 1917, the arrest of two African-American soldiers by local law enforcement officers in Houston, Texas, for disorderly conduct was followed by a rumor that one of the soldiers arrested had been killed. A mob of armed black soldiers marched on the town and, before the riot stopped, fifteen whites were killed. Sixty-three soldiers were accused of murder, mutiny and riot and were tried by general court-martial. Thirteen were sentenced to death by hanging, forty-one to life imprisonment, four to short terms, and five were acquitted. The thirteen sentenced to death were hanged immediately after the trial. When news of the swift imposition of capital punishment reached Washington, the resulting furor led to stern action and swift reform measures. The commanding general was relieved, reduced in rank and retired. The War Department prohibited the execution of death sentences before review by the Judge Advocate General.

The commander's actions were authorized by military law; the commander of a territorial department could order the execution of a death sentence for murder, rape, mutiny, desertion or espionage in time of war. The crimes technically occurred during war, although obviously far from the European front and they occurred in the racially charged climate of the Jim Crow South early in the twentieth century. But the injustice of death sentences without appeal struck a nerve.

Late in 1917, Ansell defended his effort to review the convictions in the Texas Mutiny Cases in a memorandum submitted to the Secretary of War. His defense was answered by General Crowder shortly thereafter. From Ansell's perspective, the issue was whether review of courts-martial proceedings approved by the convening commander was provided for by statute under the authority to "revise" records. Crowder saw the issue as an absence of statutory authority and a question as to whether appellate review was desirable. Senior officers opposed a commander's order being overturned by a member of the Judge Advocate General's Department and expressed fears of disastrous effects on discipline. In addition, Crowder may have been reluctant to recognize substantial defects in the 1916 Articles of War, which he had revised and guided through Congress.

The controversy between Ansell and Crowder simmered in the War Department until the Armistice in Europe in November 1918, after which Senator Chamberlain of Oregon criticized the military justice system in a Senate speech for inequality, excessive sentences and command control of the justice process and called for the establishment of an appellate tribunal to address these problems. Eventually, Senator Chamberlain introduced a reform bill, drafted by Ansell, leading to extensive hearings on the reform of military justice. Although few were adopted at the time, Ansell's proposed reforms set the agenda for military justice reform in the twentieth century.

The Ansell proposals included (1) increased specificity both as to crimes and punishments, (2) review of general court-martial charges by the Judge Advocate General's Department for legal sufficient and evidentiary support, (3) provision in a general court-martial of military counsel of the accused's choice if reasonably available, and, if circumstances warranted, civilian counsel provided at no expense to the accused, (4) a fixed number of members of a court to prevent manipulation by the authorizing commander during the course of trial, (5) authorizing enlisted members to serve on a court, (6) appointing a Court Judge Advocate to select or augment the members of the court (to lessen the influence exercised by the appointing authority), rule on questions of law and challenges to the impartiality of the court members, summarize the evidence, insure the rights of the accused at trial, approve the court's finding of guilt or substitute a finding of guilty of a lesser included offense, announce the findings of the court, and suspend any sentence except death or dismissal, (7) allowing peremptory challenges to individual members of special and general courts-martial and challenges to an array from which members were selected, (8) requiring that, except as otherwise provided by Congress, the rules of evidence applicable to trials by courts-martial should be the same as those followed in U.S. district courts, (9) immediate announcement of acquittal in open court to prevent the appointing authority from returning the findings and sentence to the court-martial for reconsideration (the War Department prohibited the practice of returning acquittals to the court for reconsideration and the upward revision of sentences in the midst of the reform debate, thereby rectifying some of the worst abuses), and (10) appellate review by a Court of Military Appeals comprised of Article III judges.

Ansell's proposals, many far ahead of their time, reflected a desire to treat military personnel charged with crimes fairly in accordance with the law. The Articles of War, in some respects unchanged from the eighteenth century, had by the end of World War I diverged considerably from civilian practice in the quality of treatment afforded an accused. Ansell played a catalytic role in prompting reform. But military justice would continue to be dispensed largely by amateurs of whatever rank, and those with legal training would have to wait their time. See generally Morgan, "The Existing Court-Martial System and the Ansell Army Articles," 29 Yale L. J. 52 (1919) and Morgan, "The Background of the

Uniform Code of Military Justice," 6 Vand. L. Rev. 169 (1953).

D. THE UNIFORM CODE OF MILITARY JUSTICE

The size of the military shrank significantly in the period between the two world wars and little attention was paid to military justice, but World War II brought with it a significant expansion in manpower and strains on the military justice system. Jonathan Lurie in *Arming Military Justice: the Origins of the United States Court of Military Appeals, 1775–1950* (Princeton, 1992), at p. 128, describes the scope of the problem as follows:

> Ill prepared to cope with what was considered in 1917–1918 to be a major increase in American armed forces, the military justice system was in a much worse position to meet the dramatic needs engendered by the Second World War. The army expanded from 1,460,000 personnel to more than 8,000,000. By 1945, the navy's ranks had doubled in size to over 4,500,000. In all, at least 12,000,000 people were subject to military justice; and at the height of the war, approximately 600,000 courts-martial were convened per year. Over 1,700,000 trials were held, more than 100 executions were carried out, and at the end of the war in 1945, some 45,000 members of the armed forces were in prison.

The unfinished business of instrumental reform of military justice and the role of the commander in the process came back to haunt the military following

World War II. Congress was flooded with complaints, and public pressure mounted for much-needed reforms in military justice. The complaints echoed those raised after World War I. These three examples are illustrative: (1) Although article 8 of the Articles of War provided that a law member from the Judge Advocate General's Department should be detailed to a general court-martial, an exception allowed an officer from another branch to be substituted. The exception often consumed the rule, and the task of assuring adherence to the law, a task for lawyers, fell to clueless amateurs who were responsible for gross, and essentially unreviewable, miscarriages of justice. (2) Command domination continued to be a problem. Commanders hectored hand-picked courts into sentencing defendants to the maximum allowable punishment and arrogated to themselves the task of setting punishment. Although allowed by the Articles, the practice contributed heavily to the perception that military justice was unduly harsh as well as unfair. (3) Indeterminate sentences continued the practice of "different spanks for different ranks." See Holtzoff, "Administration of Justice in the United States Army," 22 N.Y. U. L. Rev. 1 (1947).

Military justice reform for the Army came in two steps after World War II. The first step, the Elston Act of 1948, accommodated an on-going struggle between reformers and those who preferred the status quo by revising the Articles of War for the Army only (although the Air Force complied with it as well). The second step was the creation of one code of military justice to govern all branches of the service, a step realized with enactment of the Uniform Code of Military Justice in 1950.

The Elston Act modified the Articles of War to allow enlisted members to sit on general and special courts-martial if requested in writing by an enlisted accused. It also mandated increased use of professionally trained and qualified lawyers. The law member was required to be present throughout the trial and to rule on questions of law. In a general court-martial, if the trial judge advocate who represented the government was a lawyer, the defendant would be entitled to a lawyer. An accused who requested a lawyer would be entitled counsel during a pretrial investigation.

The Elston Act had barely entered into force when Congress undertook the process of unifying military law and procedure by creating a uniform code to govern the Army, Navy, Marine Corps, Air Force, and Coast Guard. The current operation of this code is the subject of extended treatment in the chapters on military justice, but a few of the highlights of the 1950 reform are worth mentioning here.

The Army's Articles of War served as the model, with modifications to accommodate the special needs or traditions of the Navy. Military crimes were continued in much the same way as previous codes, including peculiarly military offenses such as "conduct unbecoming an officer and a gentleman" and service discrediting conduct. The President was authorized to prescribe a table of maximum punishments for crimes as part of a revised Manual for Courts-Martial to go along with the new code.

This would end the worst abuses of the system of indeterminate sentences. Before charges could be referred to a general court-martial, the UCMJ now required appointment of an investigating officer who would make "a thorough and impartial investigation" at which an accused would have an opportunity to present evidence and cross examine witnesses. As a partial check on commanders, a court-martial convening authority was required to refer the charge to his or her Staff Judge Advocate for "consideration and advice," although the commander was not bound by the recommendation. Some effort was made to prevent a commander from exercising undue influence over courts-martial (e.g., disqualifying a commander with "personal interest" in a case and prohibiting the convening authority from censuring, reprimanding or admonishing court members or counsel with respect to the findings or sentence). The UCMJ guaranteed the right of an accused in serious cases to be represented by a lawyer. Finally, in one of the most important changes, the UCMJ created the United States Court of Military Appeals, three civilian judges appointed by the President to 15-year terms.

As this book goes to press, two issues confront military justice in the twenty-first century. These have arisen because of lax punishment for a rising tide of cases of sexual harassment and sexual abuse in the armed forces. The first issue concerns the prosecutorial function of commanders. Currently, and consistent with the history of military law, commanders initiate the prosecutorial process and appoint the court members who will pass judgment unless the accused opts for a trial by military judge alone. The second issue comes at the other end of the process. The court-martial's decision as to guilt and sentence can be reviewed and set aside by the commander. The commander cannot overturn a finding of "not guilty," but a finding of guilty can be overturned and a sentence recommendation reduced or disregarded altogether. The power of the commander remains strong, but Congress may trim that power.

Numerous excellent sources on the history of American Military Law are available for those desiring more detail. They include: William Winthrop, *Military Law and Precedents* (2d ed. 1896, reprint ed. 1920); Jonathan Lurie, *Military Justice in America: The U.S. Court of Appeals for the Armed forces, 1775–1980* (2001); William Thomas Allison, *Military Justice in Vietnam: The Rule of Law in an American War* (2007); George S. Prugh, *Law at War: Vietnam, 1964–1973* (1975); Gary Solis, *Marines and Military Law in Vietnam: Trial by Fire* (1989); Frederic L. Borch, *Judge Advocates in Combat: Army Lawyers in Military Operations from Vietnam to Haiti* (2001); Gary D. Solis, *Son Thang: an American War Crime* (1997) and *The Army Lawyer: A History of the Judge Advocate General's Corps, 1775–1975* (1975) published on the bicentennial of the Corps.

CHAPTER 2

ENLISTMENT, DISCHARGE, AND SEPARATION

A. THE ENLISTMENT CONTRACT

The end of the draft in 1973 and its replacement by a volunteer military made the enlistment contract the principal means by which individuals join the Armed Forces. Among other things, the enlistee acknowledges that he or she may be required to do things a civilian cannot be compelled to do, that the enlistment contract is governed by law that Congress is empowered to change, and that such changes will not affect the enforceability of the agreement. Additional understandings that the enlistee acknowledges disclose the uniqueness of the enlistment contract:

> a. My enlistment/reenlistment agreement is more than an employment agreement. It effects a change in status from civilian to military member of the Armed Forces. As a member of the Armed Forces of the United States, I will be:
>
> (1) Required to obey all lawful orders and perform all assigned duties.
>
> (2) Subject to separation during or at the end of my enlistment.
>
> If my behavior fails to meet acceptable military standards, I may be discharged and given a certificate for less than honorable service, which may hurt my future job

opportunities and my claim for veteran's benefits.

(3) Subject to the military justice system, which means, among other things, that I may be tried by military courts-martial.

(4) Required upon order to serve in combat or other hazardous situations.

(5) Entitled to receive pay, allowances, and other benefits as provided by law and regulation.

b. Laws and regulations that govern military personnel may change without notice to me. Such changes may affect my status, pay, allowances, benefits, and responsibilities as a member of the Armed Forces REGARDLESS of the provisions of this enlistment/reenlistment document. DD Form 4/1 (Oct. 2017).

In short, the purpose of the enlistment agreement is to transform civilians into soldiers, sailors, airmen, Marines, and members of the Coast Guard. Courts have treated the status-changing and contractual aspects of enlistment agreements differently. This differential treatment is the subject of an article by Major Udi Sagi, "Specific Performance of Enlistment Contracts," 205 Mil. L. Rev. 150 (2010).

It should be clear from the provisions set out above that an enlistment contract is enforceable despite being a personal service contract. For example, it is enforceable through the provisions of the UCMJ, Articles 85 and 86, 10 U.S.C. §§ 885 and 886, which establish the offenses of Desertion and Absence Without Leave. These provisions make it a criminal offense to absent oneself without authority from one's work assignment. Administrative statutes can suffice as well, e.g., *Baldwin v. Cram*, 522 F.2d 910 (2d Cir.1975) (providing "a way for the Army in effect specifically to enforce its personal services or enlistment contract"). The administrative statute referred to in *Baldwin* was the predecessor to 10 U.S.C. § 12303, which provides for the recall of reserve soldiers who failed to report for duty.

The seminal case with respect to enlistment contracts is *United States v. Grimley*, 137 U.S. 147 (1890) ("Enlistment is a contract, but it is one of those contracts which changes the *status*, and where that is changed, no breach of the contract destroys the new *status* or relieves from the obligations which its existence imposes.") Grimley was court-martialed for desertion and sentenced to six months imprisonment. He sought a writ of habeas corpus in federal district court, which discharged him from military custody. Grimley relied on the fact that he had misrepresented his age upon enlistment as 28 when in fact he was 40. The enlistment age limit at that time was 35, and Grimley sought to void his agreement on this ground. On appeal, the Supreme Court held that only the government could abrogate the contract on account of the misrepresentation. The Army had proper jurisdiction over Grimley based on his status as a soldier and could court-martial him for desertion.

There are essentially two avenues that an enlisted member of the Armed Services can use to challenge an enlistment agreement. The first is to raise the defense of "defective enlistment" in a court-martial proceeding. *United States v. Quintal*, 10 M.J. 532 (A.C.M.R. 1980) (recruiter misconduct); *United States v. Valadez*, 5 M.J. 470 (C.M.A. 1978) (recruiter misconduct; waiver of a non-waivable service regulation); *Lefrancois v. Mabus*, 910 F. Supp.2d 12 (2012) (failure to review a claim of "defective enlistment" was arbitrary and capricious). Alternatively, an enlistee may challenge his or her court-martial conviction by seeking a writ of habeas corpus in federal district court to challenge the exercise of military jurisdiction, as Grimley did. However, such challenges face a steep hurdle under UCMJ Article 2(c), 10 U.S.C. § 802(c) which provides:

> (c) Notwithstanding any other provision of law, a person serving with an armed force who—
>
> (1) submitted voluntarily to military authority;
>
> (2) met the mental competency and minimum age qualifications of sections 504 and 505 of this title at the time of voluntary submission to military authority;
>
> (3) received military pay or allowances; and
>
> (4) performed military duties;
>
> is subject to this chapter until such person's active service has been terminated in accordance

> with law or regulations promulgated by the Secretary concerned.

This would appear to be the exclusive remedy in federal court. *Gengler v. United States*, 453 F.Supp. 2d 1217, 1240–41 (E.D.Cal. 2006) (only a writ of habeas corpus is allowed; a servicemember cannot use the Contracts Disputes Act, the equitable estoppel doctrine, the Administrative Action Act, and the Tucker Act as causes of action against the military).

An accused must first exhaust all military appeals before seeking relief in federal court. *Parisi v. Davidson*, 405 U.S. 34 (1972). In the event there is no court-martial conviction and sentence to appeal, the servicemember must show that all available intra-service administrative remedies have been exhausted unless pursuit of intra-service remedies would be futile or cause irreparable harm. *Woodrick v. Hungerford*, 800 F.2d 1413 (5th Cir.1986) (after failing to report for active duty, Woodrick was apprehended; while being investigated for desertion, he sought habeas corpus). Accord, *Winck v. England*, 327 F.3d 1296 (11th Cir.2003) ("[A] military servicemember must exhaust all intra-military remedies before applying for a writ of habeas corpus seeking discharge from the military under the terms of his or her enlistment contract, unless the application falls within a limited number of exceptions to the exhaustion principle.").

Recent litigation over the scope of enlistment contracts has arisen from the enforcement of the Stop-Loss policy under which active duty as well as reserve component servicemembers whose enlistments are about to expire may have their terms of service extended in the interest of national security. 10 U.S.C. § 12305(a). *Santiago v. Rumsfeld*, 425 F.3d 549 (9th Cir.2005) (extension of enlistment term by a stop-loss order did not breach the terms of an Army National Guard Sergeant's enlistment contract or violate due process).

An enlistment in the Armed Forces ordinarily commits the enlistee to a definite term of service at the conclusion of which the servicemember is normally granted a discharge. While the majority of enlistments are served for the full period and terminate in discharge without complication, occasionally the government or the servicemember will desire to terminate the enlistment prior to completion of the term of service. A servicemember has no contractual right to remain in the service until the expiration of his or her enlistment. *McAulay v. United States*, 305 F.2d 836 (Ct.Cl. 1962), *cert. denied*, 373 U.S. 938 (1963). Rather, the government may terminate the enlistment contact at any time so long as there is authority for early discharge and it is accomplished consistent with procedural due process and basic fairness. *Canonica v. United States*, 41 Fed. Cl. 516, 524 (1998) ("[A]n enlisted member of the armed forces does not have a property interest in his employment because he may be discharged 'as prescribed by the Secretary' of his service. 10 U.S.C. § 1169.")

Because of the change in status brought about by an enlistment contract, formal discharge is necessary to terminate military service.

> A servicemember will not be considered to have been lawfully discharged . . . unless: (1) the member received a valid discharge certificate or a certificate of release from active duty, such as a Department of Defense Form (DD Form) 214; (2) the member's "final pay" or a "substantial part of that pay" is "ready for delivery" to the member; and (3) the member has completed the administrative clearance process required by the Secretary of the service of which he or she is a member.

United States v. Melanson, 53 M.J. 1, 2 (C.A.A.F. 2000)

Actual physical receipt of the discharge certificate (DD 214) is not required. All that the applicable statute, 10 U.S.C. § 1168(a), requires is that the discharge certificate be "ready for delivery." *Earl v. United States*, 27 Fed.Cl. 36 (1992) (no entitlement to pay and benefits after discharge notwithstanding delay in receiving certificate).

By regulation, e.g., U.S. DEP'T OF ARMY, REG. 635-200, PERSONNEL SEPARATIONS, administrative discharge is not effective until 2400 hours on the date of notification. "Under paragraph 1–31d of Department of the Army Regulation (AR) 635–200 (26 June 1996), a discharge takes effect at "2400 [hours] on the date of notice of discharge to the soldier." Even if a discharge certificate and separation orders are delivered to a member earlier in the day as an administrative convenience for the unit or the servicemember, the discharge is not effective upon such a delivery unless it is clear that it was intended to be effective at the earlier time." *United States v. Melanson,* 53 M.J. 1, 2 (C.A.A.F. 2000) (court-martial jurisdiction retained over servicemember for crime allegedly occurring after delivery but prior to 2400 hours). Pending criminal proceedings or medical treatment can extend a term of service beyond an anticipated discharge date. UCMJ, Article 802(a)(1), 10 U.S.C. § 802(a)(1).

B. DISCHARGES OF ENLISTED PERSONNEL

Separation from the service has two components. It both ends a servicemember's military obligation and usually provides a characterization of their service, which appears on their DD-214.

1. CHARACTERIZATIONS OF DISCHARGE

There are five types of discharges issued to enlisted personnel. Three are issued administratively: the honorable discharge; the general discharge "under honorable conditions;" and discharge "under other than honorable conditions" (OTH), formerly called an undesirable discharge. The remaining two—the bad conduct discharge and the dishonorable discharge—are punitive in nature and may result only from conviction by court-martial. Department of Defense Instruction ("DoDI") 1332.14 (2008).

The characterization of a discharge can have a profound effect on a former servicemember's future civilian life since it can be used by prospective employers in hiring decisions. Eligibility for veteran's benefits are affected by the type of discharge as well.

Three factors determine the characterization of a servicemember's discharge: (1) the quality of service as measured by the standards of acceptable personal conduct and performance of duty, including conduct in the civilian community; (2) the reason for separation (usually a pattern of conduct, although in some instances a single incident may be considered); and (3) the servicemember's age, length of service, grade, aptitude, and physical and mental condition.

Whenever a servicemember's record reflects acceptable military service and performance of duty, an honorable discharge is issued. An honorable discharge signifies adequate military performance. It is not a mark of distinction or meritorious service, which are generally recognized through medals and awards. An honorable discharge entitles the recipient to both tangible and intangible benefits such as veteran's benefits and favorable consideration by civilian employers.

2. SEPARATION REASONS

Regular enlisted servicemembers cannot be discharged prior to the expiration of their terms of service except as prescribed by the Secretary of their armed service, in consequence of a general or special court-martial or as otherwise provided by law. 10 U.S.C.A. § 1169. For example, the Secretary of the

Army has issued AR 635-200, Active Duty Enlisted Administrative Separations.

Separations are allowed for the convenience of the government for the following reasons: 1) to allow a servicemember to pursue educational opportunities; 2) to permit one to accept public office; 3) to alleviate dependency or hardship, so long as it is not normally incident to military service, e.g., *Rickson v. Ward*, 359 F.Supp. 328 (D.C.Cal. 1973) (upholding denial of a hardship discharge to a seaman); 4) to accommodate pregnancy or childbirth; 5) to deal with the responsibilities of parenthood where the servicemember is "unable satisfactorily to perform his or her duties or is unavailable for worldwide assignment or deployment;" 6) to address the needs of conscientious objectors; 7) to protect a surviving family member; 8) to address physical or mental conditions that do not amount to a disability but nevertheless interfere with assignment to or performance of duty such as chronic seasickness or airsickness, bedwetting (enuresis) and personality disorders. Several of these reasons require that the servicemember receive counseling regarding a deficiency prior to the initiation of separation and an opportunity to overcome the deficiency. The counseling must be appropriately documented. In addition to these grounds, the Secretary of Defense may specify additional grounds for separation for the convenience of the government.

Separation for disability is provided for by statute. 10 U.S.C. § 1203. The disability must not be the result of the member's intentional misconduct or willful neglect, and must not have been incurred during a period of unauthorized absence.

Enlistments can be defective, erroneous, and fraudulent. Separation for defective enlistment may be sought when the enlistee is under the age of 18 and enlisted without the written consent of a parent or guardian. A parent or guardian must apply to the appropriate Secretary within 90 days of the servicemember's enlistment. 10 U.S.C.A. § 1170. Separation for erroneous enlistment is appropriate when the enlistment would not have occurred if the relevant facts had been known, it was not the result of fraudulent conduct on the servicemember's part and the defect underlying the error persists. *Taylor v. United States*, 22 Ct.Cl. 335 (1991). Fraudulent enlistment occurs when a servicemember

> (1) procures his own enlistment or appointment in the armed forces by knowingly false representation or deliberate concealment as to his qualifications for that enlistment or appointment and receives pay or allowances thereunder; or
>
> (2) procures his own separation from the armed forces by knowingly false representation or deliberate concealment as to his eligibility for that separation

Article 83 UCMJ, 10 U.S.C. § 883. See *United States v. Farano*, 60 M.J. 932 (N.M.Ct.Crim.App. 2005).

A servicemember who early on demonstrates a lack of qualification or aptitude for military service because of unsatisfactory performance or conduct (or both) as evidenced by inability, lack of reasonable effort, failure to adapt to the military environment or minor disciplinary infractions may be given an Entry Level discharge. An Entry Level discharge is an uncharacterized discharge due to the short duration of service. A servicemember is in an entry level status for the first 180 days of active duty.

A servicemember who cannot perform assigned duties or whose behavior adversely affects good order, discipline or morale may be separated for unsatisfactory performance.

As noted above, enlisted servicemembers have no property interest in their employment. However, federal courts have recognized a liberty interest in their employment that "prevents the military from discharging a servicemember without due process—but only in cases where a 'stigma' would attach to the discharge." *Canonica v. United States*, 41 Fed. Cl. 516, 524 (1998).

A servicemember who has been referred to either a drug rehabilitation program or an alcohol rehabilitation program may be separated for inability or refusal to participate in, cooperate in, or successfully complete the program. Separation for misconduct is appropriate for a pattern of minor disciplinary infractions, for a pattern of misconduct, e.g., discreditable involvement with civil or military authorities, or for conduct prejudicial to good order and discipline.

If charges have been preferred with respect to an offense for which a punitive discharge is authorized, and it is determined that the servicemember is unqualified for further military service, separation at the request of the servicemember may occur in lieu of trial by court-martial. The characterization for discharge is normally under other than honorable conditions, but may be general (or under honorable conditions) if certain guidelines are met. This is commonly part of a plea bargain prior to the administrative hearing.

3. ADMINISTRATIVE DISCHARGE PROCESSES

Administrative discharge requires adherence to due process, i.e., notice and an opportunity to be heard through a process commensurate with the gravity of the situation. Two procedures are available—a notification procedure and an administrative board. A servicemember facing separation must be notified of his rights in writing as well as the factual basis of the proposed separation. In a notification procedure, the servicemember responds to the facts asserted by the government by means of submissions of letters and evidence on his or her behalf to establish suitability for continued service. By regulation, servicemembers have certain rights. These rights include (1) the right to obtain copies of documents that serve as the basis for the separation decision, including summaries of classified documents; (2) the right to submit statements; (3) the right to consult with a qualified military attorney at no expense or with a civilian counsel retained at the servicemember's expense if being heard by an administrative board; and (4) the right to request an administrative board if the servicemember has six or more years of active or reserve military service or, irrespective of time of service, is entitled to an administrative board if he or she is facing the possibility of an other-than-honorable discharge. A servicemember with six or more years of service or one facing a stigmatizing discharge characterization has a more important stake in continuing service and consequently enjoys more due process protection. In this case, the servicemember must also be notified of the result of the proposed separation, for example, whether it could result in discharge rather than release from active duty to a reserve component and the least favorable characterization for discharge authorized for the proposed separation. The procedures for administrative discharge for all services implement 32 C.F.R. Pt. 41, App. A.

A court-martial convening authority appoints the administrative board comprised of at least three experienced commissioned, warrant, or noncommissioned officers. Enlisted personnel appointed to the board must be in the grade of E-7 or above and must be senior in rank to the respondent. At least one member of the administrative board must be in the grade of 0–4 or higher, and a majority of the board members must be commissioned or warrant officers. The senior member of the board serves as the president. The convening authority can appoint a nonvoting recorder and a legal advisor to assist the board. If the enlisted respondent is in the reserves, at least one reserve officer must be included as a voting member. All voting members must be senior in grade to the respondent. Voting members of the administrative board or the legal advisor are subject to challenge for cause.

The president of the board rules on matters of procedure and evidence but can be overruled by a majority of the board. If there is a legal advisor, the advisor rules on all evidentiary matters and challenges. Evidence may be oral or written, and payment of expenses to permit attendance of witnesses is allowed. The rules of evidence do not apply before administrative boards, but evidence must be relevant and competent.

The board determines its finding in closed session with only voting members present and recommends retention or separation. If separation is decided upon, the reasons for separation must be stated and supported by a preponderance of the evidence. This is an important difference between courts-martial and administrative discharge proceedings. A court-martial is a criminal trial in which proof must be established "beyond a reasonable doubt." "Preponderance of the evidence" is a much easier standard to satisfy. That accounts for the preference by the services for administrative discharge as a means of addressing problem enlisted servicemembers as opposed to the more difficult route of court-martial.

If the board recommends separation, the record is forwarded to the separation authority which may approve the board's recommendations, approve the recommendations but suspend their execution, change the characterization of service or separation to a more favorable one, change a recommendation of transfer to the reserves or disapprove the board's recommendation and retain the servicemember.

A servicemember who has been administratively discharged can seek review before that service's Discharge Review Board (DRB). Review must be sought within fifteen years of the discharge or dismissal. 10 U.S.C. § 1553. Decisions of the DRB may be appealed on grounds of error or injustice to the service's Board for the Correction of Military Records (BCMR) within three years. 10 U.S.C. § 1552(b). This three-year statute of limitations begins to run at the conclusion of proceedings before the DRB. *Ortiz v. Sec. of Defense*, 41 F.3d 738 (D.C. Cir.1994).

Since 2016, Post-Traumatic Stress Disorder (PTSD), Traumatic Brain Injury (TBI), and Military Sexual Trauma (MST) have affected the administrative separation proceedings for servicemembers facing an OTH discharge or administrative separation in lieu of court-martial. 10 U.S.C. § 1177. PTSD is a mental health condition that presents as a psychological response to trauma. Such trauma is a common result of combat conditions either directly impacting those who experience them or indirectly impacting those in various combat support roles. TBI is caused by a bump, blow or jolt to the head or a penetrating head injury that disrupts the normal function of the brain. MST is a psychological trauma resulting from a physical assault of a sexual nature, battery of a sexual nature, or sexual harassment. Sexual harassment is defined as "repeated, unsolicited verbal or physical contact of a sexual nature which is threatening in character."

PTSD, TBI and MST have all been identified as potential contributors to misconduct that can serve as a basis for administrative separation and should be considered as possible factors in defense, mitigation or extenuation in administrative discharge proceedings if warranted by the facts.

By law, a servicemember facing an OTH or administrative separation in lieu of court-martial must undergo a medical examination prior to separation or discharge if during the previous 24 months he or she 1) has been deployed overseas in support of a contingency operation, 2) has been sexually assaulted, or 3) reasonably alleges PTSD, TBI or MST as a contributing factor to the misconduct that serves as the basis for separation. 10 U.S.C. § 1177(a)(1) and (2). The purpose of the medical examination is to "assess whether the effects of [PTSD or TBI or trauma of MST] constitute matters in extenuation that relate to the basis for administrative separation under conditions other than honorable or the overall characterization of service of the member as other than honorable." 10 U.S.C. § 1177(b).

It is important to recognize that servicemembers facing discharge may be unwilling or unable to identify the invisible wounds of PTSD, TBI, and MST that may lie behind the misconduct leading to their discharge. A military culture that prizes bravery and endurance of hardship may make servicemembers reluctant to claim PTSD, just as personal privacy and shame may prompt a refusal to disclose or explore the basis of sexual trauma. And it is true that symptoms of PTSD, TBI, or MST may not present until after separation when problems such as drug or alcohol abuse, domestic violence, maladaptation to work, family or social environments, or thoughts or attempts of suicide manifest themselves. A recent article has focused attention on the challenges in advising commanders with regard to characterizing the service of those for whom discharge is recommended. Major Bryant A. Boohar, "Combat Stress Claims: Veterans' Benefits and Post-Separation Character of Service Upgrades for "Bad Paper" Veterans After the Fairness for Veterans Act," 227 Mil. L. Rev. 95 (2019). The impact of OTH discharges on VA benefits is considered in the next section.

4. A GUIDE TO SEEKING JUSTICE FOR FORMER SERVICEMEMBERS WITH "BAD PAPER" DISCHARGES

No one should be surprised to learn that military service can be harmful to one's health. Servicemembers in combat are exposed to the risk of injury or death, or they may witness death, destruction, and torture. And those who provide support to warriors, wounded and otherwise, may sustain even lifelong harm from witnessing the horrors that combat in its various forms can inflict. E.g., Hans Pols & Stephanie Oak, "War and Military Mental Health: The U.S. Psychiatric Response in the 20th Century," 97 Am. J. Pub. Health (Published Online: October 10, 2011, https://ajph.

aphapublications.org/doi/full/10.2105/AJPH.2006.090910); Jonathan Shay, *Achilles in Vietnam: Combat Trauma and the Undoing of Character* (2010).

What may come as a surprise, however, is that not all who "have borne the battle," as President Lincoln described them in his second inaugural address, are eligible to receive Veterans' Administration (VA) benefits. Many former servicemembers are excluded by what are colloquially known as undesirable or "bad paper" discharges. As explored below, these discharges exclude servicemembers from receiving VA services because of misconduct that occurred while they were in the service, misconduct in many cases attributable to service-connected health conditions that should have been (or should now be) considered as factors in defense, mitigation or extenuation in determining their character of service.

This exclusion has created a public health crisis as former servicemembers without access to health care, counseling, and vocational services experience unaddressed issues including unemployment, mental and physical health problems, drug and alcohol abuse, domestic and other types of violence, despair and suicide.

Three conditions are of greatest concern: Post-Traumatic Stress Disorder (PTSD), Traumatic Brain Injury (TBI), and Military Sexual Trauma (MST). For example, PTSD and its effects have proven particularly insidious since, despite its devastating effects, it is difficult to recognize, and diagnose. Although unrecognized, it may contribute to incorrigible behavior, violence at work or in domestic situations, drug and alcohol abuse and other anti-social behavior. Of particular significance to Vietnam-era former servicemembers, although PTSD afflicted many thousands of them, PTSD was not even recognized in the American Psychiatric Association's Diagnostic and Statistical Manual of Mental Health Disorders (DSM) until 1980 when it was included in DSM-III. Realization by medical and mental health professionals of the nature and manifestation of the disease continued to evolve. The fifth edition of the DSM published in 2013 classified PTSD as a "Trauma- and Stressor-Related Disorder" associated with such things as irritability or aggression, risky or destructive behavior. These behaviors often provide the foundation for "bad paper" discharges.

Assessing the effects of military discharges, both administrative and punitive, i.e., through a court-martial, on VA benefits requires an understanding of both military law and the laws and procedures governing the VA. This assessment is not intended as a comprehensive guide to veterans' benefits or process for obtaining them, which is beyond the scope of this book. Those requiring such guidance are advised to seek the help of a qualified lawyer or VA benefits counselor.

Administrative discharge provides an efficient mechanism to rid the military of ineffective, maladaptive servicemembers or those guilty of misconduct incapable of remediation including drug and alcohol abuse, while courts-martial are reserved for instances of serious misconduct, comparable to felonies in the civilian world. As noted earlier, the basis for administrative discharge or separation need only be supported by a preponderance of the evidence. A punitive discharge imposed by a court-martial must meet the more stringent standard imposed in criminal proceedings—beyond reasonable doubt.

As discussed earlier, there are five service characterizations: (1) honorable, (2) general under honorable conditions, (3) other than honorable (OTH), (4) bad-conduct (BCD), and (5) dishonorable. Punitive discharges—BCDs and dishonorable discharges—can be only be imposed by a court-martial for enlisted personnel.

Uncharacterized separations can occur when enlisted personnel are administratively discharged in cases of entry level separation and void enlistment or induction. 38 U.S.C. § 105; 38 C.F.R. § 3.12(k). By regulation, the VA considers entry level separations as "other than dishonorable." Void enlistments or inductions must be reviewed to determine whether they meet this standard. Note that the armed services and the VA use different language to characterize service. While the military describes disqualifying service as "other than honorable" (OTH), the VA describes qualifying service as "other than dishonorable."

The characterization of service affects a veteran's eligibility for VA benefits. VA benefits include such things as service-connected disability compensation, health care, education assistance, non-service-connected pension, burial benefits, housing benefits and vocational rehabilitation.

VA benefits are restricted to veterans, but as pointed out above, not all former servicemembers are veterans. To be considered a veteran, a former servicemember must have performed 24 months of full-time active duty service (other than active duty for training), although in some cases less, in the Army, Navy, Air Force, Marine Corps, Coast Guard or served as a commissioned officer in the Public Health Service (PHS), National Oceanic and Atmospheric Administration (NOAA) or its predecessor, the Environmental Science Services Administration; and been discharged or separated from the military "under conditions other than dishonorable." 38 U.S.C. § 101(2); 38 C.F.R. § 3.1(d). With respect to the 24 months of service mentioned above, note that prior to September 8, 1980, there was no prescribed minimum length of service for a servicemember to have been considered a veteran. For enlistments thereafter, however, the minimum applies.

A veteran who receives an honorable discharge is eligible for all applicable VA benefits. A general discharge signifies that the veteran's military service was satisfactory, but not honorable. A general discharge entitles a veteran to all VA benefits except GI bill education benefits.

The VA criterion for veteran status requires that a former servicemember be discharged or released from military services under conditions "other than dishonorable" 38 U.S.C. § 101(2); 38 C.F.R. § 3.12(a).

"Honorable" and "General (under honorable conditions)" characterizations of military service are generally binding on the VA in determining eligibility for benefits. However, for military service characterized as OTH or a BCD imposed by a special court-martial, the VA is required to determine whether that service was "other than dishonorable." To make this assessment, the VA must develop a formal character of service determination in order to assess a former servicemember's eligibility for benefits. 38 U.S.C. § 5103A(a)(1); 38 C.F.R. § 159(c)(1).

This eligibility assessment is initiated by filing a claim with the VA using one of two forms: a VA Form 21-0966 (Intent to File) that allows a former servicemember to initiate a claim while gathering evidence to support the claim, or a VA Form 21-526EZ. Forms may be filed electronically or locally with the VA. Once filed the VA has a duty to assist the claimant in substantiating his or her claim. 38 U.S.C. § 5103A(a)(1); 38 C.F.R. § 159(c)(1). It is important to note that the VA has no authority to change or upgrade a service characterization assigned by the military. Rather, the VA review is limited to determining whether the former servicemember qualifies for VA benefits based on an assessment of relevant evidence related to the claimant's case as evaluated on the basis of VA criteria including any mitigating factors that the investigation adduces. The finding of the VA assessment will be either that the discharge is "other than dishonorable" (and the former servicemember is a veteran entitled to appropriate benefits) or "dishonorable" (and thus the former servicemember is precluded from receiving VA benefits).

There are both legal and regulatory bars to VA benefits. A former servicemember who receives a punitive discharge, such as dismissal, a BCD or a dishonorable discharge, imposed by a general court-martial generally is not eligible for veteran status. 38 U.S.C. §5303(a). If the servicemember received an OTH or BCD adjudged by a special court-martial, it may be possible to obtain veteran status. However, an OTH discharge characterization based on the following six statutory bars will preclude veteran status: (1) conscientious objection with refusal to perform duty, (2) sentencing by a general court-martial, (3) resignation by an officer for the "good of the service," (4) desertion, (5) requested release by an alien servicemember during a period of hostilities, and (6) absence without official leave (AWOL) for a continuous period of at least 180 days unless there are compelling circumstances to warrant the prolonged unauthorized absence. 38 C.F.R. § 3.12(c).

In addition to the bars established by statute, there are also five regulatory bars to VA benefits in the case of an OTH imposed as a result of the following: (1) acceptance of an undesirable discharge to escape trial by general court-martial; (2) mutiny or spying; (3) an offense involving moral turpitude, including generally, conviction of a felony; (4) willful and persistent misconduct although a discharge because of a minor offense will not, however, be considered willful and persistent misconduct if service was otherwise honest, faithful and meritorious; (5) homosexual acts involving aggravating circumstances or other factors affecting the performance of duty such as child molestation, homosexual prostitution, homosexual acts or conduct accompanied by assault or coercion, and homosexual acts or conduct taking place between servicemembers of disparate rank, grade, or status when a servicemember has taken advantage of his or her superior rank, grade, or status. However, an honorable discharge or discharge under honorable conditions issued through a military board for correction of records sets aside any statutory or regulatory bar to benefits. 38 C.F.R. § 3.12(e).

Even if a legal or regulatory bar would otherwise preclude VA benefits, a finding of insanity at the time of the offense by the VA will allow for granting benefits. There need be no direct connection between the insanity and the misconduct that led to the punitive discharge. The VA and the military use different standards to determine insanity, and it is possible for a servicemember found to be sane during a court-martial proceeding to be found insane for the purposes of receiving VA benefits. 38 C.F.R. § 3.354(a); *Gardner v. Shinseki,* 22 Vet.App. 415 (2009).

A former servicemember with an administratively imposed OTH may be entitled to service-connected health care from the Veterans Health Administration (VHA) for "any disability incurred or aggravated during active military, naval, or air service in line of duty" so long as he or she is not subject to any of the statutory bars as detailed above. 38 C.F.R. § 3.360(a); 38 C.F.R. § 3.12(c).

Health care for veterans is provided through the VHA. With some exceptions, veterans are generally required to enroll in the VA health care system in order to obtain services, which include a range of outpatient and inpatient services. 38 C.F.R. § 17.37. Veterans, otherwise qualified, are not required to be enrolled to receive readjustment counseling services through Vet Centers. Such centers address problems such as war-related psychological readjustment, PTSD counseling, family or relationship problems, lack of adequate employment or career goals, social isolation, homelessness and lack of adequate resources, psychological problems such as depression and substance abuse, military-related sexual trauma counseling, bereavement counseling, employment counseling and job referrals, preventive health care information, and referrals for VA and non-VA medical care.

Help is available on a more generous basis through the VA for Military Sexual Trauma (MST). MST is defined as "psychological trauma, which, in the judgment of a mental health professional employed by the [VHA], resulted from a physical assault of a sexual nature, battery of a sexual nature, or sexual harassment while the veteran was serving on active duty or active duty for training." Sexual harassment is defined as "repeated, unsolicited verbal or physical contact of a sexual nature which is threatening in character." Former servicemembers who experienced MST while on inactive duty training (i.e., reservists and members of the National Guard performing weekend drills) can access free MST-related health care. 38 U.S.C. § 1720D; see Fact Sheet, " Veterans Access, Choice, and Accountability Act of 2014 Military Sexual Trauma," https://www.va.gov/opa/choiceact/documents/Fact-Sheet-Military-Sexual-Trauma.pdf.

Unfavorable VA determinations may be reviewed *de novo* by a decision review officer (DRO) by filing a notice of disagreement (NOD). 38 C.F.R. § 3.2600(a). An unfavorable review at the DRO level may be appealed to the Board of Veterans' Appeals (BVA). 38 C.F.R. § 7104(a) and thence to the Court of Appeals for Veterans Claims (CAVC). 38 U.S.C. §§ 7252 (jurisdiction) and 7266 (notice of appeal). Further review is available in the Court of Appeals for the Federal Circuit and ultimately by certiorari to the U.S. Supreme Court.

Greater attention to the severe difficulties facing "bad paper" former servicemembers has led to some improvements. For example, in 2010, then-Secretary of the VA Eric Shinseki eased evidentiary requirements to provide that in assessing PTSD, the VA would not require corroboration of a stressor related to fear of hostile military or terrorist activity if a VA doctor confirms that the stressful experience recalled by a Veteran adequately supports a diagnosis of PTSD and the Veteran's symptoms are related to the claimed stressor. Previously, claims adjudicators were required to corroborate that a non-combat Veteran actually experienced a stressor related to hostile military activity. (https://www.va.

gov/opa/pressrel/pressrelease.cfm?id=1922.) In 2014, then-Secretary of Defense Chuck Hagel issued a DoD memorandum that instructed Discharge Review Boards to give "[l]iberal consideration . . . in petitions for changes in characterization of service . . . which document one or more symptoms which meet the diagnostic criteria of Post-Traumatic Stress Disorder (PTSD) or related conditions." (https://www.secnav.navy.mil/mra/bcnr/Documents/HagelMemo.pdf)

In 2016, the Fairness for Veterans Act amended 10 U.S.C. § 1553 to require military Discharge Review Boards reviewing "the discharge or dismissal (other than a discharge or dismissal by sentence of a general court-martial) of any former member of an armed force [to give] liberal consideration to the former member that post-traumatic stress disorder or traumatic brain injury potentially contributed to the circumstances resulting in the discharge or dismissal or to the original characterization of the member's discharge or dismissal." This change includes "a former member of the armed forces who, while serving on active duty as a member of the armed forces, was deployed in support of a contingency operation and who, at any time after such deployment, was diagnosed by a physician, clinical psychologist, or psychiatrist as experiencing post-traumatic stress disorder or traumatic brain injury as a consequence of that deployment [or] a former member whose application for relief is based in whole or in part on matters relating to post-traumatic stress disorder or traumatic brain injury . . . is related to combat or military sexual trauma . . . ."

This expands the "liberal consideration" requirement to embrace not only PTSD, but also TBI and MST.

Finally, the National Defense Authorization Act for Fiscal Year 2018 (NDAA 2018) extended the "liberal consideration" requirement to Boards for the Correction of Military Records for cases involving PTSD and TBI (but apparently not MST, which is not mentioned) 10 U.S.C. § 1552(h)(2)(B).

Further guidance in this area is provided in the "Memorandum from Under Secretary of Defense to Secretaries of the Military Departments, subject: Clarifying Guidance to Military Discharge Review Boards and Boards for Correction of Military/Naval Records Considering Requests by Veterans for Modification of their Discharge Due to Mental Health Conditions, Sexual Assault, or Sexual Harassment" (25 Aug. 2017) (https://dod.defense.gov/Portals/1/Documents/pubs/Clarifying-Guidance-to-Military-Discharge-Review-Boards.pdf)

The law in this area is subject to change, and those interested should check for cases, and legislative or regulatory changes that could affect the meaning and application of the "liberal consideration" standard. E.g., *Kennedy v. Esper* (D.Conn. 2018), 2018 WL 6727353.

5. CONSCIENTIOUS OBJECTOR DISCHARGES

Conscientious objector claims can arise even among those serving in an all-volunteer Armed Force. After training and deployment, servicemembers can come to understand the job of the military is to win, and that winning sometimes entails wounding and killing the enemy, collateral damage to noncombatants in harm's way and destroying property. Thoughtful self-examination may lead the person to conclude that a deeply held moral, ethical or religious objection logically should preclude involvement in war. More frequent deployments abroad, heavier post-9/11 reliance on National Guard and Reserve components, family commitments, and a desire to escape from educational obligations requiring service following extensive training at government expense, have also prompted a change of heart. E.g., *Lipton v. Peters*, 240 F.3d 1074 (Table) (5th Cir.2000) (affirming denial of a habeas corpus petition challenging the Air Force's denial of his discharge application based upon petitioner being a conscientious objector).

Federal courts have the authority to review the denial of a conscientious-objector discharge. *Parisi v. Davidson*, 405 U.S. 34 (1972) ("When a member of the armed forces has applied for a discharge as a conscientious objector and has exhausted all avenues of administrative relief, it is now settled that he may seek habeas corpus relief in a federal district court on the ground that the denial of his application had no basis in fact.") However, review of a denial of a conscientious-objector discharge is extremely narrow. *DeWalt v. Commanding Officer, Fort Benning, Ga.*, 476 F.2d 440, 442 (5th Cir.1973) (among "the narrowest known to the law"), and a denial must be sustained if the reviewing court can discern any basis in fact for it. *Silverthorne v. Laird*, 460 F.2d 1175, 1179 (5th Cir.1972). A servicemember seeking discharge as a conscientious objector must be scrupulous to follow orders, wear the uniform and observe proper military protocols during the pendency of an application for conscientious objector discharge. *Cole v. Spear*, 747 F.2d 217 (4th Cir.1984) (conscientious objector whose application was approved but not final, received bad conduct discharge for contemptuous behavior during the pendency of her application).

Processing of conscientious objector claims is governed by 32 C.F.R. Part 75 and applicable service regulations. To qualify for discharge from military service as a conscientious objector, an applicant must establish that 1) he or she is opposed to war in any form, *Gillette v. United States*, 401 U.S. 437 (1971); 2) his or her objection is grounded in deeply held moral, ethical, or religious beliefs, *Welsh v. United States*, 398 U.S. 333 (1970); and 3) his or her convictions are sincere, *Witmer v. United States*, 348 U.S. 375 (1955).

The Supreme Court has extended the concept of "religious beliefs" beyond traditional notions of organized religion to include deeply held, purely ethical or moral beliefs which represent the functional equivalent of religion in an individual's life. *Welsh v. United States*, 398 U.S. 333 (1970). In order to qualify for conscientious objector status, a servicemember's objection to participation of war of any kind must have become fixed after entry into the service. If the objection was fixed before entry into the military, the right to claim conscientious objector status is waived. The critical question is whether the servicemember's objection to participation in war "crystallized," or became manifest after entry into the service. *Czubaroff v. Schlesinger*, 385 F.Supp. 728 (E.D.Pa. 1974).

The burden of establishing a claim for conscientious objector status is on the claimant, and the burden of proof is clear and convincing evidence. This is a higher evidentiary threshold than preponderance of the evidence. Once a servicemember establishes a *prima facie* case on the three criteria above, the burden shifts to the government to refute the claim. The law is clear that once an applicant has presented a *prima facie* showing of conscientious objection to war in any form, the burden of rebuttal shifts to the military service. *Silverthorne v. Laird,* 460 F.2d 1175, 1179 (5th Cir.1972); *Maynard v. United States,* 409 F.2d 505 (9th Cir.), *cert. denied,* 396 U.S. 834 (1969). Practically speaking, this is a relatively onerous burden for the government. The service must demonstrate that the claimant held conscientious objector views prior to entry in the military. *Ward v. Volpe*, 484 F.2d 1230 (9th Cir.1973) (Tuttle, J., sitting by designation).

An applicant for discharge as a conscientious objector must avoid committing military offenses during the pendency of his or her application. Failure to do so could result in an Other Than Honorable discharge in consequence of an adverse administrative hearing or a punitive discharge (bad conduct or dishonorable) following a court-martial instead of a conscientious objector discharge. *Cole v. Spear*, 747 F.2d 217 (4th Cir.1984).

C. DISMISSAL OF COMMISSIONED OFFICERS

Like an enlisted member of the armed services, a commissioned officer has no constitutional right to remain in the service and may be separated from the military through one of several methods. Some merely terminate the officer's status in a particular military component, while others sever all connection with the military. Administrative separations of officers are much less common than enlisted separations. Ordinarily, if an officer's misconduct is serious enough to warrant an administrative discharge, it will be grave enough to warrant court-martial.

Officers can be separated by termination in some instances, by operation of law because of expiration of appointment for a designated term, by acceptance of an incompatible office or status, by conviction of certain offenses against the United States, or by appointment of a successor to an office.

One avenue of officer separation is to be dropped from the rolls. This applies to officers in regular service or in the reserves. When a servicemember is dropped from the rolls, he or she forfeits his or her military pay. 37 U.S.C. § 803. The purpose of allowing an officer to be dropped from the rolls is to address the problem of officers who have been absent without leave (AWOL) or convicted of serious crimes. Initially, the President had the authority to drop from the rolls any commissioned officer who was AWOL for at least three months. That was subsequently extended to officers confined in prison following final conviction in civil court. The authority was further extended to "any armed force" officer AWOL for at least three months or finally sentenced to confinement in a federal or state penitentiary or correctional institution. It now includes an officer both sentenced by a court-martial to more than six months' confinement and who has served at least six months of that sentence. 10 U.S.C.A. § 1161(b)(2); 10 U.S.C.A. § 1167; *Clinton v. Goldsmith*, 526 U.S. 529, 532 nn.1 and 2 (1999) (discussing dropping from the rolls).

Separation can be accomplished by retirement, either voluntary or compulsory. Officers upon termination of active duty are placed on the retired list. There are provisions for early retirement when the needs of the service require it.

Dismissal is the punitive separation of a commissioned officer convicted of a criminal offense. By statute, a commissioned officer may be dismissed only (1) by sentence of a general court-martial, (2) in a commutation of a sentence of a general court-martial, and (3) in time of war, by order of the President. 10 U.S.C.A. § 1161(a).

Under Article 4, UCMJ, 10 U.S.C. § 804, any commissioned officer dismissed by order of the President may request a court-martial in order to clear his or her name. There is no right to such a trial. The officer must apply in writing, swearing under oath that he or she has been wrongly discharged. The

President must convene the court-martial, if at all, within six months of the request. However, if the President fails to do so, or if the court-martial acquits the officer or fails to order dismissal as part of its sentence, the officer gains only a limited victory: the secretary of the service substitutes an administrative discharge in lieu of dismissal. The officer does not regain his or her military position, because the President has the sole power to appoint officers of the Armed Forces. The officer's limited victory does, however, allow him to seek reappointment by the President with full restoration of rank and benefits. An officer discharged from any armed force by administrative action or by being dropped from the rolls by order of the President has no right to trial. Article 4(d), UCMJ, 10 U.S.C. § 804(d).

Officers may be discharged for non-selection for promotion unless there is provision for their selective retention and they are retained. Their periods of retention and eligibility are governed by military departmental regulations and vary among the services.

Probationary and non-probationary officers are treated differently when involuntarily separated. A probationary officer is one who has less than five years of active commissioned service. 10 U.S.C. § 630. A probationary officer who receives a non-stigmatizing discharge such as a general discharge under honorable conditions is entitled to due process. However, the process due is limited to written notice of the grounds for discharge and an opportunity to respond; the officer is not entitled to a full adversary hearing. *Holley v. United States*, 124 F.3d 1462 (Fed.Cir.1997). Non-probationary officers have the right to an administrative hearing prior to any involuntary administrative separation. Probationary officers may be involuntarily separated from the service without any formal administrative hearing so long as they receive honorable or general discharges.

An officer may not be eliminated under other than honorable conditions without the opportunity to have a hearing before a board of inquiry. Any such hearing must be fair and impartial, but there need not be a dismissal hearing if a post-dismissal hearing is available. The officer must be notified of all statements which will be considered by the board prior to the hearing and is entitled to counsel. The officer may question witnesses who appear before the board and may request additional witnesses of his own.

An officer may resign a commission. Normally, a resignation will not be accepted unless by the requested date of separation the officer has fulfilled all applicable service obligations. If the officer's resignation is accepted, an honorable or general discharge will be issued depending on the officer's military record.

An officer may submit a resignation for the good of the service when court-martial charges have been preferred against the officer with a view toward trial by general court-martial, when the officer is under suspended sentence of dismissal.

D. SERVICE-BASED ADMINISTRATIVE REVIEW OF DISCHARGES

1. DISCHARGE REVIEW BOARDS

Congress has created two administrative bodies to review military discharges. A Discharge Review Board (DRB) is established by the secretary of each department under the authority of 10 U.S.C. § 1553 and § 70.8 (procedures). It is comprised of members who are usually high ranking active duty officers. The DRB, either on its own motion, the servicemember's motion, or the motion of a surviving spouse or next of kin, may review a discharge or dismissal, provided the action is initiated within 15 years of the issuance of the discharge. 32 C.F.R. § 70.8.

Subject to the review of the Secretary, the DRB can change a discharge or dismissal to a higher one or issue a new discharge. The review is based on the servicemember's military record and any other relevant evidence presented by the petitioner. The petitioner may appear in person, with or without counsel, and offer testimony. Generally, the petitioner must establish that the discharge was improperly or inequitably issued under the standards of law and discipline of the military department, or that new standards have been promulgated which are retroactive in application.

A DRB can review a discharge or dismissal in order to assure that a former servicemember is not deprived of a veteran's benefit because of an improper or inequitable discharge. A DRB can only review administrative discharges. It cannot review a discharge or dismissal adjudged by a general court-martial. A DRB powers are limited. Although it can recharacterize a discharge, it cannot change a date of discharge, revoke a discharge, reinstate a former servicemember to military service or recall a person to active duty.

2. BOARD FOR CORRECTION OF MILITARY RECORDS

An application for discharge review may be made to the Board for Correction of Military Records (BCMR) either initially or following an unfavorable decision by the DRB. The BCMR, established under 10 U.S.C.A. § 1552, is composed of civilian employees of the Department of Defense. See e.g., 32 C.F.R. § 581.3 (Army Board for Correction of Military Records). Other BCMRs cover the Air Force, 32 C.F.R. § 865.1 et seq.; Coast Guard 49 C.F.R. § 1.57; and Navy and Marines, 32 C.F.R. § 723.1 et seq.

BCMRs have more extensive authority than do DRBs including the authority to correct any error in a military record, and, except where procured by fraud, the correction is final and conclusive. Generally, the request for correction must be made within three years of the discovery of the error or injustice in the records, although the board may waive this statute of limitations.

Unlike the DRB, the BCMR is not subject to mandatory procedures. There is no right to a hearing, although the board may in its discretion grant a hearing. If the board rules in favor of the applicant, the board will make its recommendation to the Secretary; if it is accepted, the original discharge is vacated and the new one is made retroactive. The applicant may then file a claim for repayment of any fine paid or benefits withheld as a result of the erroneous discharge.

Despite its apparent advantages, issues have arisen with BCMR review. See Eugene R. Fidell, "The Boards for Correction of Military and Naval Records: An Administrative Law Perspective," 65 Admin. L. Rev. 499 (2013).

3. JUDICIAL REVIEW

a. Jurisdiction

Judicial review is available from denials by a service boards for the correction of military records. Three avenues of relief are available to former members of the armed forces whose effort to upgrade their discharge status has been denied by a board for the correction of military records. First, after exhausting administrative remedies, they may seek declaratory and injunctive relief against the appropriate branch of service, challenging their discharge as a violation of the Constitution, statute, or service regulations under 28 U.S.C. § 1331. *Nichols v. Hughes*, 721 F.2d 657 (9th Cir.1983). Second, they may seek judicial review of the board's action under the APA. 5 U.S.C. § 702. A district court must set aside a board's action found to be "arbitrary, capricious, an abuse of discretion, or otherwise not in accordance with law." 5 U.S.C. § 706. *Dougherty v.*

United States Navy Bd. for Correction of Naval Records, 784 F.2d 499 (3d Cir.1986). Third, a challenge can be brought in the federal court of claims under the Tucker Act for lost pay as "liquidated or unliquidated damages in cases not sounding in tort." 28 U.S.C. § 1491. For a discussion of the scope of relief available in a claims action under the Tucker Act see *Holley v. United States*, 124 F.3d 1462, 1465–1467 (rehearing denied, 1997). There is a six-year statute of limitations for such challenges. The statute begins to run from the date of discharge, and is not tolled by the preceding action before a board for the correction of military records, which is considered an optional administrative remedy and is not a mandatory prerequisite to a challenge in the court of federal claims. *Hurick v. Lehman*, 782 F.2d 984 (Fed.Cir.1986); *Martinez v. United States*, 333 F.3d 1295 (Fed.Cir.2003).

b. Exhaustion of Administrative Remedies

Generally, the courts require exhaustion of administrative remedies as a prerequisite to judicial review. The rationale is that (1) the administrative review may provide an adequate remedy, thereby saving the courts and the parties a great deal of time and money, and (2) development of the record during administrative review facilitates judicial review. The exhaustion requirement is a matter of discretion and will not be imposed where an opportunity for administrative relief is lacking or where irreparable harm caused by the delays inherent in administrative review is likely. *Dowds v. Bush*, 792 F.Supp. 1299 (D.C.D.C.1992). A former servicemember's claim for negligent infliction of emotional distress under the Federal Tort Claims Act (FTCA) was denied for failure to exhaust administrative remedies. *Smalls v. United States*, 87 F.Supp.2d 1055 (2000).

The federal courts and the military judicial system must be considered as two separate and autonomous judicial systems for exhaustion requirement purposes. Thus, a federal court should not postpone adjudication of an independent civil lawsuit within its original jurisdiction which otherwise meets the exhaustion requirements. Under these circumstances, the court should stay its hand only if the relief sought—discharge—also would be available to the petitioner with reasonable promptness and certainty through the military courts. *Parisi v. Davidson*, 405 U.S. 34 (1972).

c. Preliminary Injunction

In certain situations where a servicemember wishes to stay in the service pending either administrative review or litigation, or does not wish to continue service pending decision on a claimed entitlement to discharge, the court may grant a preliminary injunction. For example, a person who has been ordered discharged but has not yet been physically separated cannot utilize administrative review. If a court issues a stay of discharge pending administrative review, the BCMR then may review the discharge before it takes effect. The criteria for a preliminary injunction are: (1) a likelihood that the servicemember will prevail on the merits of his claim;

(2) a likelihood of irreparable injury to him or her if the injunction is not granted; (3) no substantial harm to the other parties if the injunction is issued; and (4) no harm to the public interest. *Covington v. Schwartz*, 230 F.Supp. 249 (N.D.Cal.1964), order modified by *Schwartz v. Covington*, 341 F.2d 537 (9th Cir.1965) (affirming the stay of discharge pending resolution of his petition before the Board for Correction of Naval Records).

d. Scope of Judicial Review

Consistent with the general policy of non-interference by the judiciary in military affairs, the scope of judicial review of military discharges is limited. The grounds of review are generally confined to determining: (1) whether the Secretary acted within his or her authority; (2) whether the military adhered to its statutes and regulations; (3) whether procedural due process was afforded; (4) whether the grounds for the discharge are constitutional; (5) whether there has been an administrative review; and (6) whether the review decision was arbitrary, capricious or unsupported by substantial evidence. *Ferguson v. McHugh*, 64 F.Supp.3d 33 (D.C.D.C. 2014) (sustained denial of request to change discharge in lieu of court-martial to medical retirement).

In the ordinary course, a servicemember is discharged upon the expiration of his or her term of service (ETS) and receives a discharge certificate (DD214). The processing of discharge does not happen automatically and can be delayed under some circumstances. A servicemember who is unreasonably retained on active duty has remedies, however. For example, he or she may take one or more of the following steps: (1) submit a complaint under Article 138, UCMJ, 10 U.S.C. § 938; (2) apply to the Board for the Correction of Military Records under 10 U.S.C. § 1552; (3) seek extraordinary relief from the appropriate service Court of Military Review or the C.A.A.F., *Robinson v. Abbott*, 49 C.M.R. 8 (C.M.A.1974); or, (4) assuming the exhaustion requirement has been met, file a writ of habeas corpus. *Parisi v. Davidson*, 405 U.S. 34 (1972) ("the writ of habeas corpus has long been recognized as the appropriate remedy for servicemen who claim to be unlawfully retained in the armed forces.").

e. Improper Discharge

Remedies for "improper discharge" from the military are limited. "Because no one has a right to enlist or reenlist in the armed forces unless specially granted one, an enlisted [servicemember] who has been improperly discharged is entitled to recover pay and allowances only to the date on which [his or her] term of enlistment would otherwise have expired . . . ." *Dodson v. United States*, 988 F.2d 1199, 1208 (Fed Cir.1993). There is no authority for a reviewing court to order reinstatement. For other possible remedial claims, see *Mosqueda v. United States*, 2015 WL 4498814 (Ct. of Fed. Claims 2015).

CHAPTER 3

THE MILITARY CRIMINAL JUSTICE SYSTEM

The military criminal justice system has historically been one of the largest systems for processing crimes in the United States. During World War II, for example, approximately two million courts-martial were convened, of which 60,000 were general courts-martial. Since then, a dramatic reduction in the number of uniformed servicemembers and elimination of the draft greatly reduced the size of the military criminal justice system.

In many respects, this system parallels state and federal civilian systems for dealing with crimes. Like state and federal law, military law is hierarchical, both substantively and procedurally. Substantively, the United States Constitution is at the apex of the military law system, followed by federal statutory law, regulations promulgated by the President, the secretaries of defense and of the various armed services, and rules of various commanders. Court decisions interpret these laws. Procedurally, the military court system is organized much like civilian courts: trials are conducted by courts-martial with review by two tiers of appellate courts, the first comprised of appellate military judges, the second comprised of civilian appellate judges. Judgments of the highest military court are reviewable by the Supreme Court.

In other particulars however, military law and its processes diverge from civilian criminal law. As the Supreme Court noted in *Parker v. Levy*, 417 U.S. 733 (1974), "Just as military society has been a society apart from civilian society, so military law is a jurisprudence which exists separate and apart from the law which governs in our federal judicial establishment."

A. SOURCES OF LAW

There are two basic sources of this specialized jurisprudence: the Uniform Code of Military Justice (UCMJ), which is divided into "articles" and codified in the United States Code, 10 U.S.C. §§ 801–946a and the Manual for Courts-Martial (MCM). Congress originally enacted the UCMJ in 1950, extensively revised it in 1968, and has continued to update specific provisions over the years. In 2016, Congress made significant changes to the UCMJ through the Military Justice Act of 2016. The MCM, promulgated by executive order of the President, is revised frequently. The most recent edition is 2019. An online edition is available at https://jsc.defense.gov/Portals/99/Documents/2019%20MCM%20(Final)%20(20190108).pdf?ver=2019-01-11-115724-610 as well as in searchable databases such as Westlaw.

The MCM is comprised of five Parts: Part I, the Preamble; Part II, the Rules for Courts-Martial (RCM); Part III, the Military Rules of Evidence (MRE), which correspond in many respects to the Federal Rules of Criminal Procedure and the Federal Rules of Evidence; Part IV, the Punitive Articles;

Part V, Nonjudicial Punishment Procedure; and 28 appendices. Appendix 2 contains the Uniform Code of Military Justice (10 U.S.C. §§ 801 through 946a). Earlier editions of the MCM were published periodically, e.g., 1917, 1921, 1928, 1949, 1951, 1969, and 1984. Amendments, called "Changes," were identified by the date of the edition of the MCM to which they applied. Beginning in 1995 new editions of the MCM incorporated amendments and are identified as the Manual for Courts-Martial, United States (19__ or 20__ edition). Unless otherwise noted, the edition of the MCM cited in this Nutshell is the 2019 edition.

The Department of Defense (DoD) in conjunction with the Department of Homeland Security has published supplementary materials to accompany various parts of the MCM. There is a Discussion accompanying the Preamble, R.C.M., and Punitive Articles and an Analysis along with the appendices already referred to. As noted in the Preamble, these supplementary materials are not legally binding, but are advisory only. *United States v. Lazauskas*, 62 J.J. 39 (C.A.A.F. 2005) ("MCM drafters' analysis" persuasive but not binding) (Gierke, Chief Judge concurring in the result); *United States v. Foley*, 37 M.J. 225, 828 (C.A.A.F. 1993) ("[T]he discussions that appear throughout the Manual are neither legislative nor Executive and do not purport to have the force of law.)

Another resource cited frequently is Army Regulation 27–10, Military Justice (AR 27–10). Military law incorporates regulations of the individual services, and all services publish regulations. These primary sources of law govern the disposition of cases arising in the military. Numerous resources on military law and military justice are available on Westlaw. These include publications of the Department of Defense, the Department of the Army, the Joint Chiefs of Staff, the Air Force, Navy and Marine Corps, the Military Judges' Benchbook, the Manual for Courts-Martial including subparts such as the Military Rules of Evidence, Rules for Courts-Martial, and the Uniform Code of Military Justice. It also includes published decisions by the military appellate courts in West's Military Justice Reporter and unpublished decisions as well, and numerous secondary sources of particular relevance such as the Army Lawyer, Air Force Law Review, Naval Law Review, and Military Law Review.

B. THE MILITARY COURT SYSTEM

Courts-martial are the military's courts of original jurisdiction. The UCMJ provides for appellate review within the military.

There are two levels of appellate courts within the military. There is a Court of Criminal Appeals (C.C.A.) for each service branch, previously known as the Court of Military Review until 1994. Each service Judge Advocate General appoints at least three military appellate judges to the court including a chief judge. The court may sit in one or more panels of three judges. Duly credentialed civilian attorneys may also be appointed to the C.C.A.s. Article 66, UCMJ, 10 U.S.C. § 866. The highest level appellate court within the military system is the United States Court of Appeals for the Armed Forces (C.A.A.F.), formerly designated as the Court of Military Appeals (C.M.A.) from 1951 to 1994. The five judges on the C.A.A.F. are civilians, appointed by the President and confirmed by the Senate for staggered 15-year terms. The C.A.A.F. reviews all cases in which the death penalty has been imposed or certified for review by the Judge Advocate General and where the accused petitions "on good cause shown." The C.A.A.F.'s authority is limited "to matters of law" connected to "the findings and sentence as approved by the convening authority and as affirmed or set aside . . . by the service C.C.A.s." Article 67(c), 10 U.S.C. § 867(c). The C.A.A.F. has jurisdiction to issue extraordinary writs under the All Writs Act, 28 U.S.C. § 1651(a) although the All Writs Act does not itself confer jurisdiction, *Clinton v. Goldsmith*, 526 U.S. 529 (1999) (injunction against dropping court-martialed servicemember from the Air Force rolls neither "in aid of its jurisdiction" nor "necessary or appropriate" as required by the All Writs Act) and *United States v. Denedo*, 556 U.S. 904 (2009) (Article I military courts have jurisdiction under the All Writs Act and Article 66(a), 10 U.S.C. § 866(a) to issue and review writs of corum nobis issued to challenge validity of a conviction). Decisions of the C.A.A.F. are reviewable by the U.S. Supreme Court by writ of certiorari. 28 U.S.C. § 1259.

On the following page is a chart that provides an overview of the Military Criminal Justice Court System.

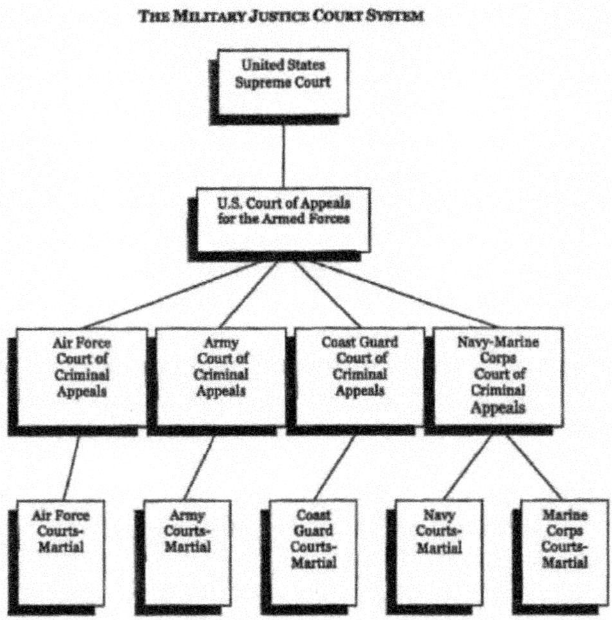

From Lisa M. Schenck, *Modern Military Justice: Cases and Materials* (3d ed. West Academic 2019), page 7. Copyright West Academic 2019, reprinted with permission.

C. OVERVIEW OF THE COURT-MARTIAL PROCESS

The military criminal justice system involves procedures for dealing with an accused that differ somewhat from civilian criminal law procedures. The criminal process, which extends from the time of initial restrictions upon the freedom of the accused through trial by court-martial, is the heart of the military criminal justice system. The remainder of this chapter considers the processes within the military for dealing with alleged offenses up to the point of operation of courts-martial. The next chapter explores operation of the courts-martial system in more detail. Before reading the remainder of this chapter and the next, however, you might find it useful to peruse the following chart, which lays out the steps of the court-martial process from the offense through the final level of appeal.

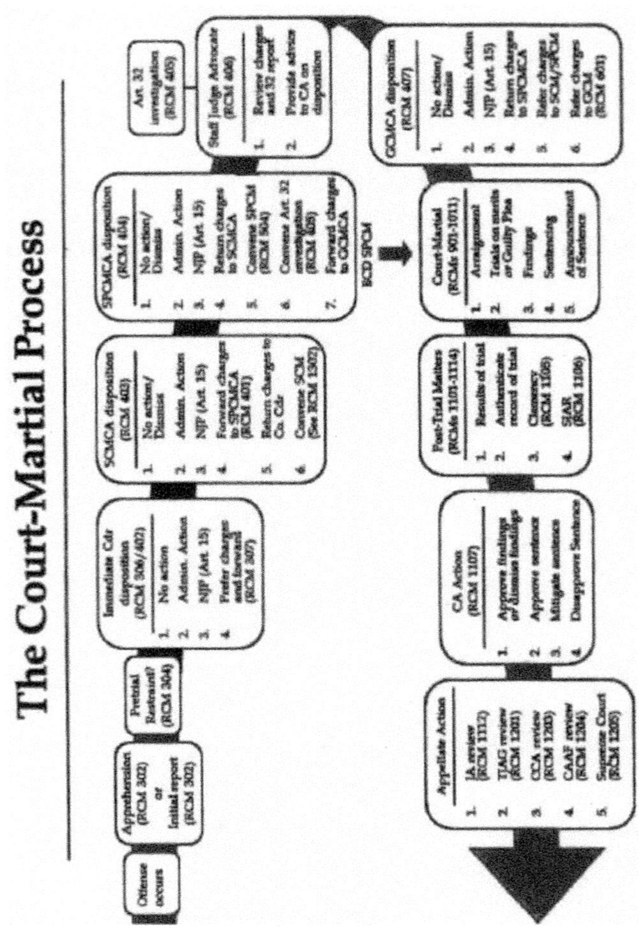

From Lisa M. Schenck, *Modern Military Justice: Cases and Materials* (3d ed. West Academic 2019), page 12. Copyright West Academic 2019, reprinted with permission.

D. INITIAL STEPS FOR DEALING WITH AN ALLEGED OFFENSE

1. ALLEGED OFFENSE

Any person can report a military offense. The report is to be forwarded to an accused's immediate commander as soon as practicable. RCM 301. An accused may be subjected to three types of pre-trial restrictions that are unique to military law. In increasing order of severity, they are arrest (sometimes called restriction), apprehension, and confinement.

2. PRETRIAL RESTRAINT

Arrest is a term of art in military law: it is simply an order, oral or written, issued by a competent authority that directs the accused to remain within certain specified limits. As Article 9(a), UCMJ, 10 U.S.C. § 809(a) says, "Arrest is the restraint of a person by an order, not imposed as a punishment for an offense, directing him to remain within certain specified limits." Arrest is either a moral or physical restraint. RCM 304(a)(3). Restriction in lieu of arrest allows for the continued performance of military duties. Restraint is allowed only upon probable cause and personal knowledge or inquiry of the arresting person. Article 9(d), UCMJ, 10 U.S.C. § 809(d); RCM 304(c). Enlisted members may be arrested by any commissioned officer or by delegates of commanding officers. Article 9(b), UCMJ, 10 U.S.C. § 809(d); RCM 304(b)(2) and (3). Officers may only be arrested by the commanding officer with authority over the accused.

Article 9(c), UCMJ, 10 U.S.C. § 809(c); RCM 304(b)(1).

Apprehension is the military counterpart to civilian arrest, for it involves "the taking of a person into custody." *United States v. Harris*, 29 M.J. 169 (C.M.A. 1989) (resisting apprehension); Art. 7(a), UCMJ, 10 U.S.C. § 807(A) ("Apprehension is the taking of a person into custody."); RCM 302(a)(1). Apprehension involves restraint on the accused's personal freedom until he or she is handed over to the proper authorities; thus, it goes beyond arrest by imposing physical restraint. Apprehension may be made by military police, when in the exercise of their duties, provided there is probable cause to believe an offense has been committed by the accused. Article 7(b), UCMJ, 10 U.S.C. § 807(b); RCM 302(b) and (c). In addition, officers may apprehend persons to control quarrels and disorders. Article 7(c), UCMJ, 10 U.S.C. § 807(C); RCM 302(c). Though it is generally inappropriate for noncommissioned officers to apprehend warrant officers or commissioned officers, this may be done if so directed by a commissioned officer to prevent disgrace to the service or escape of a serious offender. RCM 302(b)(2).

Confinement is the most severe pre-trial restriction on the accused's freedom in that it involves incarceration or placement of a guard over the accused. Article 9(a), UCMJ, 10 U.S.C. § 809(a); RCM 305(a). The confining authority, whose power to confine is defined in the same manner as the power to arrest discussed above, gives written notice to the correction officer of the name and grade of the accused along with the offense allegedly committed. Within 24 hours, the correction officer transmits this information and the name of the person ordering confinement to the commanding officer of the accused. Article 11(b), UCMJ, 10 U.S.C. § 811(b); RCM 305(h)(1). An accused arrested without a warrant must be given a prompt judicial determination (within 48 hours) of probable cause for his arrest, *County of Riverside v. McLaughlin*, 500 U.S. 44 (1991). In *United States v. Rexroat*, 38 M.J. 292 (C.M.A.1993), the Court of Military Appeals held that *McLaughlin*'s 48-hour limit applied to the military, and further that a commander's probable-cause determination under RCM 305(d) or probable-cause review under RCM 305(h) within 48 hours would satisfy *McLaughlin* if the commander qualified as a neutral and detached magistrate.

Article 12 addresses the issue of restraint of persons by the military. Confinement of servicemembers are prohibited with foreign nationals in instances where the foreign nationals are not members of the United States Armed Forces and are detained under the law of war under UCMJ art. 12 (2016), 10 U.S.C. § 812 (Supp. IV 2016).

Confinement is subject to Article 13, UCMJ, 10 U.S.C. § 813, a prophylactic rule against pretrial punishment which provides that "arrest or confinement [cannot] be any more rigorous than the circumstances require to insure his presence. . . ." *United States v. Gilchrist*, 61 M.J. 785 (A.Ct. Crim.App.2005) discusses the process for detecting when pretrial confinement conditions constitute unlawful pretrial punishment. Although the accused's pretrial confinement conditions—being temporarily housed and shackled to a cot in a barracks utility room—did not constitute unlawful pretrial confinement, they were "more rigorous" than required under Article 13, 10 U.S.C. § 813 meriting an award of confinement credit as provided for in RCM 305(k). Similarly, the pretrial marshaling of soldiers accused of drug offenses at a parade ground formation where they were called out of formation, had their unit crests removed, were shown military discourtesy when their salutes were not returned, and who were later billeted separately from their unit and given the name, "Peyote Platoon," was held to violate Article 13. *United States v. Cruz*, 25 M.J. 326 (C.M.A.1987).

A servicemember in confinement may request a military counsel, which must be provided within 72 hours. RCM 305(f). Military magistrates may be appointed to review pretrial confinement. AR 27-10, para. 8-3(a). In addition, with the 2016 amendments, military judges and military magistrates may be allowed to review matters pretrial without waiting for formal referral of charges, pre-referral warns or orders regarding electronic communications, and prereferral matters referred by an appellate court. UCMJ art. 30a(a)(1)(A)–(C) (2016), 10 U.S.C. § 830a(a)(1)(A)–(C) (Supp. IV 2016).

E. COMMANDER'S DISPOSITIONAL ALTERNATIVES

1. NO ACTION

A commander may choose to take no action or to dispose of an accused's alleged infraction by resorting to nonpunitive measures or nonjudicial punishment. The 2016 amendments required the military to establish factors to be considered in disposing of charges, to the end that justice and discipline will be furthered. UCMJ art. 33 (2016), 10 U.S.C. § 833 (Supp. IV 2016). While reported civilian crimes are dealt with exclusively through judicial processes (excluding those diverted through an exercise of discretion), military offenses may be formally dealt with through nonpunitive measures, nonjudicial punishment, and an array of judicial alternatives. This would appear strange if the conduct regulated by the UCMJ were equivalent to the conduct regulated by civilian criminal codes. However, as the Supreme Court noted in *Parker v. Levy*, 417 U.S. 733 (1974), "[The UCMJ] regulates a far broader range of the conduct of military personnel than a typical state criminal code regulates of the conduct of civilians; but at the same time the enforcement of that code in the area of minor offenses is often by sanctions which are more akin to administrative or civil sanctions than to civilian criminal ones." In short, the broad range of offenses and the specialized nature of military society govern the alternatives used to treat offenses defined by the UCMJ.

2. ADMINISTRATIVE CORRECTION MEASURES

To further the efficiency of his command or unit, a commander, i.e., a commanding officer or officer in charge, is authorized to use nonpunitive disciplinary measures when faced with minor UCMJ violations or other deficiencies. MCM, pt. V, ¶ 1.d. Such sanctions are appropriate vehicles for maintaining good order and discipline in the great majority of situations. Nonpunitive sanctions are appropriate for such deficiencies as neglect, laziness, inattention to duties, and difficulty in adjusting to military life. Nonpunitive disciplinary measures are for correction, not for punishment. Therefore, the sanction should be logically related to the offense charged and not excessive.

A commander can withhold privileges as a nonpunitive corrective measure. This could include pass privileges (the ability to leave the post), post exchange (px) or commissary privileges, on-post check cashing privileges, on-post driving privileges, or housing privileges. Appropriate regulations control the level of command appropriate to restrict or revoke privileges. Again, the restriction should correspond to the privilege abused.

Other nonpunitive sanctions are admonitions (oral or written warnings); counseling; corrective training; reductions in rank, either for misconduct or inefficiency; revocation of a security clearance; a bar to reenlistment; reclassification of one's military occupational specialty (MOS); and administrative elimination.

Some nonpunitive sanctions parallel punitive sanctions, but are not considered the same thing. Since nonpunitive sanctions are not imposed for the purpose of punishment, they are therefore not considered punitive. Servicemembers aggrieved by nonpunitive correction may seek redress through a complaint procedure, Article 138, UCMJ, 10 U.S.C. § 938, or complain to the appropriate Inspector General's office. Note that under Article 132, UCMJ, 10 U.S.C. § 932, it is illegal to misuse authority in an attempt to retaliate against a person for making a complaint or reporting a crime. Disciplining someone for making a complaint or reporting a crime is also illegal. Communicating threats is a violation of Article 115, UCMJ, 10 U.S.C. § 915.

The Military Justice Act of 2016 added new offenses. Under Article 93a, UCMJ, 10 U.S.C. § 893a (Supp. IV 2016) prohibits certain activities with a military recruit or trainee by person in position of special trust. Under Article 121a, UCMJ, 10 U.S.C. § 921a (Supp. IV 2016)), the fraudulent use of credit cards, debit cards, and other access devices is prohibited. Additionally, Article 123, UCMJ, 10 U.S.C. § 932 (2012) (amended 2016) added the new offense of using government computers for illegal purposes.

Administrative corrective measures are not always appropriate responses to UCMJ violations that come to a commanding officer's attention. Service regulations may prohibit or limit resort to these measures. Also, such measures are only appropriate for certain "minor offenses." MCM, pt. V, ¶ 1(g)(1). It is clearly inappropriate, for example, to deal with serious crimes such as rape, sexual assault, or related crimes of aggravated sexual contact or abusive sexual contact, or obviously murder, mutiny, treason, or the like through administrative corrective measures. Nonpunitive sanctions may, however, be imposed for minor criminal conduct such as shoplifting, intoxication and fighting, uttering bad checks ("check kiting"), and driving under the influence.

3. NONJUDICIAL PUNISHMENT

a. Article 15

Article 15, UCMJ, 10 U.S.C. § 815, grants authority to commanders to impose "disciplinary punishments for minor offenses without the intervention of a court-martial." Such authority is frequently exercised. Article 15 nonjudicial punishment (called "Captain's Mast" in the Navy and Coast Guard, "Office Hours" in the Marines, and simply an "Art. 15" in the Army and Air Force) is authorized on the ground that discipline and morale will be adversely affected if commanders are unable to impose punishment immediately for minor offenses. Nonjudicial punishment provides an expeditious resolution of minor infractions. It can be desirable from the perspective of an accused because it carries no stigma of criminal conviction since it is not judicially imposed. Moreover, requiring minor offenses to proceed through the court-martial system would be expensive and time-consuming. *Middendorf v. Henry*, 425 U.S. 25 at 45 ("[P]resence of counsel will turn a brief, informal hearing which may be quickly convened and rapidly concluded into an attenuated proceeding which consumes the resources of the military. . . .").

Under the authority of the Manual for Courts-Martial, MCM, pt. V, ¶ 4 and regulations issued by the armed services, e.g., AR 27-10 Military Justice, paras. 3-16 & 3-17, two types of Article 15 procedures are authorized, formal and summarized, as well as two levels of Article 15s, company grade and field grade, a reference to the rank of the commander imposing the Article 15 (O-3 and below are company grade officers, O-4 through O-6 are field grade officers, and officers above that level are general officers). Based on the evidence against an accused servicemember, the commander chooses the appropriate level of Article 15, i.e., company grade or field grade, depending on the level of punishment appropriate. A commander can refer an Article 15 up the chain of command to a commander more senior in rank in order to open the possibility of a more serious sanction if the imposing commander believes the accused is guilty of the offense charged.

A "minor offense" is one in which the maximum punishment, if tried by court-martial, would be no more than a bad-conduct discharge or confinement for one year. MCM, pt. V, ¶ 1(e). The theory of Article 15 is that the punishment imposed is primarily for corrective, not retributive, purposes.

Jurisdiction to impose nonjudicial punishment pursuant to Article 15 is dependent upon the existence of court-martial jurisdiction. The general rule for Article 15 jurisdiction is that any member of a military command is subject to Article 15 proceedings anywhere in the world, so long as the offender is attached or assigned to the command of the officer who imposes the punishment. Service regulations sometimes limit this broad jurisdictional rule, and the various services have by agreement prohibited the imposition of nonjudicial punishment upon members of other branches.

The infraction for which an Article 15 is imposed must be a crime under the UCMJ. While no specific standard of proof applies to any phase of Art. 15 proceedings, a commander considering initiating such an action must recognize that the servicemember is, in most cases, entitled to refuse the Article 15 process and demand trial by court-martial.

A table summarizing the maximum punishment imposable for enlisted members and commissioned officers is provided in AR 27-10, para. 3-19, Table 3-1. Consult the most recent edition.

The range of Article 15 punishments against officers is narrower than those against enlisted personnel, and the punishments commanding officers of lower grades may impose are more restricted than those which may be meted out by field grade, flag rank, or general officers. MCM, pt. V, ¶ 5.b. Any commander, officer in charge, or principal assistant may impose Art. 15 punishment if authorized by regulations of the Secretary concerned. MCM, pt. V, ¶ 2.

The following are examples of nonjudicial punishments authorized by the MCM:

(1) Extra duties, which entail additional work responsibilities above and beyond one's normal duties and may include fatigue duties. They cannot include anything "which constitutes a known safety or health hazard . . . or which constitutes cruel or unusual punishment or which is not sanctioned by customs of the service concerned." MCM, pt. V, ¶ 5.c.(6). Nor can they be abusive or demeaning. For example, they could not include an activity "required to be performed in a ridiculous or unnecessarily degrading manner; for example, an order to clean a barracks floor with a toothbrush." AR 27-10, para. 3-19b(5)(c). Extra duties as a punishment are imposable only on enlisted members and their extent is limited by the rank of the commander. Thus, officers below the rank of major or lieutenant commander may impose up to 14 days; those of higher rank, up to 45 days. MCM, pt. V, ¶ 5.b.(A)(ii) & (B)(ii).

(2) Restriction is described in the MCM as "the least severe form of deprivation of liberty." MCM, pt. V, ¶ 5.c.(2). It limits the places a servicemember is allowed to go and may include a requirement to report at a specific time and place to assure compliance. Enlisted members may be restricted for up to 14 days by officers below the rank of major or lieutenant commander and up to 30 days by those of higher rank. MCM, pt. V, ¶ 5.b.(A)(ii) & (B)(ii).

(3) Reduction in grade is a demotion, which results in a reduction in salary and potential change in duty assignment. It is thus more severe than extra duties or restriction. MCM, pt. V, ¶ 5.c.(7).

(4) Forfeiture of pay is a common nonjudicial punishment. It is prospective in nature applying only to pay after the date punishment is imposed. MCM, pt. V, ¶ 5.c.(8). Officers below the grade of major or lieutenant commander may order forfeiture of up to 7 days' pay for enlisted members; higher ranking officers may order forfeiture of up to one-half of one month's pay for enlisted members. Authority to order forfeiture of an officer's pay is limited to general officers and officers exercising general court-martial convening authority and the amount may not exceed one-half of 1 month's pay per month for 2 months. MCM, pt. V, ¶ 5.b.(1)(B)(ii), (2)(B)(iii).

(5) Correctional custody involves the physical restraint of a servicemember as punishment and may be combined with other punishments such as extra duties. Correctional custody may take place in a confinement facility, but is distinct from imprisonment imposed as a consequence of judicial punishment. MCM, pt. V, ¶ 5.c.(4). As with other nonjudicial punishments, officers below the rank of major or lieutenant commander may impose more limited punishment of up to 7 days, while more senior

officers may impose up to 30 days of custody. MCM, pt. V, ¶ 5.b.(2)(A)(ii) & (B)(ii).

(6) Arrest in quarters is a nonjudicial punishment imposable only on officers that "is enforced by a moral obligation rather than by physical means," and is limited to no more than 30 days. MCM, pt. V, ¶ 5.c.(3) and ¶ 5.b.(1)(B)(i).

Procedures for Article 15s vary in some respects from one branch of the service to another. For example, "Captain's mast used in the Navy and Coast Guard and office hours in the Marine Corps afford an accused a more extensive hearing in connection with the imposition of nonjudicial punishment than is customarily available in the Army and Air Force." *Dobzynski v. Green*, 16 M.J. 84 (C.M.A. 1983), 87n.4 (citations omitted) (Everett, C.J., dissenting). Perhaps most striking is the difference among the service branches regarding the burden of proof applied in administering Article 15s. The Army, for example, requires the commander to find the servicemember guilty "beyond reasonable doubt." AR 27-10, para. 3-16(d)(4), 3-18(*l*). The Air Force encourages commanders to apply a less demanding version of the "beyond reasonable doubt" standard. U.S. Dep't of Air Force, Instr. 51-202, Nonjudicial Punishment para. 3-4). The Navy, Marine Corps, and Coast Guard apply a "preponderance of the evidence" standard. U.S. Dep't of Navy, JAGINST 5800.7F, Manual of the Judge Advocate General (JAGMAN) sec. 0110(b); U.S. Coast Guard, Commandant Instr. Manual 5810.1E, Nonjudicial Punishment art. 1.D.1.f. See David A. Schlueter, *Reforming Military*

Justice: An Analysis of the Military Justice Act of 2016, 49 St. Mary's L.J. 1, 28 and n.158.

A commander acting under Article 15 must notify the accused of the offense of which he or she has been accused, of the commander's intention to proceed under Article 15 with respect to the accusation, and of the maximum punishment that could be imposed as a consequence of the Article 15. The notification must also inform the servicemember of the following rights:

1. The right to remain silent. The servicemember need not say anything. Anything said may be used against him or her.

2. The right to consult with counsel, time off to consult with counsel, and information about where to receive assistance from the JAG office. There is no right to representation by a military attorney, however.

3. The right to refuse the Article 15 and to demand trial by court-martial unless attached to or embarked on a vessel. (Note that there is a naval exception to the right to refuse nonjudicial punishment. Article 15(a), 10 U.S.C. § 815(a).) An accused is not entitled to know what level court-martial the commander will recommend (i.e., summary, special or general) if the Article 15 is refused. Note that refusing nonjudicial punishment carries the risk of imposition of

a more severe punishment at court-martial. E.g., *United States v. Bass*, 11 M.J. 545 (A.C.M.R. 1981) (accused offered an Article 15 demanded trial by court-martial sentenced to 8 years confinement and dishonorable discharge, punishment far in excess of that imposable in an Article 15).

4. The right personally to present one's case in the commander's presence, unless the commander is unavailable or under extraordinary circumstances.

5. The right to call witnesses, if reasonably available.

6. The right to present evidence in defense, extenuation, and mitigation.

7. The right to request the presence of a spokesperson who may but need not be a civilian lawyer. Both the spokesperson and the accused may speak. Particularly if the accused is young or inexperienced, requesting a spokesperson is a good idea. Even innocent persons have trouble confronting accusations by themselves and unaided.

8. The right to an open hearing. Hearings are normally open, but the accused may request that his or hers be closed.

9. The right to examine available evidence.

10. The right to appeal.

Notification of these rights is required in a formal Article 15. See DA Form 2627, AR 27-10, Figure 3-2, p. 11 and para. 3-18.

Use of a summarized Article 15 is permitted when the appropriate punishment imposed will not exceed 14 days extra duties, 14 days restriction and an oral reprimand or admonition. MCM, pt. V, ¶ 4c.(1)(B) and (G); AR 27-10, para. 3-16. The rights of the accused in a summarized Article 15 are fewer in view of the limitations on the deprivations he or she can suffer upon a finding of guilt. The goal is an expeditious resolution of the matter with spare but adequate procedural safeguards. Because the type of Article 15, summarized or formal, is limited by the maximum punishment that can be imposed, a more senior commander would generally not elect to use a summarized procedure.

Under Army practice, a summarized Article 15 is handled utilizing DA Form 2627-1. A summarized Article 15 may be imposed by any commander, but only upon enlisted personnel. Because of the limitation on the punishment that can be imposed, the procedure is appropriate only for very minor offenses. The notice required is normally 24 hours and the commander may delegate the task of notification. There is no right to consult with a military lawyer. There is no open hearing and no entitlement to a spokesperson. The accused has a right to call witnesses and to be heard. There is a right to appeal to the next higher commander within 5 days. See AR 27-10, Form 2627-1, Figure 3-1, p. 9.

One of the more important aspects of the Article 15 process is the disposition of the record of the Article 15. Adverse information such as an Article 15 can affect military career advancement possibilities. AR 27-10, para. 3-6. Under Army practice, for those in the rank of E-4 and below, records of a formal Article 15 are kept in the unit and destroyed upon transfer from the unit or after 2 years. For those in the rank of E-5 and above, at the commander's election, the original record of the Article 15 (DA Form 2627) can be kept in the unit records and destroyed upon transfer from the unit or after 2 years or it can be made a part of the soldier's Official Military Personnel File (OMPF). The OMPF has two portions, a restricted fiche and a performance fiche. The restricted fiche is not normally reviewed by career managers and selection boards, which make assignment, school and promotion selections. The performance fiche is used for career decisions. Placement in the restricted fiche has less adverse impact on one found guilty in an Article 15. A non-commissioned officer (NCO) can have only one Article 15 in a restricted fiche. Any subsequent Article 15s would go into the performance fiche.

An accused who does not demand a court-martial receives merely an informal hearing before the commanding officer. His or her rights to a public hearing, to an advocate (in some branches, a lawyer), to present matters in defense, extenuation or mitigation, to present and directly examine his witnesses, and to appeal any punishment to a superior commander are reiterated at this hearing. However, the option to consult counsel prior to accepting an Article 15 punishment does not create either a Sixth Amendment right to counsel or constitute the "appointment" of counsel, since nonjudicial punishment by definition is not a criminal proceeding. *United States v. Kendig*, 36 M.J. 291 (C.M.A. 1993). Subsequent to reiteration of the rights of the accused, evidence is presented to the commander, who decides the question of guilt and, if necessary, imposes punishment.

Appeals of two sorts may follow imposition of Article 15 punishment. First, the commander or a superior to the commander may suspend, set aside, remit or mitigate any punishment. MCM pt. V. ¶ 6. Second, one punished under Article 15 who thinks the punishment is unjust or disproportionate to the offense may thereafter appeal within five days of imposition of punishment. This appeal, addressed to the commander's superior, must be in writing and must state the reasons for regarding the punishment as unjust or disproportionate. The appellate authority cannot increase the punishment imposed. MCM, pt. V, ¶ 7. Before acting on such an appeal, the superior must refer the case to a Judge Advocate or to a lawyer in the Department of Homeland Security for review and advice. There is no further appeal beyond the commander's superior and no judicial review exists of Article 15 determinations.

Submission to Article 15 punishment does not always bar subsequent court-martial for the same misconduct. In the usual case, where nonjudicial punishment is imposed for a minor offense and the court-martial concerns the same minor offense, the "former punishment" bars trial of the same offense. RCM 907(b)(2)(D)(iv); *United States v. Fretwell*, 29 C.M.R. 193 (C.M.A. 1960) (distinguishing "former punishment" from double jeopardy under the Fifth Amendment). However, if the original offense was "serious" rather than "minor," a court-martial could be initiated notwithstanding Article 15 punishment because there was no prior judicial proceeding. Article 15(f), UCMJ, 10 U.S.C. § 815(f); MCM, pt. V, ¶ 1(e); *U.S. v. Gammons*, 51 M.J. 169 (C.A.A.F. 1999). The accused is entitled to introduce evidence of punishment imposed by nonjudicial punishment at sentencing. Double jeopardy attaches at the introduction of evidence. *United States v. Easton*, 71 M.J. 168, 176 (C.A.A.F. 2012). Article 44 also provides that "no person may, without his consent, be tried a second time for the same offense." Article 44(a), UCMJ, 10 U.S.C. § 844(a). Jeopardy attaches at a different point depending on the court. In a court-martial by a military judge alone, jeopardy attaches after the introduction of evidence and the case is ended or dismissed for lack of evidence or witnesses. Article 44(c)(1), UCMJ, 10 U.S.C. § 844(c)(1). In a court-martial with members, jeopardy will attach when the members take their oath under Article 42, after challenges have been completed, and the members are impaneled. Article 44(c)(2), UCMJ, 10 U.S.C. § 844(c)(2).

Servicemembers, with the exception of those "attached to or embarked in a vessel" as noted above, have a right to decline nonjudicial punishment. Article 15(a), UCMJ, 10 U.S.C. § 815(a). As a consequence, a servicemember within the exception can receive nonjudicial punishment for an offense even if he or she has been acquitted by a court-martial of that offense. In such an instance neither former punishment nor former jeopardy will serve as a bar. *Jones v. Commander, Naval Air Force, U.S. Atlantic Fleet*, 18 M.J. 198 (C.M.A. 1984) (denying extraordinary relief for a "legal error" which occurred when nonjudicial punishment was imposed on a conspiracy charge which, if the charge and specification had been referred to court-martial, the government would have been collaterally estopped from prosecuting). Note also that the UCMJ makes no provision for the judicial review of the legality of punishments imposed under Article 15, 10 U.S.C. § 815. *Dobzynski v. Green*, 16 M.J. 84 (C.M.A. 1983).

The lack of procedural protections for the accused and the absence of judicial review over Article 15 punishment have raised questions as to whether Article 15 violates due process requirements of the Fifth Amendment to the United States Constitution. Some argue that most constitutional problems with Article 15 procedure are overcome because the offender may demand trial by court-martial before punishment is imposed. Others disagree, arguing that the right to demand court-martial does not save Article 15 from due process infirmities because an accused demanding a court-martial runs the risk of incurring more severe punishment as noted earlier. In addition, the accused may suffer not only the Article 15 punishment itself, but also serious administrative consequences resulting from that punishment. For example, in *Bennett v. Tarquin*, 466 F.Supp 257 (D.Haw.1979), sailors found "guilty" of use and possession of marijuana were punished under Article 15 with restrictions, reductions in rank, and fines. In addition, this punishment led to automatic removal under Navy regulations from nuclear submarine duty, which cost the sailors their monthly submarine pay and their eligibility for a reenlistment bonus.

There is as yet no definitive resolution to the due process question. However, *Middendorf v. Henry*, 425 U.S. 25 (1976), provides some guidance. In *Middendorf*, the Court held that there was no constitutional right to counsel at a summary court-martial, in part because the accused could have demanded a special or general court-martial at which he would have been entitled to counsel. Congress clarified this in the 2016 amendments by that a summary court-martial conviction is not a criminal conviction. Due process is implicated, however, in the decision whether or not to accept nonjudicial punishment in lieu of a court-martial. *Fairchild v. Lehman*, 814 F.2d 1555, 1559 (Fed.Cir.1987). There is no constitutional right to representation by counsel at a summary court-martial or by extension a nonjudicial punishment hearing under Article 15, 10 U.S.C. § 815. There is, however, a right to consult with counsel prior to electing between nonjudicial punishment and trial by court-martial:

> The consequences of a decision to accept either an Article 15 or a summary court-martial disciplinary action under Article 20 involve due process considerations. Believing as we do that only a legally trained person can supply the

> requisite quantum of information necessary for an informed decision, we believe it mandatory that the individual to be disciplined must be told of his right to confer with an independent counsel before he opts for disposition of the question at either of the above levels.

United States v. Booker, 5 M.J. 238, 243 (C.M.A. 1977) (disapproved in a limited aspect not pertinent to the point by *U.S. v. Booker*, 5 M.J. 246 (C.M.A. 1978)).

The right to consult with counsel in this circumstance has been described as "a practical means of implementing the right to decline nonjudicial punishment which Congress granted accused persons. . . ." *United States v. Mack*, 9 M.J. 300, 320 (C.M.A. 1980) (Everett, C.J.). Acceptance of nonjudicial punishment in lieu of court-martial must be based on an intelligent waiver informed by counsel. In *Fairchild*, for example, the accused was erroneously told he "could not receive an adverse discharge" if he accepted an Article 15. However, his nonjudicial punishment included an other-than-honorable discharge. The *Fairchild* court concluded that an accused cannot "execute an intelligent waiver of his statutory right to trial when he has been misinformed of the consequences of electing nonjudicial punishment by counsel provided by the military." 814 F.2d 1555, 1560.

b. Article 139

The topic of claims for loss involving the military is beyond the scope of this Nutshell. An article by

Colonel R. Peter Masterton, "Claims Office Management," 2011-SEP *Army Lawyer* 48, provides a helpful overview of the various federal claims statutes implicated and in some instances their interrelationship with Article 139. A provision in Article 139, UCMJ, 10 U.S.C. § 939, which allows claims against servicemembers who willfully damage or destroy or wrongfully take the property of others, is treated here because liability under Article 139 affects servicemember conduct that would constitute a violation of one or more punitive articles of the UCMJ.

Procedure under Article 139 is governed by regulation, e.g., AR 27-20 Claims, paras. 9-1 through 9-10. Any individual, civilian or military, or any entity, public or private, with an interest in property may file a claim. Article 139 covers claims for tangible or intangible personal property and real property that is willfully damaged, wrongfully taken or withheld through larceny, forgery, embezzlement, fraud, misappropriation or similar offense but not breach of a fiduciary or contractual duty. Claims for loss from negligent acts, for personal injury or death, or from acts or omissions of military personnel acting within the scope of their employment are not included nor are claims for theft of services, even if such theft constitutes a violation.

The claim is processed by the local military claims office, but it is investigated by the offender's unit. With some exceptions, claims are forwarded to the special court-martial convening authority (SPCMCA) with jurisdiction over the servicemember or members who appoints an investigating officer. If the claim is meritorious and the servicemember fails to make restitution, the investigating officer submits findings and recommendations to the SPCMCA who in turn submits the claim for legal review. Once a claim is verified, the offender's SPCMCA may approve assessments up to $5000, a General Court-Martial Convening Authority (GCMCA) may approve assessments up to $10,000, and service branch claims authorities such as the United States Army Claims Service can approve assessments above these amounts.

A claim is either approved or disapproved by the approval authority. The approval authority is not bound by the findings or recommendations of the investigating officer. An offender may request reconsideration unless the approval authority determines that the delay entailed will result in substantial injustice. If the claim is found warranted, the claim will be paid directly from the pay of the servicemember responsible for the loss or damage (or allocated among servicemembers of a unit found responsible for the loss). A request for reconsideration is the only path available for review open either to a claimant or the servicemember offender; there is no right of appeal provided for Article 139 claims.

c. Administrative Separation

Administration separation is another option available to a commander to address servicemember misconduct. It can be sought as an alternative to or in addition to nonjudicial punishment or trial by court-martial. Administrative discharge is, as its name implies, an administrative rather than a judicial procedure.

An enlistment in the armed services or issuance of an officer's commission creates a service obligation that is terminated by a discharge. 10 U.S.C. § 1168(a). Most servicemembers will receive an "honorable discharge," one of the five types of discharges. Occasionally, however, the government will wish to administratively separate a servicemember prior to the completion of a term of service or service obligation. In such an instance, two other characterizations of discharge in addition to an honorable discharge are possible: a "general discharge under honorable conditions" and an "other than honorable discharge" (formerly called an "undesirable discharge"). These forms of discharge are distinguished from punitive discharges—a "dishonorable discharge" and "bad-conduct" discharge—that can only be imposed by a court-martial. Congress has authorized each branch of service to issue and characterize administrative discharges pursuant to regulations promulgated by the Secretary of each military department and limited the discharge of regular enlisted servicemembers to those pursuant to such regulations, to general or special court-martial or as otherwise provided by law. See 10 U.S.C. § 1169, discussed at greater length in Chapter 2.

d. Forward Charges to Superior Commander

Charges are initiated when information is brought to the attention of military authorities concerning an offense suspected to have been committed by a person subject to the UCMJ. Charges are written and may be made only by one subject to the Code. Article 30(a), UCMJ, 10 U.S.C. § 830(a). Charges are usually made directly to the commanding officer authorized to impose Art. 15 punishment; if not, by commanders at higher echelons. RCM 307.

The commander, after receiving a charge, has broad discretion concerning its disposition. First, the commander may order a preliminary inquiry. This is an informal investigation of the charges, and involves little more than interviewing witnesses, collecting, marking, and securing physical evidence, and developing information sufficient to dispose of the charges intelligently. Second, the commander may dismiss trivial charges or charges unsupported by the evidence. Third, he or she may impose Art. 15 nonjudicial punishment, unless his superiors have directed otherwise. Fourth, the commander may prefer charges by swearing to the truth of the charge. Finally, the commander may forward charges too serious for Art. 15 disposition or administrative elimination to the officer exercising summary court-martial jurisdiction over the accused. When this is done, the accused must be informed of the charges and the summary court-martial officer should be provided with a summary of the evidence and the commander's recommendation for disposition. The summary court-martial commander may make any of the dispositions open to the Art. 15 commander; additionally, he or she may refer the charge for trial by summary court-martial, or forward the charge with a recommendation for special, or general court-martial, depending on the severity of the offense.

e. Convene a Court-Martial

When the commander is also the accuser or the accused, he or she is precluded from serving as the convening authority. *United States v. Tittel*, 53 M.J. 313 (C.A.A.F. 2000) (violation of a "routine, administrative type of order" would not violate a personal interest of a superior officer so to make him or her an "accuser") (Effron, J. concurring in part and in the result). An accuser is disqualified from convening a general or special court-martial. RCM 503(c)(1). The case of *McKinney v. Jarvis*, 46 M.J. 870 (Army Ct.Crim.App. 1997) canvasses the disqualifications of an accuser. Note, however, that an accuser can convene a summary court-martial. RCM 1302(b).

F. COMMAND INFLUENCE OVER MILITARY JUSTICE

1. COMMAND INFLUENCE AND DUE PROCESS

The Constitutional basis for a separate judicial system for military-related crimes is Art. I, § 8, which gives Congress the authority "to make Rules for the Government and Regulation of the land and naval Forces." The rationale for Congress' enactment of the

UCMJ pursuant to this authorization is that the military has special needs for order, discipline, and efficiency that make resort to civilian courts for trial of military-related matters inappropriate. Aspects of the military justice system, however, related to the pervasive role of a commander in the system created the possibility and perception of unfairness to an accused. Unlawful command influence can be either actual or apparent. *United States v. Allen*, 33 M.J. 209, 212 (C.M.A. 1991)("We will not presume that a military judge has been influenced simply by the proximity of events which give the appearance of command influence in the absence of a connection to the result of a particular trial.")

The case of *Curry v. Secretary of the Army*, 595 F.2d 873 (D.C.Cir.1979) explored the many bases for perceptions of unfairness in the military justice system but ultimately concluded "that the system of military justice, as presently constructed, is the sole means capable of satisfying the unique needs of the armed services" and further finding it to be "constitutionally permissible." Robert E. Curry, a soldier, was convicted by court-martial of two homicides and sentenced to hard labor, reduction to the lowest enlisted grade and a dishonorable discharge. Having exhausted his routes of review in the military appellate courts and separately in the Board for Correction of Military Records, Curry collaterally attacked his conviction on constitutional grounds alleging denial of his Fifth Amendment right to due process. Curry's due process challenges were based primarily on the role of the commander in the military justice system in general, and on his trial in particular. The commander plays a central role in the military justice process that could suggest prejudice to an accused. For example, as Judge Tamm notes

> The convening authority, who is generally the commanding officer, . . . participates in various levels of the court-martial process. He determines whether charges should be referred to the court-martial [Article 34, UCMJ, 10 U.S.C. § 834], selects the members of the court-martial [Article 25(d)(2), UCMJ, 10 U.S.C. § 825(D)(2)] and details the military judge [Article 26(a), UCMJ, 10 U.S.C. § 826(a)], and details the prosecuting and defense counsel [Article 27(a), UCMJ, 10 U.S.C. § 827(a)]. The convening authority also reviews the court-martial record [Article 60, UCMJ, 10 U.S.C. § 860]. He can approve the findings and sentence [Article 64, UCMJ, 10 U.S.C. § 864], return for reconsideration and appropriate action specifications dismissed without a finding of not guilty [Article 62(a), UCMJ, 10 U.S.C. § 862(a)], or disapprove findings of guilty and the sentence imposed [Article 64, UCMJ, 10 U.S.C. § 864].
>
> Curry further argued that [T]he convening authority having initiated the prosecution, has an interest in the result of the case and is therefore constitutionally incapable of insuring that the accused receives a fair and impartial trial . . . is likely to appoint individuals to serve as counsel and court members who generally are more inclined to find an accused guilty than would a random sampling of military personnel

> . . . [particularly given that they] are dependent upon him for their promotions, their efficiency ratings, their assignments of duty, and their furloughs.

595 F.2d 873, 875–6.

Judge Tamm concludes that although "the system established in the UCMJ would be inconsistent with due process if instituted in the context of a civilian criminal trial," it strikes a "constitutionally permissible" balance in the context of the demands of military justice that satisfies the requirements of the Fifth Amendment's due process clause.

The competing interests of command and its perquisites on the one hand and the interests of justice present special challenges. One area of special concern is that of unlawful command influence. A commander's influence can corrupt the fairness of due process to the point where it becomes unlawful. Another issue concerns the power of a commander serving as a convening authority to review the decisions of courts-martial. For perspective on lawful command influence, see Colonel James F. Garrett, et al., "Lawful Command Emphasis: Talk Offense, Not Offender; Talk Process, Not Results," Army Lawyer, Aug. 2014, 4.

2. UNLAWFUL COMMAND INFLUENCE

A commander's influence is pervasive in military life and is at the heart of the concept of command. Concomitantly, however, as Chief Judge Gierke has emphasized: "[B]ecause the inherent power and influence of command are necessary and omnipresent facets of military life, everyone involved in both unit command and in military justice must exercise constant vigilance to protect against command influence becoming unlawful." *United States v. Harvey*, 64 M.J. 13, 17–18 (C.M.A., 2006). The evil of unlawful command influence, which corrupts the integrity of the military justice system and erodes confidence in it, both by servicemembers and the public at large, are well recognized. An important role for military judges and lawyers is policing unlawful command influence. The keys, as the *Curry* opinion in the previous section explains, are the safeguards provided by Congress to unlawful expressions of "command influence," or the improper interference by a superior in command with the independent judgment of persons responsible for passing judgment on an accused. As Chief Judge Everett pointed out in *United States v. Thomas*, 22 M.J. 388, 393 (C.A.A.F.1986), *cert. denied*, 479 U.S. 1085 (1987): "Command influence is the mortal enemy of military justice."

Numerous safeguards against unlawful command influence are provided by law. For example, convening authorities and commanders are expressly prohibited from censuring, reprimanding, or admonishing a court-martial or other military tribunal or court member, military judge or counsel, and all persons subject to the UCMJ are prohibited from improperly attempting to influence or coerce the processes of military justice with respect to findings or sentencing or a commander's actions in convening, approving or reviewing a court-martial. Article 37,

UCMJ, 10 U.S.C. § 837 and RCM 104(a)(1) and (2). In addition, as the Curry court notes, "before ordering a trial, the convening authority must consult [the] staff judge advocate concerning the sufficiency of the charges and the availability of the evidence," and the staff judge advocate must conclude "there is probable cause to believe that the accused committed the offense charged" [Article 34, UCMJ, 10 U.S.C. § 834]. Note particularly in this regard that "a prime motivation for establishing a civilian Court of Military Appeals was to erect a further bulwark against impermissible command influence." *United States v. Thomas*, 22 M.J. 388, 393 (C.A.A.F. 1986). The 2016 amendments now provide that in a special court martial, the accused shall be provided a military lawyer. However, in a general court-martial, non-lawyer/non-JAGs may serve if they are determined to be competent by the Judge Advocate General. Generally, procedural safeguards against command influence guarantee an accused to representation by a military lawyer both at trial [Article 27(a) and (b), UCMJ, 10 U.S.C. § 827 (a) and (b)] and on appeal [Article 70, UCMJ, 10 U.S.C. § 870] or civilian counsel at the accused's expense. And, as the Curry court concludes, "Finally, and most importantly, Article 37 of the UCMJ broadly prohibits the improper use of command influence [and] Article 98 makes a violation of Article 37 a military offense" [10 U.S.C. §§ 837 and 898]. 2016 amendments now provides that in a special court martial, the accused shall be provided a military lawyer. However, in a general court-martial, non-lawyer/non-JAGs may serve if they are determined to be competent by the Judge Advocate General.

The "last sentinel" to protect a court-martial from unlawful command influence is the military judge. *United States v. Rivers*, 49 M.J. 434 at 443 (C.A.A.F. 1998). Procedurally, the defense bears the burden of raising the issue of unlawful command influence. "[T]he threshold for this is low. The test is 'some evidence' of 'facts which, if true, constitute unlawful command influence, and that the alleged unlawful command influence has a logical connection to the court-martial in terms of its potential to cause unfairness in the proceedings.'" *United States v. Harvey*, 64 M.J. 13, 18 (C.A.A.F. 2006).

Once an issue of unlawful command influence is raised, initially the burden of persuasion is on the prosecution to show beyond a reasonable doubt that that there was no unlawful command influence or that the unlawful command influence did not affect the findings or the sentence imposed. *United States v. Biagase*, 50 M.J. 143 (1999). Biagase sets forth the analytical framework for deciding issues involving unlawful command influence: "[O]nce the issue of unlawful command influence is raised, the Government must prove beyond a reasonable doubt: (1) that the predicate facts do not exist; or (2) that the facts do not constitute unlawful command influence; or (3) that the unlawful command influence will not prejudice the proceedings or did not affect the findings and sentence."

Unlawful command influence is proscribed by Article 37, and violations of Art. 37 can be punished under Art. 98 (noncompliance with procedural rules). As noted, responsibility for avoiding unlawful command influence is the responsibility of all involved in military justice, with significant responsibility falling on the military judge, the "last sentinel." When unlawful command influence is raised on appeal, a *DuBay* hearing may be warranted. In *U.S. v. DuBay*, 37 C.M.R. 411 (C.M.A. 1967) the court discussed the hearing warranted when the defendant raises an issue of command influence as follows:

> Whenever an issue of command influence is raised [on appeal,] the record will be remanded to a convening authority other than the one who appointed the court-martial concerned and one who is at a higher echelon of command. That convening authority will refer the record to a general court-martial for another trial. Upon convening the court, the law officer will order an out-of-court hearing, in which he will hear the respective contentions of the parties on the question, permit the presentation of witnesses and evidence in support thereof, and enter findings of fact and conclusions of law based thereon. If he determines the proceedings by which the accused was originally tried were infected with command control, he will set aside the findings or sentence, or both, as the case may require, and proceed with the necessary rehearing. If he determines that command control did not in fact exist, he will return the record to the convening authority, which will review the findings and take action thereon, in

accordance with Articles 61 and 64 of the Uniform Code of Military Justice. The convening authority will forward the record, together with his action thereon, to the Judge Advocate General for review by a board of review, in accordance with Article 66 of the Code. From the board's decision, the accused may appeal to the Court of Military Appeals on petition, or the decision may be certified to the Court by the Judge Advocate General, under the provisions of Article 67 of the Code.

In *United States v. Baker*, 65 M.J. 691 (A.Ct. Crim.App.2007), a case dealing with effective assistance of counsel and the responsibilities of counsel confronting the problem of potential client perjury, the court ordered repeated *DuBay* hearings seeking factual clarification. The *DuBay* methodology is clear in that case. On *DuBay* hearings see Major Grace M. W. Gallagher, "Don't Panic! Rehearings and *DuBay*'s Are Not the End of the World," Army Lawyer, June 2009, 1.

Neither the UCMJ nor the MCM provide procedures for collateral, post-conviction attacks on guilty verdicts. Instead, a military defendant must rely on other procedures to protect his or her rights. The *DuBay* evidentiary hearing is one such device. Remand to a Court of Criminal Appeals for consideration of affidavits submitted by the parties is another. *United States v. Henry*, 42 M.J. 231, 238 (1995). See also *United States v. Murphy*, 50 M.J. 4 (C.A.A.F.1998) (considering trial record and affidavits).

The role of a reviewing court is to determine de novo beyond a reasonable doubt whether the military judge was successful in purging any residual taint from the unlawful command influence. Some cases, for example, where the unlawful command influence rendered the entire trial process fundamentally unfair, dismissal with prejudice can be an appropriate remedy, e.g., *United States v. Gore*, 60 M.J. 178 (C.A.A.F. 2004) (military judge's dismissal of charges against an accused was an appropriate remedy for illegal command influence whereby a convening authority acted to prevent witnesses from testifying on behalf of, and cooperating with accused; military judge did not abuse his discretion).

Policing improper command influence can, however, be an awkward and difficult task. See *United States. v. Dugan*, 58 M.J. 253 (C.A.A.F. 2003) in which the commander held a Commander's Call at which he discussed the problem of drugs in a way and at a time that may have influenced the members of the court as they were considering what sentence to recommend. The Dugan court recalled a similar case, *United States v. Brice*, 19 M.J. 170 (C.M.A. 1985) in which a new trial was ordered because "members of an ongoing court-martial attended a Commandant's meeting where drug problems in the military were discussed." The Court struggles to delineate a line between proper leadership by a commander and unlawful activity:

> We do not in any way wish to be viewed as condemning the contents of the Commandant's remarks since the drug problem in the military

> demands command attention; nor do we feel that such remarks necessarily constitute illegal command influence. Instead, we base our decision on the confluence of subject and timing, particularly as they affect the minds—however subtly or imperceptibly—of the triers of fact. . . .

In many instances, this uncertain boundary may be an invitation to commanders to venture on their own to tiptoe through a minefield. Several cases offer cautionary guidance in this regard, e.g., *United States v. Treakle*, 18 M.J. 646 (A.C.M.R. 1984) (first of 3d Armored Division cases dealing with unit-wide unlawful command influence); *United States v. Cruz*, 20 M.J. (A.C.M.R. 1985) (1st Armored Division case), rev'd in part on other grounds, 25 M.J. 326 (C.M.A. 1987). For a recent treatment of unlawful command influence see Lieutenant Colonel Mark L. Johnson, "Unlawful Command Influence—Still with Us; Perspectives of the Chair in the Continuing Struggle Against the 'Mortal Enemy' of Military Justice," Army Lawyer, Jun. 2008, 104, 112. ("The prevention of unlawful command influence is a primary reason we exist as a JAG Corps today, and is certainly the main reason Congress created the Court of Appeals for the Armed Forces (CAAF)."

The effects of unlawful command influence can be felt both individually by an accused as well as institutionally by the impact on the public's perception of the fairness of the military justice system. In *United States v. Boyce*, 76 M.J. 242 (C.A.A.F. 2017), the U.S. Court of Appeals for the Armed Forces discussed these two types of unlawful command influence: "*actual* unlawful command influence and *the appearance of* unlawful command influence." (76 M.J. 242 at 247) As discussed above, the *actual* form of unlawful command influence occurs "when there is an improper manipulation of the criminal justice process which negatively affects the fair handling and/or disposition of a case." (76 M.J. 242 at 247) Additionally, however, the *appearance* of unlawful command influence can occur when "the influence of command [places] an 'intolerable strain on public perception of the military justice system.'" (76 M.J. 242 at 248, citations omitted).

Appellate review of unlawful command influence claims is de novo. (76 M.J. 242 at 249) The standard applied to weigh the public perception focuses "upon the perception of fairness in the military justice system as viewed through the eyes of a reasonable member of the public." (at 248) Assessing such an appearance requires no showing of prejudice to the accused. However, once an accused demonstrates by some factual evidence a presence of unlawful command that is logically connected to his or her case (76 M.J. 242 at 249 n.6), the burden shifts to the government to rebut the allegation. (76 M.J. 242 at 249). The "government bears the burden of proving beyond reasonable doubt that either the predicate facts proffered by the appellant do not exist, or the facts as presented do not constitute unlawful command influence." (76 M.J. 242 at 249)

One form of unlawful command influence is "court stacking," which is defined as "assigning members to—or excluding members from—a court-martial panel in order to 'achieve a particular result as to findings or sentence.'" *United States v. Riesbeck*, 77 M.J. 154, 165 (C.A.A.F. 2018). Although courts-martial are not subject to the Sixth Amendment's jury trial requirements, there are legal restraints designed to insure a military accused of a fair trial. *United States v. Kirkland*, 53 M.J. 22, 24 (C.A.A.F. 2000) (a military defendant has a right to trial by a "fair and impartial" panel). The role of the commanding officer who refers the charges against an accused convenes the court-martial that will try the accused also selects and details the court members who will sit in judgment as noted earlier. UCMJ Articles 22 and 23, 10 U.S.C. §§ 822, 823; R.C.M. 501–503.

Member selection is governed by the criteria in UCMJ. Article 25, 10 U.S.C. § 825 and R.C.M. 501–503. Specifically, R.C.M. 502(a)(1) directs the selection of persons who "in the opinion of the convening authority are best qualified for the duty by reason of their age, education, training, experience, length of service, and judicial temperament." Selection of members based on other criteria are mostly forbidden, e.g., selection on the basis of sex. *United States v. Riesbeck*, 77 M.J. 154 (C.A.A.F.2018) (unlawful court stacking based on gender where the victim is female and the defendant is male; "the seven-member panel was composed of five women, four of whom were victim advocates—persons trained to provide support and counseling to victims of rape and sexual assault—and two men;" and the panel selection occurred "in an atmosphere of external pressure to achieve specific results in sexual assault cases"). However, a convening authority is allowed to depart from the prescribed selection criteria "in one limited circumstance: when seeking in good faith to make the panel more representative of the accused's race or gender." *United States v. Riesbeck*, 77 M.J. 154, 163 (C.A.A.F.) citing *United States v. Crawford*, 15 C.M.A. 31, 41, 35 C.M.R. 3, 31 (1964) (intentional selection of a black servicemember on a panel judging a black accused held permissible because if it is discrimination, "it is discrimination in favor of, not against, an accused."); *United States v. Smith*, 27 M.J. 242 (C.M.A. 1988) ("a convening authority may take gender into account in selecting court members if he [or she] is seeking in good faith to assure that the court-martial panel is representative of the military population.") In addition, the 2016 amendments left the commander in charge of the selection process. Article 25 was also amended in 2016 which provided that a convening authority must appoint at least the number of members required for each court—twelve members in a capital case, eight in a non-capital general court-martial, and four in a special court-martial. UCMJ art. 25(e)(3) (2016), 10 U.S.C. § 825(e)(3) (Supp. IV 2016).

The *appearance* of unlawful command influence is not dependent on whether the senior influencer in a position of authority over the principals involved in a court-martial even knows of the existence of the accused's case. "No showing of knowledge or intent on the part of government actors is required in order for an appellant to successfully demonstrate that an appearance of unlawful command influence arose in a specific case." (*United States v. Boyce*, 76 M.J. 242 at 251) The evil against which the *Boyce* case is directed is a stain on the reputation of the military justice system arising from a public perception of unfairness. The goal, as claimed by the *Boyce* court's majority, is to conform military justice to the standard set by the U.S. Supreme Court: "Federal courts have an independent interest in ensuring that . . . legal proceedings appear fair to all who observe them." *Wheat v. United States*, 486 U.S. 153, 160 (1988).

The facts of *Boyce* illuminate how perceptual problems arise. The accused was tried and convicted by a general court-martial on specifications of sexual assault. His trial was overshadowed by the question whether the actions of the General Court-Martial Convening Authority (GCMCA) in his case, Lieutenant General Craig A. Franklin, a three-star general, as well as those of the Secretary of the Air Force and of the Chief of Staff of the Air Force resulted in the appearance of unlawful command influence. Early in 2013, in an unrelated case, Lieutenant General Franklin, the Commander of the Third Air Force, used his clemency authority to set aside the findings and sentence of a lieutenant colonel convicted of aggravated sexual assault. Franklin's clemency action caused backlash from both Congress and the media over his lax treatment of sexual assault cases. Then on September 3, 2013, Franklin again dismissed sexual assault allegations in another case. On December 20, 2013, Deborah Lee James was appointed as Secretary of the Air Force. On December 27, 2013, Franklin was notified by the

Chief of Staff of the Air Force "that the new Secretary had 'lost confidence' in him and that he had two options: voluntarily retire from the Air Force at the lower grade of major general, a two-star, or wait for the Secretary to remove him from his command in the immediate future." It took Franklin only three hours to decide on retirement at a lower grade. On the very same day that Franklin was pushed into giving up his command, he received the referral package on Boyce, who was accused of one specification of rape on several occasions and two specifications of assault consummated by battery. As GCMCA, on January 6, 2014, Franklin referred Boyce's sexual assault case for general court-martial. The question before the C.A.A.F. was whether there was an appearance of unlawful command influence as a result of the publicity and evidence of possible pressure regarding referral of Boyce's sexual assault charges. That court concluded that there was an appearance of unlawful command influence warranting reversal of the findings and sentence in Boyce's case and return of the case to the Judge Advocate General of the Air Force and a rehearing.

Note that the authority of a GCMCA not to refer charges for court-martial in cases where a sex-related offence has been alleged by a victim has been affected by changes in the law subsequent to the *Boyce* case. Pub. L. 113-66 as amended Pub. L. 113-291 note under 10 U.S.C. § 834 ("The Secretary of Defense shall require the Secretaries of the military departments to provide for review of decisions not to refer charges for trial by court-martial in cases where a sex-related offense has been alleged by a victim of the alleged offense.")

The *Boyce* approach was applied by the U.S. Army Court of Criminal Appeals in *United States v. Bergdahl*, 79 M.J. 512 (A.C.C.A.2019), another case attended by substantial pre- and post-trial publicity. On 30 June 2009, then-SGT Beaudry Robert "Bowe" Bergdahl walked away from his observation post in Afghanistan and was captured by the Taliban and held captive for five years. Significant military resources were devoted to searching for him, and some individuals were seriously injured in that search. In May 2014, he was exchanged for five Taliban detainees, who had been held at the U.S. detention facility in Guantanamo Bay, Cuba. Bergdahl was returned to military duty and assigned eventually to the Fifth Army Headquarters. Court-martial jurisdiction was retained at the four-star level and the facts and circumstances of his absenting himself from his post investigated. At the conclusion of his Article 32 investigation in October 2015, the preliminary hearing officer recommended that his case be referred to a "straight special" court-martial not empowered to adjudge a discharge and that jail time would be inappropriate. The AR 15-6 investigation concluded that Bergdahl had left his post with intent to shirk important service, but also carried a recommendation of no jail time. Charges were preferred and he was tried by a military judge sitting as a general court-martial. After a lengthy trial that lasted almost two years, Bergdahl entered pleas of guilty desertion to shirk hazardous military duty (Article 85, UCMJ, 10 U.S.C. § 855) and misbehavior before the enemy (Article 99, UCMJ, 10 U.S.C. § 899). Bergdahl was sentenced to a dishonorable discharge, reduction to the grade of E-1, and forfeiture of $1,000 per month pay for ten months.

The decision to exchange the five Taliban detainees for Bergdahl was subject to public criticism. During the investigative phase of proceedings, the late Senator John McCain called the exchange "ill-founded" and a "mistake [that put] the lives of American [servicemembers] at risk" concluding that if no punishment is imposed on Bergdahl, "we're going to have a hearing in the Senate Armed Services Committee." In addition, while Donald Trump was campaigning for the presidency, he had this to say:

> It's like Sergeant Bergdahl, right? So we trade a dirty rotten traitor, where five or maybe even six people were killed when he deserted and we knew that they were killed and we knew he was a traitor. [And,] Don't forget, with Bergdahl we lost at least five people and I watched the parents on television, I've seen the parents, I've met one of the parents, who're devastated, ruined, destroyed. And they were killed going out to try and bring him back, and they lost five people, probably six, by the way. But at least five people.

(79 M.J. 512 at 518). In sharp contrast to Trump's fantastical account, the court dryly notes in a footnote that, although some of the servicemembers searching for Bergdahl did suffer serious injuries,

"The government produced no evidence that anyone was ever killed searching for appellant [Bergdahl]." (at 518n.3)

Bergdahl entered his guilty pleas to desertion and misbehavior before the enemy on 16 October 2017. On that same day, now-President Trump, the Commander-in-Chief, stated at a press conference:

> Well, I can't comment on Bowe Bergdahl because he's—as you know, they're—I guess he's doing something today, as we know. And he's also—they're setting up sentencing, so I'm not going to comment on him. But I think people have heard my comments in the past.

(79 M.J. 512 at 519)

The court concluded that although comments made by the President of the United States and Commander in Chief on day accused's sentence was announced constituted some evidence of unlawful command influence, they did not create the appearance of unlawful command influence. Furthermore, the statements of Senator McCain and of candidate Trump were statements of private citizens that cannot be considered either actual unlawful command influence or its appearance. *Bergdahl* shows how the *Boyce* factors for assessing the appearance of unlawful command influence can be applied.

Three recent cases have changed the application of the concept of unlawful command influence in the military justice system. *United States v. Boyce*, 76 M.J. 242, 248 (C.A.A.F. 2017) abolished the requirement to find prejudice to an accused in cases involving the appearance of unlawful command influence. *United States v. Barry*, 78 M.J. 70 (C.A.A.F. 2018) eliminated the requirement of intent to unlawfully influence in cases alleging actual unlawful command influence. It also weakened the requirement of action under the "mantle of command authority" as a prerequisite for finding unlawful command influence. Until the decision in *Barry*, an individual accused of committing unlawful command influence must have acted with the "mantle of command authority." Under this concept, unlawful command influence was a product of the use of rank or status to improperly influence the military justice process. *United States v. Stombaugh,* 40 M.J. 208, 211 (C.M.A. 1994) (abuse of "the mantle of official command authority"). After *Barry*, even though the influencer is not a commander, convening authority or SJA, a violation can occur. The *Barry* court found that the language of Article 37(a), UCMJ, 10 U.S.C. § 837(a), "does not require one to operate with the imprimatur of command" although it "may be a relevant factor" in determining Article 37 violations. 78 M.J. 70, 76 and 77n.3. The third case that enters into the mix of unlawful command influence is *United States v. Bergdahl*, 79 M.J. 512 (A.Ct.Crim. App.2019). That court's analysis of the status of Senator John McCain in relation to the claim of unlawful command influence reflects the breadth of that doctrine's reach after the *Barry* court's contraction of the requirement of a "mantle of command authority." The *Bergdahl* court concluded that contrary to the conclusion of the military judge who tried Bergdahl, McCain was properly subject to the UCMJ as a retired member of a regular component of the armed forces, Article 2, UCMJ, 10 U.S.C. § 802 (a)(B)(4), and thus subject to the strictures of Article 37(a), UCMJ, 10 U.S.C. § 873(a), which proscribes coercing or influencing "the action of court-martial or any other military tribunal of any member thereof, in reaching the findings or sentence in any case . . . ." Although the court concluded that there was no logical connection between McCain's statement and any potential unfairness in Bergdahl's court-martial, the sheer breadth of exposure in a post-*Barry* world revealed in *Bergdahl* identifies a problem. There have been calls for Congress to address some of these issues. See Colonel John Loran Kiel, " 'So You're Telling Me There's a Chance': Why Congress Should Seize the Opportunity to Reform Article 37 (UCI) of the UCMJ," 227 Mil. L. Rev. 1 (2019).

CHAPTER 4

COURTS-MARTIAL

A. TYPES OF COURTS-MARTIAL

There are three types of court-martial procedures: the summary court-martial, the special court-martial, and the general court-martial. Article 16(a), UCMJ, 10 U.S.C. § 816(a), RCM 201(f).

1. SUMMARY COURT-MARTIAL

There are four alternatives available to address misconduct apart from a criminal trial by court-martial. In addition to corrective measures, nonjudicial punishment under Article 15, and administrative separation, the UCMJ authorizes Summary Court-Martial. Article 20, UCMJ, 10 U.S.C. § 820. By law, a trial by summary court-martial is not a criminal trial: "A summary court-martial is a non-criminal forum. A finding of guilty at a summary court-martial does not constitute a criminal conviction." Article 20(b), UCMJ, 10 U.S.C. § 820(b). RCM 1301(b). It is therefore the most limited of the three different types of courts-martial. Only enlisted personnel accused of non-capital offenses may be tried by summary court-martial. An accused must consent to trial by a summary court-martial. Punishments are limited as well. A summary court-martial cannot discharge a servicemember nor impose a sentence of confinement for more than one month, hard-labor without confinement for more than 45 days, restriction to specified limits for more than two months, or forfeiture of more than two-thirds of one month's pay. Article 20, UCMJ, 10 U.S.C. § 820.

The summary court-martial is primarily designed to try criminal cases promptly, although it should "thoroughly and impartially inquire into both sides of the matter." RCM 1301(b). The accused in a summary court-martial has a right to consult with military counsel prior to trial, but does not have a right to be represented by a military defense counsel at the hearing. An accused may be represented by a civilian attorney, so long as there is no expense to the government.

A summary court-martial consists of one impartial commissioned officer who serves as judge. Art. 16(d), UCMJ, 10 U.S.C. § 816(d). Summary courts-martial follow an inquisitorial rather than the adversarial model of criminal justice. The judge, who acts in some respects like an examining magistrate in countries following the Napoleonic Code, has an active, not a passive, role; the role or even presence of adversarial counsel is minimized; and the protections accorded the accused in civilian trials or special and general courts-martial are substantially diminished. As the Supreme Court has expressed it, "the presiding officer acts as judge, fact finder, prosecutor, and defense counsel." *Middendorf v. Henry,* 425 U.S. 25 (1976). Indeed, the summary court-martial is so similar to an Art. 15 proceeding that expanded use of nonjudicial punishment has greatly decreased the use of summary courts-martial.

An accused member of an armed service can refuse trial by a summary court-martial. If the accused consents to summary court-martial, the charges are read and the accused is asked to plead to each charge. If the individual pleads guilty, the court must explain the meaning and effect of the plea. The court will not accept a guilty plea unless the accused understands the meaning and effect of the plea and it believes the accused is guilty. RCM 910 and RCM 1304(b)(2)(D). If the court doubts that the accused's guilty pleas are made voluntarily and with understanding, or if at any time during trial any matter arises that is inconsistent with a guilty plea and that cannot be resolved, the court shall enter not guilty pleas regarding the specific charges affected. RCM 1304(b)(2)(D)(iii).

During the hearing on the merits, witnesses testify under oath, the accused may cross-examine witnesses, and the trial is public. As in civilian courts, the accused may testify or remain silent. When the evidence is in, the court makes its findings and announces them. Before a sentence is imposed, however, the accused may submit further evidence, make an unsworn statement, and correct the record as to previous convictions and personal data—all with an eye towards convincing the court of extenuating and mitigating factors. The court then imposes sentence, which cannot exceed the maximum punishments set forth above.

The denial of appointed counsel in summary courts-martial was an issue when the Supreme Court considered *Middendorf*, supra. The Court held that "even were the Sixth Amendment to be held applicable to court-martial proceedings, the summary court-martial provided for in these cases was not a criminal prosecution within the meaning of that Amendment." And likewise found no Fifth Amendment violation, again, because the proceeding is not criminal in nature. Justice Marshall dissented in *Middendorf* arguing that the summary court-martial carries a risk of "the stigma of a criminal conviction" that is not present in nonjudicial punishment. And further that "any timesaving [resulting from the use of a summary court-martial is overcome by] the presiding officer's being something less than an adequate substitute of independent defense counsel." It may be time to reconsider the summary court-martial.

2. SPECIAL COURTS-MARTIAL

Special courts-martial can sit with a judge alone or with a judge and members. Art. 16, UCMJ, 10 U.S.C. § 816. A special court-martial consisting of a military judge and members is impaneled as provided in Art. 25(e)(3), UCMJ, 10 U.S.C. 825(E)(3) Art. 29(d)(2)(c).

The maximum punishments imposable by a special court-martial include a bad conduct discharge, confinement for not more than one year, hard labor without confinement for not more than three months, and forfeiture of pay not exceeding two-thirds pay per month or forfeiture of pay for no more than one year. If the special court-martial consists of a military judge alone, neither a bad-conduct discharge, nor confinement for more than six months, nor forfeiture of pay for more than six months may be adjudged. Article 19(b), UCMJ, 10 U.S.C. § 819(b). The special court-martial is typically used to try matters that in a civilian criminal context would be considered misdemeanors. A member of the armed services cannot refuse trial by a special court-martial.

The jurisdiction of the special court-martial extends over all persons subject to the UCMJ; but it is seldom used for officers. For limits on sentencing see RCM 1003.

A special court-martial usually is presided over by a military judge. the trial is generally recorded verbatim, and counsel must be appointed to ensure that the accused effectively exercises his right to call witnesses, to cross-examine adverse witnesses, and to remain silent. RCM 501(a)(1)(A); 502(d)(5) & (6). However, a military judge, with the consent of the parties, will be able to designate a military magistrate to preside over the court-martial. Art. 19(c), UCMJ, 10 U.S.C. § 819(c).

A special court-martial may impose the following sentences: a bad-conduct discharge, one year of confinement, hard labor without confinement for up to three months, forfeiture of two-thirds pay and benefits for one year. However, a bad conduct discharge, confinement for more than six months, or forfeiture of pay for more than six months cannot be imposed unless all three of these conditions—military judge, verbatim recording, and defense counsel—have been satisfied. RCM 201(f)(2)(B)(ii); RCM 1103(c).

3. GENERAL COURTS-MARTIAL

The general court-martial is the highest and most powerful trial court in the military criminal law system. It has the power to try any person subject to the UCMJ for any offense punishable by the UCMJ and may impose punishments which include the death penalty, dishonorable discharge, total forfeiture of all pay and allowances, confinement, and, of course, lesser punishments. RCM 201(f)(1). Additionally, when local civil authority is displaced by military occupation, general courts-martial may try persons subject to trial by military tribunal under the law of war. See Ex parte Milligan, 71 U.S. 2, 127 (1866) (discussing the occasions for martial rule).

General courts-martial consist of a military judge and no fewer than five members, unless the accused requests trial by military judge alone. RCM 501(a)(1)(A). In death penalty cases, however, a military judge may not sit alone. Procedures for general courts-martial parallel those for special courts-martial. The only notable differences are that in general courts-martial (1) appointed trial lawyers are always certified military lawyers and (2) military judges are always detailed. RCM 1103(b)(2)(B). Procedures for both special and general courts-martial are examined later in more detail.

B. THE MILITARY JURY SYSTEM

There is no set number of members to a court-martial so long as the statutory minimums are met. For general courts-martial, no fewer than five members are impaneled (Article 16(1)(A), UCMJ, 10

U.S.C. § 816(1)(A)), unless the case is capital, in which case there may be no fewer than twelve (Article 25a, UCMJ, 10 U.S.C. § 825a). For a special court-martial, no fewer than three members are necessary (Article 16(2)(A), UCMJ, 10 U.S.C. § 816(2)(A)), and for a summary court-martial, only a commissioned officer (Article 16(3), UCMJ, 10 U.S.C. § 816(3)) is required. For whatever reason, it is also more common in military than civilian practice to try criminal cases before the military judge alone upon request of the accused than it is to have a judge-only civilian criminal trial.

In courts-martial, unanimous verdicts are not required except in death penalty cases, and no one may be sentenced to life imprisonment or confinement for more than ten years except by a three-fourths vote. A finding of guilty requires at least three-fourths of the vote. Reconsideration of a guilty verdict in order to decrease the sentence may be made by any lesser vote if the reconsideration is not opposed by the number of notes required for a three-fourths majority. Article 52, UCMJ, 10 U.S.C. § 852 (Supp. IV 2016).

In military practice, the convening authority is authorized to select for the jury those members of the armed forces who are "best qualified for the duty by reason of age, education, training, experience, length of service, and judicial temperament." Article 25(d)(2), UCMJ, 10 U.S.C. § 825(D)(2); RCM 502(a)(1). There is no requirement that court-martial members represent a "fair cross-section" of the military community. In addition, either trial or defense counsel's voir dire may challenge an unlimited number of court members for "cause," which includes prior contact with the case as accuser, witness, counsel, or investigating officer, as well as rigidity of opinions concerning guilt or penalty, and racial or other class prejudice. The basic test is that excusing the members would be appropriate "in the interest of having the trial and subsequent proceedings free from substantial doubt as to legality, fairness, and impartiality." RCM 912(f)(1)(N). A similar standard is applied in the recusal of a military judge.

A special court-martial consists of not less than three members and in practice always involves a military judge. The accused, after learning the military judge's identity, may request in writing a trial by the judge alone. RCM 903(c)(2)(A). Members of a special court-martial may be from the convening authority's command or made available by their commander, even if they are members of an armed force different from that of the convening authority or the accused. RCM 503(a)(3). The Discussion accompanying RCM 503(a)(3) notes: "Members should ordinarily be of the same armed force as the accused. When a court-martial composed of members of different armed forces is selected, at least a majority of the members should be of the same armed force as the accused unless exigent circumstances make it impractical to do so without manifest injury to the service." Commissioned or warrant officers on active duty and enlisted personnel on active duty from units other than those of the accused may serve on special courts-martial. UCMJ Article 25, 10 U.S.C. § 825; RCM 502(a)(1).

Only commissioned officers may try another commissioned officer. When an enlisted person is on trial, he may request orally on the record or in writing that at least one-third of the special court-martial members be enlisted personnel. This request must be honored unless eligible enlisted personnel from other units cannot be obtained because of physical conditions or military exigencies. RCM 503(a)(2). Those excused for cause from service on the court-martial are: accusers, witnesses, investigating officers, counsel for any party, arrested or confined servicemembers, those who have acted or will act in conjunction with the convening authority or a reviewing authority, or those junior to the accused in grade or rank (unless this is unavoidable).

The convening authority generally should assign the "best qualified" people (by age, education, training, experience, length of service, and judicial temperament) available to serve on the court. RCM 502(a)(1). In 1991, the USCMA affirmed this standard by reversing a sentence based on the finding that a subordinate to the convening authority had "stacked" the pool of potential court-martial members. *United States v. Hilow* 32 M.J. 439 (C.M.A. 1991). The court held that since the accused had pleaded guilty, and the plea was not affected by the stacking, the accused merely needed to be resentenced. However, the court noted that the right to trial by fair and impartial members is the cornerstone of the military justice system and any deviation from this standard creates the appearance of injustice.

C. JURISDICTION OF COURTS-MARTIAL

Broadly speaking, jurisdiction is the power to try a case. In the military criminal law system, jurisdiction of a court-martial exists when (1) the court is properly convened and the membership of the court accords with the UCMJ requirements; (2) the court has the power to try the person accused; and (3) the offense charged is triable by the court under the UCMJ. *United States v. Choy*, 33 M.J. 1080 (A.C.M.R. 1992). Courts-martial must be convened and constituted in accordance with law in order to have jurisdiction. The membership of courts-martial has been described above, and only brief preliminary attention need be paid to the convening of a court-martial. More detailed consideration of jurisdiction over the person and jurisdiction over the offense is required. Finally, the relationship between Status of Forces agreements and court-martial jurisdiction will be addressed.

1. CONVENING A COURT-MARTIAL

After a preliminary inquiry, RCM 303, and due consideration of administrative, non-punitive and nonjudicial alternatives, a commander may determine that a matter is serious enough to warrant trial by court-martial. The commander recommends trial up the chain of command to the Convening Authority. The Convening Authority is a person authorized by the UCMJ to create a court-martial by assigning members of the court and referring charges to it. The persons so authorized vary depending upon the type of court-martial convened. Thus, general courts-martial may only be convened by very senior officers such as territory, division, separate brigade, fleet, or air command commanders, or by the President of the United States, the Secretary of Defense, the Secretary of the armed force concerned, or an officer designated by the President or Secretary. UCMJ, Article 22, 10 U.S.C. § 822. Special courts-martial may be convened by any of the above as well as by commanding officers of districts, garrisons, forts, camps, stations, air fields, wings, groups, squadrons, vessels, bases, detached units, and the like. UCMJ, Article 23, 10 U.S.C. § 823. Summary courts-martial may be convened by any of the above plus commanding officers of detached companies. UCMJ, Article 24, 10 U.S.C. § 824.

A commanding officer who is the accuser of the person charged may not convene a general or special court-martial. The accusing officer must refer the charges to a superior commanding officer. UCMJ, Article 22(b) & 23(b), 10 U.S.C. §§ 822(b) & 823(b); RCM 504(c). For a summary court-martial, the accusing officer may either convene the court-martial or refer the charges to superior authority. UCMJ, Article 24(b), 10 U.S.C. § 824(b), RCM 1302(b).

The process of convening a court-martial is straightforward. A convening order that designates the kind of court, place and time it is to meet and members of the court, is issued by the convening authority. MCM, Appendix 6; RCM 504(d). When appropriate, the military judge and members of the prosecution and defense are also listed. Duration of court-martial sessions should not be unduly protracted. *United States v. Ward*, 48 C.M.R. 617 (A.C.M.R.1974).

2. JURISDICTION OVER PERSONS

All U.S. citizens are normally entitled to criminal trial in Art. III federal courts or state courts with full Constitutional protections. Since courts-martial operate under legal and Constitutional limitations not identical to those binding these courts, specific Constitutional and statutory authorization must be found for subjecting citizens, whether civilians or servicemembers, to the authority of military tribunals.

a. Civilians

The general rule that court-martial jurisdiction does not extend over civilians was established long ago. In *Ex parte Milligan*, 71 U.S. 2 (1866), a civilian was tried and convicted by a military commission for conspiracy, insurrection, and other crimes relating to an alleged plan to organize a secret military force in Indiana to aid the Confederacy during the Civil War. On petition for habeas corpus, the Supreme Court held that the military commission was without jurisdiction, stating: "This court has judicial knowledge that in Indiana the Federal authority was always unopposed, and its courts always open . . . and no usage of war could sanction a military trial there for any offense whatever of a citizen in civil life, in nowise connected with the military services." The important factors which led the Court to provide the full Constitutional safeguards of civilian courts were that Milligan: (1) was a citizen of a Union state not under military siege; (2) could have been tried, convicted, and punished in civilian court for these crimes; and (3) was not connected with the military services. These rationales are the core of four "exceptions" to the general rule that military court-martial jurisdiction does not extend to civilians.

Exception 1: Civilians of belligerent nations at war with the United States are subject to trial by court-martial or other authorized form of military tribunal when the United States occupies that belligerent's territory. Upon the premise that the occupying nation has a duty to maintain the security of the inhabitants while the war continues, the Supreme Court has, for example, upheld military jurisdiction over civilians in territories seized from Mexico, *Leitensdorfer v. Webb*, 61 U.S. 176 (1857), and sanctioned such authority over Confederate civilians in Louisiana during the Civil War. *United States v. Reiter*, 27 F.Cas. 768 (No. 16,146) (Provisional Court, D.La. 1865) (upholding jurisdiction of Provisional Court, established by President Lincoln in New Orleans, to try defendant Augustus Reiter convicted of murder; John Louis of arson); see also *The Grapeshot*, 76 U.S. (9 Wall.) 129 (1869) (jurisdiction of the Provisional Court upheld in an admiralty case as well as the authority of Congress to transfer jurisdiction to a Circuit Court at the end of hostilities).

Exception 2: "Unprivileged enemy belligerents" who commit hostile acts without identifying themselves as belligerents may be detained as POWs and tried by specialized military tribunals governed by the rules set forth in the 2009 Military Commissions Act. 10 U.S.C. §§ 948a–950t (Supp. III 2009). These tribunals operate under rules based on the UCMJ, with some modifications to protect classified information. They have jurisdiction over thirty-two defined offenses, most of which are traditional war crimes but some of which (such as material support for terrorism) are arguably newer war crimes.

Congress initially authorized the use of military detention to fight terrorism in the Authorization to Use Military Force of 2001, Pub. L. No. 107-40, 115 Stat. 224 (2001) ("[T]he President has authority to use all necessary force . . . to deter and prevent acts of international terrorism"). Congress affirmed that authority in 2012 National Defense Authorization Act. (AUMF "includes the authority for the Armed Forces of the United States to detain [members of al-Qaeda, the Taliban, or "affiliated forces"] . . . pending disposition under the law of war." The 2012 National Defense Authorization Act, § 1021(a), Pub. L. No. 112-81, § 1021(a), 125 Stat. 1298 (2011)). See also, Presidential Policy Directive/PPD-14, 2012 WL 62771 (Feb. 28, 2012).

The Supreme Court has upheld the government's authority to detain and try such unprivileged belligerents in *Ex parte Quirin,* 317 U.S. 1 (1942). In *Quirin,* German nationals, including a dual-national

Hans Haupt, who attempted sabotage against the U.S. during World War II were permitted to be tried by military commission. The Court said:

> The spy who secretly and without uniform passes the military lines of a belligerent in time of war, seeking to gather military information and communicate it to the enemy, or any enemy combatant who without uniform comes secretly through the lines for the purposes of waging war by destruction of life or property, are familiar examples of belligerents who are generally deemed not be entitled to the status of prisoners or war, but to be offenders against the law of war subject to trial and punishment by military tribunals.

This rationale is broad enough to encompass trial by courts-martial of even U.S. citizens who serve as "spies" or "enemy combatants" in this country during time of war. Building on *Quirin,* in *Hamdi v. Rumsfeld*, 542 U.S. 507 (2004), the Supreme Court upheld military commission jurisdiction over a U.S. citizen captured on the battlefield in Afghanistan, though it also held that a U.S. citizen must have a "meaningful opportunity" to challenge designation as an "enemy combatant."

Exception 3: Private contractors "serving with" or accompanying an armed force during a declared war or contingency operation are subject to courts-martial. UCMJ, Article 2(a)(10), 10 U.S.C. § 802(a)(10). The jurisdiction of the military to try civilians has waxed and waned. Prior to the founding of this country, the British Articles of War of 1765 provided for jurisdiction over "[a]ll Suttlers and Retainers to a Camp, and all persons whatsoever serving with Our Armies in the Field." British Articles of War of 1765, section XIV, art. XXIII, *reprinted in* William Winthrop, *Military Law and Precedents* 941 (2d ed., Government Printing Office 1920). The first American Articles of War enacted in 1775 included this language from the British Articles. American Articles of War of 1775, art. XXXII, *reprinted in* Winthrop, *Military Law and Precedents* (at 956). The Articles retained that language with only minor modifications until enactment of the Uniform Code of Military Justice in 1950.

Jurisdiction over a foreign national working as a civilian contractor in Iraq was upheld in *United States v. Ali,* 71 M.J. 256 (C.A.A.F. 2012) under Article 2(a)(10). Ali disputed the application of Article 2 insofar as it requires service to be "in time of war." In *United States v. Averette,* 41 C.M.R. 363 (C.M.A. 1970), the term "time of war" in Article 2(a)(10) had been held to refer only to a "war formally declared by Congress." And since undeclared wars had become the norm after World War II, the application of Article 2 to civilian contractors was limited. However, in 2007 Congress amended the language of Article 2 to read "[i]n time of *declared* war or *contingency operation,*" effectively nullifying *Averette.* 2007 National Defense Authorization Act, Pub. L. No. 109-364, § 552, 120 Stat. 2217 (2006) (emphasis added). As the *Ali* court concluded:

> Thus, in its current form Article 2(a)(10) provides jurisdiction "[i]n time of declared war or contingency operation, [over] persons serving with or accompanying an armed force in the field." Neither Ali nor the Government disputed the military judge's finding that Operation Iraqi Freedom in which Ali served as an interpreter was a contingency operation as that term is defined in 10 U.S.C. § 101(a)(13) (2006) (defining a "contingency operation" as "[A] military operation that—(A) is designated by the Secretary of Defense as an operation in which members of the armed forces are or may become involved in military actions, operations, or hostilities against an enemy of the United States or against an opposing military force; or (B) results in the call or order to, or retention on, active duty of members of the uniformed services under section 688, 12301(a), 12302, 12304, 12304a, 12305, or 12406 of this title, chapter 15 of this title, or any other provision of law during a war or during a national emergency declared by the President or Congress.").

A number of decisions by lower courts have upheld court-martial jurisdiction over civilians accompanying or serving with the armed forces "in the field." See *Perlstein v. United States*, 151 F.2d 167 (3d Cir.1945); *In re Berue,* 54 F.Supp. 252 (S.D.Ohio 1944); *In re Di Bartolo,* 50 F.Supp. 929 (S.D.N.Y. 1943); *McCune v. Kilpatrick*, 53 F.Supp. 80 (E.D.Va. 1943). These include training operations preliminary to actual wartime combat, *Hines v. Mikell*, 259 F. 28 (4th Cir.1919), and operations of a merchant ship transporting troops and supplies to a battle zone. *McCune v. Kilpatrick*, 53 F. Supp. 80 (E.D.Va.1943).

Exception 4: Jurisdiction over military dependents is a more complex exception fraught with unresolved questions over whether it is an exception. Historically, during peacetime, civilians have not been subject to trial by court-martial. *Willenbring v. Neurauter*, 48 M.J. 152, 157 (C.A.A.F. 1998) ("both the Supreme Court of the United States and this Court have insisted that courts-martial not exercise jurisdiction beyond that granted by the applicable statutes. As a matter of constitutional law, the Supreme Court has held that Congress may not extend court-martial jurisdiction to cover civilians who have no military status in peacetime, even if they are accompanying United States forces overseas as employees or dependents.")

Beginning with *United States ex rel. Toth v. Quarles*, 350 U.S. 11 (1955) (military jurisdiction over former servicemember invalid), the Supreme Court invalidated the assertion of military jurisdiction over a variety of civilians. After first holding that the trial of civilians accompanying the armed forces abroad during peacetime did not violate an accused's constitutional right to trial by jury, *Kinsella v. Krueger*, 351 U.S. 470, 475 (1956), on rehearing, in *Reid v. Covert*, 354 U.S. 1 (1957), the Court subsequently held the trial by court-martial of two military wives accused of murdering their servicemember husbands to be unconstitutional. Justice Black's plurality opinion rejected any power in the military to try civilians in peacetime because courts-martial lacked the constitutional requirement of trial by jury, an independent judiciary, grand jury indictment and any indication that the Bill of Rights applied to them. Concurring opinions by Justice Frankfurter and Justice Harlan limited the ruling to capital cases. *Reid* paved the way for additional exclusions of civilians from the ambit of military justice, e.g., *Kinsella v. United States ex rel. Singleton*, 361 U.S. 234 (1960) (civilian dependent, non-capital offense); *Grisham v. Hagan*, 361 U.S. 278 (1960) (civilian employee, capital offense); *McElroy v. United States ex rel. Guagliardo*, 361 U.S. 281 (1960) (civilian employees, non-capital offenses). This created a jurisdictional gap whereby civilians, military contractors and military dependents, who could not be subjected to military jurisdiction also could not be subject to federal jurisdiction which at that time did not extend extraterritorially and might not be subject to host nation jurisdiction if the host country was indifferent to the crime, say where both the accused perpetrator and victim were foreign.

Congress responded to this gap by enacting the Military Extraterritorial Jurisdiction Act of 2000 (MEJA) which, extended federal jurisdiction over crimes committed abroad by civilians who are "accompanying or employed by" the U.S. military. 18 U.S.C. §§ 3261–3267. (Initially, the MEJA contained a jurisdictional gap of its own in that civilian employees of non-military federal entities would appear exempt from the MEJA. In response to this gap, the 2005 Defense authorization Act expanded the jurisdictional scope of the MEJA to include civilian employees, contractors or subcontractors, and their employees, of the Department of Defense or "any other Federal agency, or any provisional authority, to the extent such employment relates to supporting the mission of the Department of Defense overseas." Pub. L. No. 108-375, § 1088, 118 Stat. 1811, 2066–2067 (2006). It remains unsettled, however, whether these provision would, for example, necessarily cover contractors of the State Department, FBI or CIA.)

The MEJA covers crime involving conduct engaged in outside the United States by members of the Armed Forces or by persons employed by or accompanying the Armed Forces abroad that would be a felony if it had occurred in the United States. § 3261. This allows prosecutions of two groups: first, persons employed by or accompanying the Armed Forces outside the United States, or second, persons who are members of the Armed Forces and are subject to the UCMJ at the time the conduct occurred. Servicemembers, who are subject to the UCMJ, can be punished under the MEJA only if they are indicted with at least one civilian. Thus, absent a charge of conspiracy or similar offense in conjunction with a civilian co-defendant, military jurisdiction over the servicemember is exclusive. Indictment with a civilian co-defendant opens the possibility of trying the servicemember in federal court under the MEJA. In the event of approval of a motion for separate trials of the co-defendants, the servicemember could still be tied in federal court. § 3261. The Department of Justice could, however, dismiss the complaint against the servicemember and allow him or her to be tried by court-martial. § 3261(d) of the MEJA covers the problem of the discharged servicemember who is no longer subject to the UCMJ, as was the case in *United States ex rel. Toth v. Quarles*, 350 U.S. 11 (1955) (crime committed abroad and discovered only after the accused was discharged from the military).

Jurisdiction over civilian contractors under the MEJA can be asserted either in a federal district court under federal criminal law or under the UCMJ in a court-martial, as in the *Ali* case above, depending on the circumstances. In *United States v. Brehm*, 2011 WL 1226088 (E.D.Va.2011), the defendant, a citizen of South Africa, who at the time of the alleged attack, was employed by DynCorp International LLC ("DynCorp"), a civilian contractor for the U.S. Department of Defense supporting the U.S. military effort in Afghanistan, was charged in a two-count indictment with assault. He allegedly attacked another civilian, a citizen of the United Kingdom employed in Kandahar by Global Strategies, a private corporation that contracts with the U.S. Agency for International Development ("USAID"). The federal court upheld jurisdiction under the MEJA.

The decision in *Reid v. Covert*, 354 U.S. 1 (1957), discussed above, which disallowed court-martial jurisdiction over a military dependent spouse, was grounded in part on the fact that the situs of the two crimes, England and Japan, were at peace and there was no wartime exigency. Military jurisdiction in time of war is unquestioned. For example, even Justice Black's plurality opinion in *Reid* concedes that "the extraordinary circumstances present in an area of actual fighting" adequately sustain jurisdiction over civilians present there. *Reid v. Covert*, 354 U.S. 1, 33–34 (1957).

Two factors may conspire to weaken the bright line that seemed to emerge from *Reid* and its progeny. First, changes in the UCMJ, Article 2(a)(10), 10 U.S.C. § 802(a)(10) which now confers court-martial jurisdiction: "In time of declared war or a contingency operation, persons serving with or accompanying an armed force in the field." As noted in *Ali*, 71 M.J. 256 (at 262), the term "contingency operation" has no defined meaning, and would in light of the open-ended nature of the Authorization for the Use of Military Force (AUMF), Pub. L. No. 107-40, § 2(a), 115 Stat. 224 (2001) appear to sweep dependents "accompanying an armed force" into military jurisdiction. While it could be argued that the phrase "in the field" could limit Article 2, again *Ali*, rejects a narrowing construction: "We see no reason not to adopt this interpretation of "in the field," which requires an area of actual fighting, for our analysis of Article 2(a)(10)."

Jurisdiction under the MEJA is concurrent, as *Ali* notes, 71 M.J. 256, 270) ("MEJA expressly provides for concurrent jurisdiction with courts-martial") and the better practice would appear to be to defer to federal court jurisdiction under the MEJA as two commentators suggest. E.g., Captain Brittany Warren, "The Case of the Murdering Wives: Reid v. Covert and the Complicated Question of Civilians and Court Martial," 212 Mil. L. Rev. 133, 192n. 4 (2012):

> "A civilian dependent, however intimately connected to the service, is not part of the armed forces because he or she does not serve a historically military function in a hostile area. It is far more difficult to argue that the civilian contractor providing direct logistical or operational support to combat operations in Afghanistan is not "part of" the armed forces as that phrase was traditionally understood."

See also John F. O'Connor, "Contractors and Court Martial," 77 Tenn. L. Rev. 751, 790 (2010) ("[T]he current existence of a readily available means to try civilians in federal court under MEJA severely undermines any claim by the military that it needs court-martial jurisdiction.") Prosecution under the MEJA was not an alternative in *Ali*, however, because Ali was an Iraqi citizen serving in Iraq, and as Senior Judge Effron, concurring in part and in the result, notes, "Ali was not subject to Article III jurisdiction under MEJA. See 18 U.S.C. §§ 3267(1)(C), 3267(2)(C) (excluding host-country nationals from coverage under MEJA)." 71 M.J. 256 (at 280). For a detailed analysis of the MEJA see Glenn R. Schmitt, "Closing the Gap in Criminal Jurisdiction Over Civilians Accompanying the Armed Forces Abroad—A First Person Account of the Creation of the Military Extraterritorial Jurisdiction Act of 2000," 51 Cath. U. L. Rev. 55 (2001).

b. Military Persons

Beginning with the first Article of War on June 30, 1775, the United States has always provided for a military justice system to discipline members of its armed forces. In *Dynes v. Hoover*, 61 U.S. 65 (1857), the Supreme Court acknowledged Congress' power to provide for trial and punishment of military offenses. The source of this power is Art. I, § 8 of the United States Constitution that authorizes Congress to make rules for the governing of the land and naval forces.

The jurisdiction of a court-martial depends upon the "military status" of the accused. In *Solorio v. U.S.*, 483 U.S. 435 (1987), the Court held that "the proper exercise of court-martial jurisdiction over an offense [depends] on one factor: the military status of the accused." The Court rejected earlier decisions such as *O'Callahan v. Parker*, 395 U.S. 258 (1969) requiring that the crime also be "service connected" and held that a court-martial was proper even though the offenses, sexual abuses of two minors, were committed off-base in the accused's privately owned home.

The difficulty is in ascertaining an accused person's status: is the accused in the court-martial proceeding a person who can be regarded as falling within the term "land and naval forces"? *Kinsella v. U.S. ex rel. Singleton*, 361 U.S. 234 (1960). Though there is no litmus test of military status, some indicia include accepting a position in writing, swearing to the oath of service, wearing a uniform, performing military duties, being paid according to rank, and being entitled to a pension. *Ex parte Reed*, 100 U.S. 13 (1879); UCMJ, Article 2(c), 10 U.S.C. § 802(c).

Few categorization problems have arisen with respect to persons currently serving full-time active military duty. Moreover, while at their service academies cadets and midshipmen are subject to the jurisdiction of military tribunals. The problems of application focus on (1) entry into the military, (2) persons performing part-time military service, and (3) exit from the military.

i. Entry into the Military

With the end of the draft and the advent of all-volunteer Armed Forces, the primary focus on the acquisition of military jurisdiction deals with the enlistment contract. That contract is treated in detail in Chapter 2. Jurisdiction over enlisted servicemembers attaches when a valid enlistment contract is signed. *U.S. v. Williams*, 302 U.S. 46 (1937). The seminal case with respect to enlistment contracts is *United States v. Grimley*, 137 U.S. 147 (1890), which explains the unique aspect of the military enlistment contract: Although "[e]nlistment is a contract, . . . it is one of those contracts which changes the [party's] *status*, and where that is changed, no breach of the contract destroys the new *status* or relieves from the obligations which its existence imposes." This language is reflected in Article 2(b), UCMJ, 10 U.S.C. § 802(b):

> The voluntary enlistment of any person who has the capacity to understand the significance of enlisting in the armed forces shall be valid for purposes of jurisdiction . . . and a change of status from civilian to member of the armed

forces shall be effective upon the taking of the oath of enlistment.

At one time, technical aspects of the enlistment process allowed for invalidation of some enlistment contracts for fraud or duress. However, subsequent changes in Article 2(b), UCMJ, 10 U.S.C. § 802(b) which confers jurisdiction over "any person who has the capacity to understand the significance of enlisting" have largely eliminated those problems.

ii. Part-Time Servicemembers

The status of persons performing part-time military service has been considered by courts in several contexts. For example, ROTC students have been held not subject to court-martial jurisdiction (because they are given a deferment from induction) even though service academy members may be tried by military tribunals. Article 2(a)(2), UCMJ, 10 U.S.C. § 802(a)(2). *Allison v. United States*, 426 F.2d 1324 (6th Cir.1970) (Senior ROTC student, who died of natural causes during training while at summer camp, not automatically eligible for death coverage under Servicemen's Group Life Insurance).

Members of reserve components lawfully called to active duty for an initial training period or for delinquency in fulfilling inactive duty requirements may be subjected to court-martial. Article 2(a)(1), UCMJ, 10 U.S.C. § 802(a)(1). Inactive reservists subject to proceedings under Articles 15 or 39 may be ordered to active duty involuntarily for investigation, court-martial, or nonjudicial punishment only if the offense was committed while the member was on active duty or inactive-duty for training (IDT). *U.S. v. Ernest*, 32 M.J. 135 (C.M.A. 1991); Article 2(d)(2), 10 U.S.C. § 802(d)(2). The general courts-martial convening authority or the Secretary of the particular armed force may order a reservist to active duty. Article 2(d)(4), UCMJ, 10 U.S.C. § 802(d)(4). Additionally, reservists on IDT are subject to court-martial jurisdiction. Article 2(a)(3), UCMJ, 10 U.S.C. § 802(a)(3).

A reservist challenging military jurisdiction must first exhaust his military remedies before litigating in federal district court. *Murphy v. Garrett*, 729 F.Supp. 461 (W.D.Pa.1990) On remand, the Court of Military Appeals held that there is jurisdiction to require a reservist to report for active duty to stand trial by court-martial. *Murphy v. Garrett*. 29 M.J. 469 (C.M.A. 1990). In interpreting the term "active duty" in Article 2(d)(2)(A), the court held: "[t]he fact that his regular service was terminated by the issuance of an Honorable Discharge and that his reserve service commences upon the simultaneous issuance of a new commission does not divest his armed force of jurisdiction." Chief Judge Everett provides a useful background of the history of the interpretation of the term "active duty" as it applies to reservists, *Murphy v. Garrett*. 29 M.J. 469, 472 (C.M.A. 1990).

Article 3(d), UCMJ, 10 U.S.C. § 803(d) now allows jurisdiction over a member of a reserve component, despite termination of a period of active duty or IDT, for an offense committed during that period of active duty or IDT. RCM 204 provides more specific guidance regarding jurisdiction over reservists. A reserve member must be on active duty before commencement of an Article 32 investigation at a general or special court-martial. A reservist so ordered to active duty may be kept in that status to serve any adjudged confinement or other restriction on liberty. However, that member may not be retained on active duty after service of the confinement or other restriction. All punishment remaining unserved when the member is released from active duty may be carried over to subsequent periods of IDT or active duty. RCM 204(b)(1). In contrast, a reservist may be tried by summary court-martial either while on active duty or IDT. But a summary court-martial conducted during IDT may be held only during normal periods of such training, and the accused may not be held beyond such training periods for trial or service of punishment. Moreover, a member of a reserve component at the time disciplinary action is initiated, who is alleged to have committed an offense while on active duty or IDT, is subject to court-martial jurisdiction regardless of any change between active and reserve service.

For a discussion of military jurisdiction over Army Reserve soldiers attending inactive duty training (IDT) during the "gap" between "sign out" and "sign in" see Major T. Scott Randall, "Saturday Night Jurisdiction Over Reserve Soldiers," Army Lawyer, June 2013, 31.

iii. Former Servicemembers

There is no jurisdiction over one whose military status has been completely terminated before commission of an offense. RCM 204(d). However, several exceptions exist to the general rule that court-martial jurisdiction over servicemembers ceases upon termination of military status.

First, jurisdiction extends to all offenses committed during the incarceration of a person who is in the custody of the military serving a sentence imposed by court-martial, even though the offense was committed after the prisoner's status as a servicemember ended. *Kahn v. Anderson*, 255 U.S. 1 (1921).

Second, jurisdiction which attaches by apprehension, arrest, confinement or filing of charges continues in effect even after the servicemember's status later terminates. *Messina v. Commanding Officer*, 342 F.Supp. 1330 (S.D.Cal.1972).

Third, if military status terminates but there is "immediate" re-enlistment, the short gap between periods of military status does not sever military ties and jurisdiction remains over offenses committed on a previous tour of duty. *United States v. Gallagher*, 22 C.M.R. 296 (C.M.A.1957).

Fourth, retired members of regular armed forces components who are entitled to receive pay technically remain in the military service and may be tried by court-martial. *U.S. v. Tyler*, 105 U.S. 244 (1881). However, this jurisdiction was limited to permit court-martial dismissal but not confinement of retired officers. *United States v. Hooper,* 26 C.M.R. 417 (C.M.A.1958), *Hooper v. United States,* 326 F.2d 982, 987 (Ct.Cl.1964) (upholding dismissal and consequent loss of entitlement to pay; "We are not concerned with the authority of a court-martial to order the confinement of a retired officer and our holding does not reach that issue."); *United States v. Allen,* 31 M.J. 572 (N.M.C.M.R.1990) (pretrial confinement of retired servicemember otherwise subject to court-martial jurisdiction), affirmed on other grounds, 33 M.J. 209 (C.M.A.1991).

Finally, jurisdiction over a servicemember exists until the member's military status is terminated by formal discharge, regardless of any delay (even if unreasonable) by the government in discharging that person at the end of an enlistment. *United States v. Poole,* 30 M.J. 149 (C.M.A. 1990).

Discharge normally terminates court-martial jurisdiction over a former servicemember. Two cases provide the underpinnings for this conclusion. First, *United States ex rel. Hirshberg v. Cooke,* 336 U.S. 210 (1949) held as a matter of statutory law that under then-existing statutes governing military jurisdiction, discharged servicemembers—"whether reenlisted or not"—were not subject to court-martial jurisdiction for prior-service offenses. The second case, *United States ex rel. Toth v. Quarles,* 350 U.S. 11 (1955), involving a crime committed abroad and discovered only after the accused was discharged from the military, was decided on constitutional grounds and held court-martial jurisdiction had been improperly exercised over the accused. Congress has repeatedly addressed the "*Hirshberg* jurisdictional gap" under which crimes perpetrated during a prior period of service could not be prosecuted by courts-martial if the accused servicemember reentered military service. See RCM 202(a)(2)(B) and the excellent discussion in *Willenbring v. Neurauter*, 48 M.J. 152 (C.A.A.F.1998):

> Articles 2(d), 3(a), and 3(d) should be read in harmony, in conjunction with RCM 204(d), as follows: First, Article 2(d) authorizes a reservist to be ordered to active duty to face trial by court-martial for both current-service and prior-service offenses, including offenses committed while a member of a regular component; second, when there has been a complete termination of military status, the version of Article 3(a) applicable to offenses occurring before October 23, 1992, permits a reservist, like a regular component member, to be tried for prior-service offenses only if the offenses cannot be tried in a civilian court and if confinement for 5 years or more is authorized for the offense; and third, Article 3(d) makes clear that the mere movement of a reservist on and off active duty does not terminate jurisdiction whenever a period of active duty terminates.

Court-martial jurisdiction in Willenbring's case cited above, *Willenbring v. Neurauter*, 48 M.J. 152 (C.A.A.F.1998), concerned three rape offenses committed in the late 1980s and tried by court-martial in the 1990s. Willenbring subsequently, unsuccessfully challenged military jurisdiction by habeas corpus. *Willenbring v. United States*, 559 F.3d 225 (4th Cir.2009). The conclusion of Willenbring's odyssey is worth noting:

> In the late 1990s, Willenbring was indicted in North Carolina for six unrelated crimes—four rapes and two kidnappings—and the Army did not seek to exercise jurisdiction over those offenses. North Carolina placed Willenbring in pretrial confinement for those offenses on November 1, 1996, and later released him to the Army after the court-martial specifications were preferred. On January 8, 1999, Willenbring was convicted of the North Carolina charges and sentenced to life imprisonment, a sentence he is currently serving.

Willenbring v. United States, 559 F.3d 225, 228 n.6.

The "*Toth* jurisdictional gap," involving crimes committed abroad by discharged servicemembers, as discussed above, has been resolved by enactment of the Military Extraterritorial Jurisdiction Act of 2000 (MEJA) which, extended federal jurisdiction over crimes committed abroad by civilians who are "accompanying or employed by" the U.S. military. 18 U.S.C. §§ 3261–3267.

A note on the vitality of *Willenbring* is in order. The opinion by Judge Effron in that case is in three parts. Part III addresses issues raised by the appellant concerning the applicable statute of limitations for the crime of rape. Specifically, the appellant argued for dismissal of the rape charges against him on the ground that they were barred by the 5-year statute of limitations in Article 43(b)(1). The Government argued that there was no time limit because the under Article 129(a) rape was punishable by death, and such crimes were a statutory exception under Article 43(a). Appellant had argued inter alia that the Supreme Court's decision in *Coker v. Georgia*, 433 U.S. 584 (1977) that the Constitution's Eighth Amendment precluded imposition of the death penalty for "rape of an adult woman" meant that the military was precluded from enforcing the language in Article 120 to try him for rape "at any time without limitation." *Willenbring* rejected this argument. In *United States v. Mangahas*, 77 M.J. 220 (C.A.A.F. 2018) the Court of Appeals for the Armed Forces changed course on the narrow issue of the statute of limitations for rape and held two prior cases, including *Willenbring* were "overruled to the extent that they hold that rape was punishable by death at the time of the charged offense." In particular, the *Mangahas* court was concerned with *Willenbring's* failure to engage in an analysis of the Supreme Court's *Coker* decision: "This failure to incorporate and analyze applicable Supreme Court precedent further undermines the precedential value of *Willenbring*." *Id.* at 224. In *United States v. Briggs*, 141 S. Ct. 467 (2020) the Supreme Court reviewed the cases of three military servicemembers convicted of rape. The question presented was whether he applicable statute of limitation in these cases was "without limitation" under Art. 43(a), 10 U.S.C. § 843(a) or five years under Article 43(b), 10 U.S.C. § 843(b). Pursuant to the decision in *Mangahas* respondents had argued that the Court's decision in

Coker meant that when all applicable law was taken into account, their rape charges could not be considered "punishable by death." In an opinion by Justice Alito, the Court rejected this argument and abrogated the decision in *Mangahas*. This leaves the decision in *Willenbring* untouched with respect to its treatment of military jurisdiction over former servicemembers.

3. JURISDICTION OVER OFFENSES

The law concerning the appropriate type of court-martial is simple at both ends but complex in the middle. Just as summary courts-martial may only try enlisted personnel, they are also limited to trial of relatively minor offenses. General courts-martial, at the other extreme, may try not only any person subject to the UCMJ, but any offense made punishable by the Code. The sole limitation on this broad jurisdiction is that a general court-martial composed of a military judge alone may not try capital cases.

Between these extremes is the special court-martial, which may try any non-capital offense punishable by the Code. What constitutes a "non-capital offense" is complicated because: (1) some offenses are capital only if committed "in time of war" (e.g., desertion, assaulting or willfully disobeying a superior commissioned officer, improperly using a countersign, spying, or misbehaving as a sentinel); (2) the President has the power, as yet unexercised, to limit punishments to less than death; (3) the convening authority may direct that the case be treated as non-capital; and (4) a sentence previously imposed, which is less than death, may not be increased to death upon retrial.

4. SPECIAL MILITARY JURISDICTION CONSIDERATIONS

As with civilian criminal trials, substantial prosecutorial discretion exists for commanders, and trial by court-martial is not required even if court-martial jurisdiction exists. Courts-martial have exclusive jurisdiction over purely military offenses. RCM 201(d)(1); *U.S. v. Espinosa*, 789 F.Supp.2d 681 (E.D. Va. 2011). But, where an act violates both military and local criminal law, foreign (depending on the terms of the relevant SOFA, see infra) or domestic, the accused may be tried by court-martial or by the appropriate civilian tribunal. RCM 201(d)(2). In that case, the determination of which tribunal will exercise jurisdiction rests with the nation, state, or agency concerned—it is not a right of the accused. RCM 201(d)(3). However, a court-martial proceeding will be dismissed if the accused has previously been tried by a federal civilian court for the same offense. RCM 907(b)(2)(C)(i). However, the accused may be tried by both a court-martial and a *state* civilian court for the same offense. This authority is rarely exercised and service regulations generally require approval of the service secretary to try an accused for an offense previously tried by a state court.

Under the UCMJ, military authorities, in their discretion, "may" deliver upon request a member of the armed forces accused of an offense against civilian authority to the civilian authorities for trial. Art. 14(a), UCMJ. But when such delivery interrupts the execution of the court-martial sentence, the offender shall be returned to military custody for the completion of his sentence upon request of the proper military authority. Art. 14(b), UCMJ, 10 U.S.C. § 814(b). In practice, however, crimes committed in the civilian community by service personnel most likely will be investigated and prosecuted through a cooperative effort between military and civilian authorities.

a. Double Jeopardy

The Double Jeopardy Clause of the Fifth Amendment proscribes trying a servicemember for the same conduct both by court-martial and in civilian federal court. *Grafton v. United States*, 206 U.S. 333 (1907). As the *Willenbring* case, at least in its habeas corpus iteration, reveals, criminal conduct by servicemembers may be prosecuted either in state or federal court or by court-martial. A memorandum of understanding between the Department of Justice and the Department of Defense, DoD Directive 5525.7 (January 22, 1985), MCM, Appendix 3, establishes a presumption that servicemembers will be tried before courts-martial rather that in federal district court for crimes prosecutable under the UCMJ. *United States v. Espinosa*, 789 F.Supp.2d 681, 684n. 6 (E.D.Va.2011) (the Department of Defense will investigate, and the military department concerned will prosecute by court-martial, crimes committed on military installations by individuals subject to the Uniform Code of Military Justice).

As noted earlier, nonjudicial punishment under Article 15, UCMJ, 10 U.S.C. § 815, is no bar to subsequent court-martial for serious crimes because the nonjudicial punishment is appropriate only for minor offenses. *United States v. Pierce*, 27 M.J. 367 (C.M.A.1989) (nonjudicial punishment does not preclude subsequent court-martial of a servicemember accused of a serious offence). However, a court has held that it is unconstitutional to try a servicemember in federal court for conduct that had previously received nonjudicial punishment under Article 15. *United States v. Espinosa*, 789 F.Supp.2d 681 (E.D. Va. 2011) (fundamentally unfair and is barred by the Due Process Clause of the Fifth Amendment). Both state and federal prosecutors prefer to allow the military to prosecute erring servicemembers.

Prosecution for the same conduct in both state court and in a court-martial, although rare, is legally permissible, and the Double Jeopardy Clause is no bar. E.g., *United States v. Lanza*, 260 U.S. 377 (1922); *United States v. Schneider*, 34 M.J. 639 (A.C.M.R. 1992). In *Schneider*, the accused was convicted of attempted murder of his wife and two specifications of conduct unbecoming officer and gentleman by committing perjury and by having improper affair with another woman; he was acquitted of attempted murder in state court and a similar issue of perjury was resolved in his favor. The *Schneider* court held that the doctrine of collateral estoppel doesn't apply in military criminal law, and "prosecution of an offense in state court does not normally bar a federal prosecution of the same criminal matter." For a discussion of state and court-martial prosecutions for the same conduct see Major Charles L. Pritchard, Jr., "The Pit and the Pendulum: Why the Military Must Change Its Policy Regarding Successive State-Military Prosecutions," Army Lawyer, Nov. 2007, 1.

b. Assimilative Crimes Act

The Assimilative Crimes Act, 18 U.S.C. § 13, makes state law applicable to conduct occurring on lands reserved or acquired by the Federal government as provided in 18 U.S.C. § 7(3), when the act or omission is not made punishable by federal law. Prosecutions instituted under this statute are not to enforce the laws of the state, but rather to enforce federal law. The Assimilative Crimes Act covers minor violations as well as a number of serious criminal offenses defined by state law such as burglary and embezzlement. State criminal laws enacted after the adoption of the Assimilative Crimes Act are considered prospectively incorporated. The prospective incorporation of state law was upheld in *United States v. Sharpnack,* 355 U.S. 286 (1957). State law is assimilated only when no "enactment of Congress" covers the conduct.

Because of its unlimited applicability, the UCMJ is not considered an "enactment of Congress" within the meaning of 18 U.S.C. § 13. *See United States v. Walker*, 552 F.2d 566 (4th Cir.1977), *cert. denied*, 434 U.S. 848 (1977) (drunk driving). *See also Franklin v.*

United States, 216 U.S. 559 (1910). Thus, military personnel who commit acts on an enclave subject to federal jurisdiction which are not made an offense by federal statutes other than the UCMJ may be prosecuted in district court for violations of state law assimilated by 18 U.S.C. § 13, even though they are also subject to court martial. However, dual prosecution both in federal court and by court-martial is constitutionally precluded by the Double Jeopardy Clause. See *Grafton v. United States*, 206 U.S. 333 (1907).

c. Removal Jurisdiction

In limited instances, both civil and, particularly for purposes here, criminal cases against military servicemembers are removable to federal court:

> A civil or criminal prosecution in a court of a State of the United States against a member of the armed forces of the United States on account of an act done under color of his office or status, or in respect to which he claims any right, title, or authority under a law of the United States respecting the armed forces thereof, . . . may at any time before the trial . . . be removed for trial into the district court of the United States for the district where it is pending in the manner prescribed by law. . . .

28 U.S.C. § 1442a

Compare *People of Puerto Rico v. Santos-Marrero*, 624 F.Supp. 308 (D.Puerto Rico 1985) (reckless driving involving a military convoy driver) with *State of Georgia v. Westlake,* 929 F.Supp. 1516 (M.D.Ga. 1996) (vehicular homicide case involving military convoy driver; removal denied and remanded to state court). *Westlake* held that removal under the statute requires defendant to assert colorable defense based upon federal law; no basis existed for removal of defendant's case under the statute; and the statute could not serve as basis for district court's exercise of "arising under" jurisdiction.

Removal jurisdiction does not extend to servicemembers whose activities bear only an attenuated connection to military service, for example to a retired member of the Armed Forces merely charged with driving under the influence. *Florida v. Simanonok*, 850 F.2d 1429 (11th Cir.1988) (for a state criminal prosecution to come within 28 U.S.C. § 1442a, according to the Supreme Court, "[t]here must be [a] causal connection between what the officer has done under asserted official authority and the state prosecution.")

5. STATUS OF FORCES AGREEMENTS AND COURT-MARTIAL JURISDICTION

Under international law, a state has jurisdiction over persons and events occurring within its borders. When members of an American armed service are in a foreign country in other than hostile circumstances, as for example when they are based or stationed abroad, they would be subject only to the domestic law of the foreign state unless treaties or other international agreements between the United States (the sending state or country in this example) and the foreign state (the host or receiving country) provide otherwise. Such an agreement is called a Status of Forces Agreement (SOFA). A SOFA is a pact between nations specifying which nation has jurisdiction in particular situations. For example, when a United States servicemember commits an offense within a foreign country, should the accused be tried in a court-martial or in a court of the host country? Because such questions have great potential for international dispute, it is not surprising that countries have tried to resolve them in advance of actual cases. Some SOFAs are based on treaties, while others are in less formal international agreements such as base leases. Executive agreements are binding as a matter of international law even though they lack the formality of a treaty. *United States v. Belmont*, 301 U.S. 324 (1937) ("an international compact . . . is not always a treaty which requires the participation of the Senate [but can be] a protocol, a modus vivendi, a postal convention," etc.).

One typical and important SOFA is the one between all the parties to the North Atlantic Treaty. Agreement Between the Parties to the North Atlantic Treaty Regarding the Status of their Forces" ["SOFA Treaty"]. T.I.A.S. No. 2846, 4 U.S.T. 1792, 1953 WL 44517 (August 23, 1953). Art. VII of this SOFA provides that the United States retains court-martial jurisdiction over all offenses committed by persons subject to such jurisdiction and that the host country has jurisdiction over all armed servicemembers, civilian components, and dependents with respect to offenses committed in the host country punishable by its laws. When one contracting nation does not have laws that punish a certain offense, the other country gets exclusive jurisdiction over the accused. More important are the rules laid down for jurisdiction where the laws of both countries apply: (1) the United States gets primary jurisdiction when its personnel harm United States property or its personnel, or if the offense is duty-related; and (2) the host nation has primary jurisdiction in all other cases. Should the nation having primary jurisdiction decide not to prosecute, it is obligated to notify the other nation as soon as practicable.

SOFAs are not purely jurisdictional; they also provide some guarantees to accused persons. For example, when an accused has been tried by one nation, the other nation cannot retry him for the same offense. However, the United States military authorities may bring disciplinary charges against a servicemember even if he is tried by the other nation. NATO SOFA, Art. VII § 8. Where trial is by the host nation, the accused is guaranteed a speedy trial, pretrial notice of the charges, the right to confront witnesses, compulsory process, legal representation, an interpreter, and the right to have a United States representative present at trial. There is no right to trial by jury. NATO SOFA, Art. VII § 9.

Although the NATO SOFA provides substantive guarantees to an accused, it does not confer standing for example, to sue for the assertion of primary jurisdiction by a host nation in order to avoid imposition of the death penalty, *United States v. Murphy*, 50 M.J. 4 (C.A.A.F.1998) or to challenge the admissibility of evidence obtained by unreasonable search and seizure, *United States v. Whiting*, 12 M.J. 253 (C.M.A.1982).

D. FORMAL INVESTIGATION

Before a charge may be referred to a general court-martial for trial, a formal Article 32 investigation is required. 10 U.S.C. § 832. RCM 405. This investigation has two purposes. First, it screens charges prior to trial by a general court-martial, impartially weighing the facts to determine whether the case should be brought to trial. *United States v. Bramel*, 29 M.J. 958 (A.C.M.R.1990). In this respect, it parallels indictment by grand jury in the civilian trial process. However, this investigation need not follow grand jury procedures, since the Fifth Amendment exempts members of the Armed Services from the Constitutional requirement of indictment. Second, it provides the defense with some discovery and gives the defendant an opportunity for an early exoneration from charges. In this sense, it bears some resemblance to a civilian preliminary examination.

The Article 32 investigation commences when the commander appoints an investigating officer, who need not be an attorney. Because the Article 32 investigation is required to be "thorough and impartial," an accuser may not serve as the investigating officer. *U.S. v. Cunningham*, 30 C.M.R. 402 (C.M.A. 1961).

At the conclusion of the investigation, the investigating officer prepares a written report to the convening authority. This report includes a summary of testimony taken, other evidence, a statement concerning the likely mental state of the accused, a statement concerning availability of witnesses, and a recommendation of whether or not the accused should be tried.

The Article 32 investigation is a crucial pretrial procedure that accords an accused of important safeguards. The accused is entitled to representation by counsel. Article 32(b), UCMJ, 10 U.S.C. § 832(b). The investigating officer must forward any request for military counsel to the commander who directed the investigation. RCM 405(d)(2)(B). Alternatively, upon request, the accused must be given a reasonable time to obtain civilian counsel. RCM 405(d)(2)(C). During the investigation, the accused may cross-examine witnesses and testimony must be under oath. However, Article 32(b) provides only for the right of cross-examination and does not provide for any right of confrontation. Therefore, an Article 32, pretrial investigation, while an important right, is not the equivalent of a trial for purposes of the Confrontation Clause. Because the investigation is advisory, strict rules of evidence are not applied and the Article 32 investigating officer is not required "to decide difficult legal questions." *United States v. Bramel*, 29 M.J. 958, 964 (A.C.M.R.1990)

Under RCM 405(h)(3), Article 32 hearings are normally open to the press and public unless, on a case-by-case basis, "cause shown outweighs the value of openness." *ABC, Inc. v. Powell*, 47 M.J. 363 (C.A.A.F. 1997). The remedy in *Powell* was a writ of mandamus in the C.A.A.F. Similar remedies were denied, however, in *Assange and Wikileaks v. United States and Lieutenant Colonel Paul Almanza*, 71 M.J. 100 (C.A.A.F.2012) (summary disposition) and in *Center for Constitutional Rights v. United States*, 72 M.J. 126 (C.A.A.F. 2013). *Center for Constitutional Rights* (CCC) was an appeal of a summary denial of a writ of mandamus and prohibition by the Army Court of Criminal Appeals, based on a narrow reading of that court's jurisdiction in light of the decisions in *Clinton v. Goldsmith*, 526 U.S. 529 (1999) and *United States v. Denedo*, 556 U.S. 904 (2009). *CCC* questioned the continuing validity of *Powell*, see 72 M.J., 126, 129. This history was reviewed in *Bergdahl v. Burke*, 2015 WL 5968401 (Army Ct. Crim.App. 2015). Supervision of the court-martial process by Article III courts would seem the only sure way to assure constitutionally guaranteed access for the press and public.

E. PRE-TRIAL ASPECTS OF COURTS-MARTIAL

1. GENERAL PRETRIAL PROCESSES

The convening authority initiates the pretrial stages of the court-martial appointing court-martial members, the military equivalent to jurors.

Immediately after the convening authority's action, trial and defense counsel are detailed by their respective superiors. In both general and special courts-martial, counsel must be qualified attorneys. Additionally, counsel must be certified as competent to perform such duties in a general court-martial.

Following counsels' appointments, responsibility shifts from the convening authority to the attorneys. Defense counsel should consult with the accused, and arrange for the attendance of witnesses at trial. Both trial and defense counsel have equal opportunity to obtain witnesses and an accused has a right to compel the attendance of witnesses in his or her behalf. Article 46, UCMJ, 10 U.S.C. § 846. The right is not absolute; it depends on a showing of relevance and materiality. "However, once materiality has been shown the Government must either produce the witness or abate the proceedings." *United States v. Carpenter*, 1 M.J. 384 (C.M.A. 1976); RCM 703(b).

Generally, the rules applicable to subpoenaing witnesses in civilian trials also apply in courts-martial. However, unlike the civilian accused, the military defendant need not be indigent in order to have the costs of obtaining witnesses borne by the government, where the expected testimony would raise doubts concerning the defendant's guilt. In *United States v. Sweeney*, 34 C.M.R. 379 (C.M.A. 1964), the court decided that character witnesses (two of defendant's former superior officers) should be subpoenaed at government expense. Since the character of an alleged co-conspirator testifying under immunity was impeached, the core of Sweeney's defense was his own good character and reputation. The court essentially balanced the equities, looking at the relevance of the testimony, the responsibilities of the witnesses sought, and the lack of readily available alternative sources of similar testimony.

Pretrial discovery is considerably more liberal in the military than in state and federal criminal proceedings. Generally, even evidence not required to be produced will be disclosed. It is also less formal than in civilian processes. Information is often obtained upon request, without resort to court processes. The basic sources for the rules of discovery in military proceedings are the MCM, the Jencks Act, and the Federal Rules of Criminal Procedure.

RCM 701(a)(1) summarizes trial counsel's disclosure responsibilities. The papers accompanying the charge sheet, including the report of the Article 32 investigation, are also available to the defense. Defense counsel's disclosures are treated in RCM 701(b)(1) and (2). Upon request, the defense may inspect evidentiary material in the hands of the military authorities relevant to the defense's preparation or which trial counsel intends to use as evidence. RCM 701(a)(2). Additionally, when a general court-martial is recommended, defense counsel is supplied with a copy of the substance of all testimony taken at the Article 32 investigation. Evidence favorable to the accused including evidence which reasonably tends to negate the guilt of the accused, reduce its degree or would reduce the punishment must be disclosed. RCM 701(a)(6) codifies and expands the civilian criminal procedure rule of *Brady v. Maryland*, 373 U.S. 83 (1963) (prosecutorial duty to disclose exculpatory evidence), which is based upon the due process clause of the Fifth Amendment.

Trial counsel also is required to notify the defense of any records of prior convictions of the accused of which trial counsel is aware and plans to offer for any purpose. RCM 701(a)(4). Finally, upon request, the defense may inspect any information that trial counsel will present at presentencing proceedings as well as notify the defense of the witnesses to be called at those proceedings. RCM 701(a)(5).

The Jencks Act, 18 U.S.C. § 3500, requires production at trial of pre-trial statements of government witnesses. Such statements may substantially assist defense counsel on cross examination. In *United States v. Albo*, 46 C.M.R. 30 (C.M.A. 1972), the Jencks Act was held applicable to courts-martial. Under its terms, after a Government witness testifies on direct examination, the defense is entitled to the production of documents that are (1) statements of the witness as defined by the statute, (2) in the possession of the Government, and (3) related to the subject matter of the witness's testimony. If a statement meets the statutory criteria, the defense has a right to its production without any showing that the document is inconsistent with the testimony of the witness or that it would be useful for impeachment.

To the extent they are not displaced by the UCMJ or inconsistent with military justice, the Federal Rules of Criminal Procedure apply in courts-martial proceedings. For example, statements of the defendant in the government's possession or control may be inspected, copied, or photographed by defense counsel. Fed.R.Crim.P. 16(a)(1)(A); Mil. R. Evid.

304(d)(1). Defense counsel is also entitled to a copy of the defendant's prior criminal record and the results of physical or mental examinations which are material to the defense or intended for use by the government as evidence. Fed.R.Crim.P. 16(a)(1)(B), (C), and (D). RCM 701(a)(2)(B) & (4).

As in civilian criminal cases, there are some limitations on discovery in courts-martial proceedings. The most important limitations, contained in Military Rules of Evidence, 501–506, and 513, relate to privileged information. Military secrets, state secrets, and classified material are not discoverable, and defense counsel is required to notify the prosecution before any potential disclosure of classified information, so that the government has an opportunity to assert its privilege as to that information. Mil. R. Evid. 505(h)(1). Likewise undiscoverable are attorney work product or confidential communications between husband and wife, penitent and clergy, attorney and client, and, with some exceptions, psychotherapist and patient. All these limitations, of course, may be waived. Although confidential psychotherapist-patient communications are largely protected, there is no physician-patient privilege for military medical records.

2. SPEEDY TRIAL

The Sixth Amendment to the Constitution guarantees that "the accused shall enjoy the right to a speedy trial." In Federal courts, this right has been implemented by the Speedy Trial Act, 18 U.S.C.A.

§ 3161, which establishes time periods for indictment and trial, sets out delays excluded from the computation, and specifies sanctions for impermissible delay. However, the Speedy Trial Act does not apply to military tribunals. 18 U.S.C. § 3172(2). Instead, the speedy trial rights of servicemembers are governed by the Sixth Amendment, Article 10, UCMJ, 10 U.S.C. § 810, and RCM 707. The confluence of these rights is sorted out in *United States v. Mizgala*, 61 M.J. 122 (C.A.A.F. 2005): "Article 10 creates a more exacting speedy trial demand than does the Sixth Amendment." Indeed, "unreasonable delay in disposing of criminal charges in the military is unlawful." Article 98, UCMJ, 10 U.S.C. § 898 ("Any person subject to this chapter who—(1) is responsible for unnecessary delay in the disposition of any case of a person accused of an offense under this chapter; or (2) knowingly and intentionally fails to enforce or comply with any provision of this chapter regulating the proceedings before, during, or after trial of an accused; shall be punished as a court-martial may direct."). An accused's rights under "Article 10 [are] not restricted by RCM 707" since "[I]n the area of subconstitutional speedy trial, Article 10 reigns preeminent over anything propounded by the President." citing *U.S. v. Kossman*, 38 M.J. 258, 261 (C.M.A. 1993).

The *Mizgala* court identifies an important distinction between the Speedy Trial Act and a servicemember's rights under Article 10:

The Speedy Trial Act imposes the burden of proof upon an accused to support a motion to dismiss. 18 U.S.C. § 3162(a)(2) (2000). Under Article 10, the Government has the burden to show that the prosecution moved forward with reasonable diligence in response to a motion to dismiss. *United States v. Brown*, 28 C.M.R. 64, 69 (C.M.A. 1959). This distinction is additional proof of the importance of Article 10 to the incarcerated servicemember.

Under RCM 707, an accused is entitled to trial within 120 days after notice to the accused of referral of charges, the imposition of restraint, or a reservist's entry into active duty to stand trial by court-martial, whichever occurs first. RCM 707(a), 905(c)(2)(B), and 907(b)(2)(A). However, that time frame is not determinative with respect to the government's compliance with speedy trial requirements. Again from *Mizgala*, "Article 10 and RCM are distinct, each providing its own speedy trial protection. The fact that a prosecution meets the 120-day rule of RCM 707 does not directly 'or indirectly' demonstrate that the Government moved to trial with reasonable diligence as required by Article 10."

Military court interpretations of Art. 10 have imposed more rigorous speedy trial requirements than the Sixth Amendment demands. *U.S. v. Powell*, 49 M.J. 460 (C.M.A. 1975). These decisions have required more than the normal Sixth Amendment balancing of (1) length of delay, (2) reasons for delay, (3) timely assertion of speedy trial right, and (4) prejudice to the accused. *Barker v. Wingo*, 407 U.S.

514 (1972). Moreover, military law protects the defendant against government delays in pressing charges, while the Sixth Amendment does not protect an accused against pre-indictment government delays. *U.S. v. Marion*, 404 U.S. 307 (1971). In the military, government accountability for expediting the process begins with pretrial restraint or preferral of charges, whichever occurs first. RCM 707; *U.S. v. Ward*, 1 M.J. 176 (C.M.A. 1975). However, civilian restraint of the accused for non-military offenses is not charged against the government.

The *Mizgala* court offers the following "framework to determine whether the Government proceeded with reasonable diligence [which] includes balancing the following four factors: (1) the length of the delay; (2) the reasons for the delay; (3) whether the appellant made a demand for a speedy trial; and (4) prejudice to the appellant."

These additional provisions concern speedy trial. Article 10, UCMJ, 10 U.S.C. § 810 requires that immediate steps be taken to inform any person placed in arrest or confinement of the charges and that the charges be promptly tried or dismissed. Article 10(b)(2) requires the President to promulgate regulations concerning the prompt referral of charges, including forwarding of charges. An accused is entitled to trial within 120 days after notice to the accused of referral of charges, the imposition of restraint, or a reservist's entry into active duty to stand trial by court-martial, whichever occurs first. RCM 707(a), 905(c)(2)(B), and 907(b)(2)(A).

According to *U.S. v. Kossman*, 38 M.J. 258 (C.M.A. 1993), military judges have broad powers of discretion to determine if the speedy trial requirement has been satisfied [and] can readily determine whether the government has been foot dragging on a particular case, under the circumstances then and there prevailing."

Procedurally, the right to a speedy trial is implemented by the defendant and defense counsel. There is no automatic entitlement to expeditious process; the defendant must raise the issue. Normally, the issue is raised upon a motion to dismiss under RCM 907(b)(2)(A). After a hearing on the motion, the judge makes a finding of fact and conclusions of law on the speedy trial issue.

Counsel for the accused, when moving for speedy trial relief, "should provide the court with a chronology detailing the processing of the case." RCM 707(c)(2). The remedy for the prosecution's failure to afford a speedy trial is dismissal of the charges. RCM 707(d). If there is a deprivation of the accused's right to a speedy trial, the dismissal will be with prejudice. The proper determinants for this are the *Mizgala* court's framework set out above.

3. PLEAS TO CHARGES

The accused has three basic choices of pleas: guilty, not guilty, or guilty of a lesser offense. Pleas of no contest or nolo contendere, which admit the sufficiency of evidence to prove guilt without actually admitting guilt although allowed in federal court, are not allowed in a court-martial. Pleas are first entered at arraignment but may be received up until the time of trial. Arraignment is a watershed because without consent of the accused no additional major alterations to the charges may be added following arraignment. RCM 601(e)(2); 603(d). Additionally, after arraignment, the accused can be tried even though absent from trial. RCM 804(b).

If the accused introduces a "not guilty" plea, all matters are placed in issue and the prosecution at trial must prove the accused's guilt beyond a reasonable doubt. A "guilty" plea admits every element of the crime specified, and if accepted is equivalent to a conviction. A "guilty of a lesser offense" plea generally occurs as a result of a pretrial agreement entered into between the convening authority and the accused.

If the accused makes an irregular plea or no plea at all, a plea of not guilty is entered and the court proceeds on that basis. Article 45(a), UCMJ, 10 U.S.C. § 845(a); RCM 910(b). Moreover, if the accused pleads guilty and later raises matters inconsistent with a guilty plea, or if it appears that the accused improvidently or through lack of understanding entered the guilty plea, the court will enter a plea of not guilty. Art. 45(a), UCMJ, 10 U.S.C. § 845(a); RCM 910(h)(2). At any time up to announcement of the sentence, a guilty plea may be withdrawn by the accused. RCM 910(h)(1). Finally, military law does not permit any pleas of guilty to a charge for which the death penalty may be adjudged. Article 45(b), UCMJ, 10 U.S.C. § 845(b); RCM 910(a)(1).

4. PRETRIAL AGREEMENTS (PLEA BARGAINS)

Plea bargaining is "an essential component of the administration of justice," in military as well as civilian criminal cases. *Santobello v. New York,* 404 U.S. 257 (1971). Plea bargains in the military are referred to as pretrial agreements. All pretrial agreements must be in writing and signed by the accused, defense counsel, and the convening authority. RCM 705(d)(2) and (3). Note that pretrial agreements are concluded with the convening authority, not the judge (as in civilian trials). A convening authority has a range of options in a pretrial agreement. For example, pursuant to a pretrial agreement, the convening authority may agree to limit the sentence to that set forth in the agreement; to refer the accused's case to a particular level of court-martial; or refer what could be a capital (death penalty) case as a noncapital case (in which the death penalty is not an option).

Either side may initiate plea negotiations and propose terms. Before signing, defense counsel should be satisfied that the accused, if tried, would probably be found guilty. *United States v. Care,* 40 C.M.R. 247 (C.M.A. 1969) ("[T]he court-martial records [must] reflect fully an awareness by an accused pleading guilty of what he is admitting that he did and intended and of the law that applies to his acts and intentions.") Defense counsel has a duty to pass on any plea bargain offers from the government to the accused. *Missouri v. Frye,* 566 U.S. 134 (2012). In addition, any pretrial agreement between the convening authority and the accused will be carefully scrutinized before being accepted by the military judge in lieu of a full-fledged trial of the facts. RCM 910(f). Further protection against abuse of the plea bargaining process in the military is the so-called "providence inquiry." The procedure is most fully articulated in *United States v. Care*, 40 C.M.R. 247 (C.M.A. 1969):

> [T]he record of trial . . . must reflect not only that the elements of each offense charged have been explained to the accused but also that the military trial judge or the president [of the court] has questioned the accused about what he did or did not do, and what he intended (where this is pertinent), to make clear the basis for a determination by military trial judge or president whether the acts or the omissions of the accused constitute the offense or offenses to which he is pleading guilty. . . . The record must also demonstrate the military trial judge or president personally addressed the accused, advised him that his plea waives his right to a trial of the facts by a court-martial, and his right to be confronted by the witnesses against him. . . .

The providence inquiry is conducted by the military judge out of the presence of the court. Should the providence inquiry disclose matters inconsistent with the accused's plea, the military judge "must either resolve the inconsistency or reject the plea." *United States v. England*, 2009 WL 6842645 (A.Ct. Crim.App. 2009) (military judge did not abuse his discretion in rejecting accused's plea of guilty to the offense of conspiracy to commit maltreatment because of conflicting testimony of alleged conspirators showed no "meeting of the minds" among them). After rejection of PFC Lynndie R. England's guilty plea, she was convicted by a general court-martial and sentenced to a dishonorable discharge, three years confinement and reduction to Private E1. The judge may immediately enter a finding of guilty after accepting a plea of guilty. RCM 910(g). If the plea is to a lesser offense, the judge should not enter a finding until the evidence is received on the lesser offense.

The common errors committed during providence inquiries include: failure to inform the accused that his constitutional rights are waived by a guilty plea; misunderstanding by the accused concerning the maximum sentence; failure to list the elements of the offense to which the accused pleads guilty; and failure to develop a factual basis for the plea through responses of the accused to questions by the judge. Moreover, the trial judge dealing with such a plea should inquire carefully into the terms and conditions of any pretrial agreement, "assuring on the record that an accused understands the meaning and effect of each condition as well as the sentence limitations imposed." *United States v. Elmore*, 1 M.J. 262 (C.M.A. 1976). But "[w]here the plea bargain encompasses conditions which the trial judge believes violate either appellate case law, public policy, or the trial judge's own notions of fundamental fairness, he or she should move to strike such provisions from the agreement with the consent of the parties." The judge is authorized to strike any conditions in the agreement which violate "appellate case law, public policy, or the trial judge's own notions of fundamental fairness. (Fletcher, Chief Judge concurring in the result), Id.

Problems arise when the judge too readily accepts or rejects the pretrial agreement. Acceptance of the sentencing terms of a pretrial agreement, for example, should not be done until the judge first announces sentence based on the rest of the plea following a providence inquiry. RCM 910(f)(3). On the other hand, if the judge refuses to accept the plea of guilty, the accused may seek to have the judge who has seen the plea recused from presiding over the trial. *United States v. Cockerell*, 49 C.M.R. 567 (A.C.M.R. 1974) ("[A] judge should recuse himself to protect both the rights of the government and the accused, whenever a plea of guilty has been found to be improvident, if he has any doubt as to his ability to render justice to either side. Any doubt should be resolved in favor of recusal.")

F. TRIAL

There are relatively few important procedural differences between civilian and military trials, and some of the obvious ones are matters of form rather than substance. For example, courts-martial are conducted by attorneys who are uniformed officers of the armed services; this includes the military judge, trial and defense counsel.

The Sixth Amendment right to an open, public trial applies to court-martial proceedings: "Without question, the sixth-amendment right to a public trial is applicable to courts-martial." *United States v. Hershey*, 20 M.J. 433, 435 (C.M.A. 1985). Military regulations provide that "courts-martial shall be open to the public [and the] 'public' includes members of both the military and civilian communities." RCM 806(a).

The Discussion to RCM 806(a) notes that provision should be made for "members of the press." Press access to court-martial proceedings was discussed earlier in connection with Article 32 hearings. Generally speaking, court-martial proceedings are normally open to the press and public unless, on a case-by-case basis, "cause shown outweighs the value of openness." *ABC, Inc. v. Powell*, 47 M.J. 363 (C.A.A.F. 1997). Although military judges have the power to exclude members of the press and public from court-martial proceedings in appropriate cases, that decision is subject to judicial review in order to protect the rights that the Sixth Amendment assures. The remedy in *Powell* was a writ of mandamus in the C.A.A.F. Similar remedies were denied, however, in *Assange and Wikileaks v. United States and Lieutenant Colonel Paul Almanza*, 71 M.J. 100 (C.A.A.F.2012) (summary disposition) and in *Center for Constitutional Rights v. United States*, 72 M.J. 126 (C.A.A.F. 2013). *Center for Constitutional Rights* was an appeal of a summary denial of a writ of mandamus and prohibition by the Army Court of Criminal Appeals, based on a narrow reading of that court's jurisdiction in light of the decisions in *Clinton v. Goldsmith*, 526 U.S. 529 (1999) and *United States v. Denedo*, 556 U.S. 904 (2009). In light of *Center for*

Constitutional Rights, the most promising route to challenge closure of court-martial proceedings would appear to be by writ of mandamus or other compulsory process in federal district court. Unless *Center for Constitutional Rights* is reversed, supervision of the court-martial process is left to Article III courts which clearly lack the jurisdictional handicaps complained of by the C.A.A.F. majority in *Center for Constitutional Rights*. The right of the press and public to access to court-martial proceedings is clear. *ABC, Inc. v. Powell*, 47 M.J. 363 (C.A.A.F. 1997) ("We have consistently held that the Sixth Amendment right does apply to a court-martial.") In *Center for Constitutional Rights* the court was troubled by the standing of nonparties to assert a conceded constitutional right to public access to a court-martial in instances where the accused has not asserted a right to a public trial. The alternative, forcing nonparties who clearly can claim a constitutionally grounded right to access into pursuing their rights in a forum outside the military justice system, raises unresolved issues about the integrity of a system which, through a very narrow construction of its jurisdiction, is unable to enforce the provisions of their own governing rules, even rules grounded in the Constitution. Congress may wish to address this issue.

1. TRIAL PROCEDURES

The presiding officer sets the time and place for trial. After all court personnel have assembled but before the court is called to order, the presiding officer determines whether (1) the convening order is valid; (2) a quorum is present; (3) the accused is present; and (4) counsel are qualified. Unless arraigned at a previous Article 39(a) session, the accused is informed of the charges and asked to plea.

The members of the court are then seated according to rank, the court is called to order, and the court is sworn in. Witnesses can be excluded from the courtroom at the request of the prosecution or defense, or the military judge may order exclusion sua sponte. MRE 615. The charge is read, and members of the court are challenged, if at all, by trial counsel and then defense counsel. Race, ethnicity, and gender are impermissible grounds for challenging court members and shaping the military panel to one's liking. *United States v. Cruse*, 50 M.J. 592 (A.Ct.Crim.App. 1999). There are an unlimited number of challenges for cause, and one peremptory challenge for each party. Article 41, UCMJ, 10 U.S.C. § 841; RCM 912(f)–(g). If a military judge is present, he or she determines challenges for cause; if not, then a simple majority vote of the members of the court decides challenges for cause. RCM 912(f)(3), (h). In *United States v. White*, 36 M.J. 284 (C.M.A. 1993) the C.M.A. ruled that judges should grant challenges for cause liberally, and appellate courts should not overrule lower court challenge determinations.

The court members are provided a copy of the charges and are informed of the plea made to each charge. If the plea is "not guilty," counsel may make an opening statement. Following the opening statement, if any, the evidence is presented. Ordinarily, the prosecution's witnesses are examined first, followed by the defense witnesses, then by each side's rebuttal witnesses. RCM 913.

At the conclusion of the presentation of evidence, the prosecution and then the defense counsel may present their arguments. RCM 919. Occasionally, these arguments raise issues, for example, whether prosecutorial arguments exceeded the bounds of earnest and forceful presentation, *United States v. Doctor*, 21 C.M.R. 252 (C.M.A. 1956) (failure to object in the trial arena where the harmful effects, if any, might be ameliorated by prompt instructions, normally raises the doctrine of waiver and precludes an accused from asserting a claim of error on appeal).

At the close of argument, the presiding officer instructs the members of the court on the applicable law. Article 51(c), UCMJ, 10 U.S.C. § 851(c). The members then meet alone to determine the guilt or innocence of the accused. A substantial body of law has given necessary detail to the bare requirement of Article 51(c) that the presiding officer instruct court members concerning their general responsibilities and the elements of the offense. For example, the military judge should define any terms with special meanings, tailor all instructions to the facts, and give such other explanations, descriptions or directions as may be necessary and which are requested by a party or which the military judge decides should be given. RCM 920(e). The military judge may summarize and comment on the evidence as long as it is an accurate, fair, and dispassionate statement of what the evidence shows.

The military judge has the authority to enter contrary findings of not guilty after the court members' verdict in order to set aside findings of guilty that are incorrect as a matter of law. Article 51(b), UCMJ, 10 U.S.C. § 851(b). For example, consider a case in which an accused was acquitted of a charge alleging sale of marihuana, but found guilty of the charge of conspiracy to sell marihuana. Because the sale was the only overt act alleged in the conspiracy charge, the court members' verdict was inconsistent and the conspiracy charge, as a matter of law, could not stand. The military judge who is responsible for ruling "upon all questions of law . . . arising during the proceeding," would otherwise be compelled to submit legally erroneous findings of guilty (in this case, of a conspiracy). *United States v. Kelly*, 12 M.J. 509 (A.C.M.R. 1981).

2. SENTENCING PROCEDURES

If there is a finding of guilty, the sentence is imposed at a second stage of the court-martial proceeding. Like the findings stage, the second stage is adversarial: first prosecution and then defense counsel present evidence relevant to sentencing and make arguments to the court. RCM 1001(a). Evidence in aggravation admissible by the prosecution at sentencing includes prior civilian convictions, including pleas of nolo contendere, evidence of "hate crime" motivation (i.e., that the accused intentionally selected any victim or any property as the object of the offense because of the actual or perceived race, color, religion, national origin, ethnicity, gender, disability, or sexual orientation of any person), and character evidence of the accused. (RCM 1001(b)(3)–(5)). The military judge must advise the accused of the right to present matters in extenuation and mitigation. RCM 1001(a)(3). The accused may testify under oath on his or her own behalf, but may be cross-examined or impeached. The accused also has the option of making an unsworn statement, oral, written, or both, which is not subject to cross-examination. RCM 1001(c). The accused may also choose simply to have counsel argue on his or her behalf.

After receiving instructions from the court concerning the sentence, such as the maximum sentence possible, the trier of fact determines a sentence. RCM 1005 & 1006(a). All evidence admitted during the trial and reasonable inferences therefrom may be considered in determining the appropriate sentence. RCM 1001(f)(2). When a decision has been reached, the court is opened, and the accused is informed of the sentence. The judge then reviews the sentence for proper form and adjourns the court after sentence is adjudged. If there is no agreement on a sentence by the required number of jurors, the military judge may declare a mistrial; the case is returned to the convening authority who may direct a rehearing on the sentence. RCM 1006(d)(6).

Defense counsel may then prepare a recommendation for clemency to be submitted to the convening authority. Any members of the court who desire to do so may sign the recommendation and state their reasons for signing. The recommendation properly may include matters not admissible at trial and should not merely cumulate evidence considered at trial.

Military sentences are not executed when adjudged. However the accused will normally begin serving any adjudged confinement immediately and forfeitures will normally take effect 14 days later. Article 57, UCMJ, 10 U.S.C. § 857. Except when a sentence of death is adjudged, the convening authority has the discretion to suspend or remit a sentence. RCM 1108(b).

If the sentence includes a dishonorable or bad-conduct discharge, dismissal of a commissioned officer or cadet, or a punishment of death, the sentence is executed when approved by the convening authority. RCM 1113(a)–(c). Otherwise, the sentence is not executed until approved by a Military Court of Criminal Appeals, which exercises all the traditional authority of appellate courts as well as "[a]wesome, plenary, de novo power of review. . . ." *United States v. Cole*, 31 M.J. 249 (C.M.A. 1990). Subsequent to review by the service C.C.A., the C.A.A.F. may, upon petition, review the case as well. The C.A.A.F. may decline review altogether; moreover, so long as there is some competent evidence, it will not reevaluate the facts of a particular case.

3. EVIDENCE IN COURTS-MARTIAL

Article 36(a), UCMJ, 10 U.S.C. 836(a) states in part that in military trials, procedures "may be prescribed by the President by regulations which shall, so far as he considers practicable, apply the principles of law and the rules of evidence generally recognized in the trial of criminal cases in the United States district courts. . . ." These regulations, which specify many evidentiary rules in detail, also expressly state that courts-martial shall apply "the rules of evidence generally recognized in the trial of criminal cases in the United States district courts and . . . , when not inconsistent with . . . , the rules of evidence at common law." MRE 101(b). The President has set out the rules of evidence applicable to courts-martial in the Military Rules of Evidence (MRE). They are based on the Federal Rules of Evidence and amendments to the Federal Rules are automatically incorporated into the Military Rules 18 months after their Federal Rule effective date, unless the President takes affirmative action to prevent their incorporation. MRE 1102.

When evidence regulations conflict with the UCMJ, the regulations must give way. *United States v. Eggers*, 11 C.M.R. 191 (C.M.A. 1953). Further, when either conflicts with a constitutional principle, the constitutional right governs. For example, in *United States v. Jacoby, 29 C.M.R. 244* (C.M.A. 1960), an accused successfully argued that her Sixth Amendment right to confront the witnesses against her was violated by former UCMJ Art. 49, which allowed admission into evidence of depositions taken upon written interrogatories.

While a detailed discussion of all issues of evidence in courts-martial is beyond the scope of this book, a discussion of some major points is in order. For a detailed analysis of the Military Rules of Evidence consult Appendix 22, MCM, "Analysis of the Military Rules of Evidence."

First, neither the prosecution nor the defense need present at trial all available evidence or present evidence in any particular order. However, failure to present evidence known to and within the sole control of one party may lead to adverse inferences being drawn against that party. Moreover, while the court generally must refrain from becoming an advocate in a court-martial proceeding, it may play an active role in obtaining further evidence from the parties. RCM 801(c); MRE 614.

Second, court-martial counsel generally present evidence in the sequence in which the relevant events occurred. The prosecution presents its case first, attempting to establish every essential element of the offense. Thereafter, the defense often moves for a finding of not guilty, which, if denied, is followed by defense evidence concerning justification, denial, or affirmative defense. The prosecution is afforded an opportunity to rebut the defense's case-in-chief, and the defense may present evidence in surrebuttal. Finally, additional rebuttal evidence is allowed in the discretion of the military judge, as is evidence requested by the military judge or members. RCM 913(c).

Third, either prosecution or defense counsel may make an offer of evidence to which the opposing party may object. Failure to object at trial to admission of evidence is generally deemed, upon appeal, to waive objections relating to admission, especially where a party consciously chooses not to object, asserts a position inconsistent with reliance on an objection, or appears to invite error by failing to object. MRE 103(a); RCM 905(e).

The primary objections to admissibility are irrelevancy, hearsay, and illegality. Relevancy, of course, depends on the charges brought and the circumstances sought to be presented. MRE 401–403. MRE 801's definitions of hearsay is taken verbatim from the Federal Rules of Evidence. MRE 803 thereafter sets forth extensive categories of exceptions, which parallel exceptions to the Federal Rule with the necessary modifications for adaptation to military practice. Analysis of MRE 803, Appendix 22, MCM.

Finally, once evidence has been admitted in a court-martial, it is the role of the trier of fact to draw conclusions from the evidence. Simply stated, some evidence will appear more indicative of particular conclusions than other evidence. Several so-called presumptions, which demand certain conclusions absent contrary evidence, deserve separate treatment. The "presumption of innocence" reiterates the fundamental proposition that to obtain a conviction in a criminal trial, the prosecution must demonstrate the defendant's guilt beyond a reasonable doubt. See RCM 920(e)(5)(A). The "presumption of sanity" simply absolves the government from proving the defendant's sanity until such time as the defendant presents credible evidence questioning his or her sanity. See RCM 916(k)(3)(A). Finally, the "presumption of competency of witnesses" merely indicates that witnesses' testimony usually will be believed unless context, demeanor, internal contradictions and so forth indicate that it should be disbelieved. MRE 601.

CHAPTER 5

REVIEW OF COURTS-MARTIAL

Both civilian and military appellate review processes are designed to correct errors in individual cases and establish a body of law for application to subsequent cases. However, the military review system is more protective of the rights of convicted persons than state or federal review systems because several military reviews are automatic. Moreover, some military reviews correct factual errors and exercise clemency as well as reviewing questions of law and "clearly erroneous" factual findings. Appointment of new counsel at government expense to handle appeals also encourages a thorough and detached review of the court-martial trial process. Finally, defense counsel is mandatory when requested by the accused, when the United States is represented by counsel, or when the Judge Advocate General (TJAG) has sent the case to the C.A.A.F.

The military appellate process involves mandatory review by the convening authority, often with the advice of a staff judge advocate (SJA). RCM 1106. Additionally, further reviews may be appropriate by superiors of the convening authority, TJAG, the Court of Criminal Appeals, and the C.A.A.F. In rare cases, subsequent review by civilian federal courts is also appropriate. For an overview of the appellate review processes and the court structures referred to in this chapter, review Charts 1 and 2 in Chapter 3.

A. CONVENING AUTHORITY ACTION

Until the commander who convened the court-martial affirms the court's actions, the findings and sentence, with the exception of any confinement or forfeitures, do not take effect. Art. 57(c), UCMJ, 10 U.S.C. § 857(c); RCM 1113(a). An announced sentence containing an error may be corrected by a subsequent announcement made prior to adjournment. RCM 1007(b).

Following the trial the record of the proceedings is submitted automatically to the convening authority. Article 60(a), UCMJ, 10 U.S.C. § 860(a); RCM 1101(a). The commander may not disturb any finding of not guilty, RCM 1107(b)(4), but has the discretion to disapprove all or any portion of a finding of guilty and to reduce, mitigate, or disapprove any sentence or portion of a sentence. Art. 60(c)(2), UCMJ, 10 U.S.C. § 860(c)(2); RCM 1107(c)–(d). Unlike in federal court, neither the commander nor the court-martial can "correct" upwards a previously announced sentence. *U.S. v. Baker*, 32 M.J. 290 (C.M.A. 1991); Art. 60(e)(2)(c), UCMJ ("In no case . . . may the record be returned for increasing the severity of the sentence unless the sentence prescribed for the offense is mandatory").

The long-established power of senior commanders to overturn convictions and dismiss charges has prompted criticism from advocacy groups and members of Congress because of the handling of sexual assault cases, most notably the decision by Air Force commander, Lt. Gen. Craig A Franklin to dismiss the conviction of Lt. Col James Wilkerson who was found guilty in November 2012 of aggravated sexual assault and sentenced to one year imprisonment. Proposed legislation supported by Secretary of Defense Chuck Hagel would scale back the power of a court-martial convening authority to overturn a guilty verdict returned by a court-martial in serious cases like sexual assault. Other contemplated legislation would require commanders who make changes in cases involving minor offenses to explain the basis for their decisions in writing. Charlie Savage, "Amid Criticism, Pentagon Is Seeking Overhaul of the Court-Martial System," NY Times (April 9, 2013), 2013 WLNR 8593836.

The commander must evaluate all aspects of the trial, calling upon the SJA in appropriate cases. RCM 1107(b)(3). In this process, the commander should weigh the evidence, pass on the credibility of witnesses, ensuring that the accused is guilty beyond a reasonable doubt, and ensure that each aspect of the sentence accords with his or her notions of justice. This review, a hybrid between trial and appellate process, is heavily weighted in favor of the defendant. Reductions of sentences by convening authorities are common. Additionally, ambiguous sentences can be corrected post adjournment in special sessions called by the military judge. RCM 1109(c)(1). However, following adjournment there are limitations placed on the ability to correct errors in announced sentences. *United States v. Jones,* 34 M.J. 270, 271 (C.M.A. 1992).

A convening authority who is biased or has become so involved in the prosecution as to give the appearance of impropriety, is obligated to pass the record on to a superior field commander for review. For example, when the convening authority grants immunity to one involved in a crime with the accused, that action raises some doubt as to his or her ability to be impartial. In that case, someone else should review the record to avoid even the appearance of bias. However, the mere granting of immunity is not equivalent to actual bias, and each case must be examined to determine if such bias exists. *United States v. Lilly*, 7 M.J. 701 (N.C.M.R. 1979).

B. JUDGE ADVOCATE REVIEW

Before acting on the record of trial by a general court-martial or a special court-martial that adjudged a sentence of bad conduct discharge or one-year confinement, a convening authority must refer the case to the SJA for a written opinion. Art. 60(d), UCMJ, 10 U.S.C. § 860(d); RCM 1106(a). The purposes of this evaluation are to advise the convening authority concerning the legal posture of the case and to apprise appellate agencies, in condensed form, of the trial proceedings and results.

Cases involving acquittals are given very limited SJA review. The SJA merely provides an opinion concerning the existence of court-martial jurisdiction and determines the propriety of the court's appointment. However, no such review is required. RCM 1112(b).

Cases involving convictions are given much more thorough SJA review. This review must be in writing and must contain concise information regarding: (1) the findings and sentence adjudged by the court-martial; (2) a summary of the accused's service record, including length and character of service, awards received, and any records of nonjudicial punishment and previous convictions; (3) a statement of the nature and duration of any pretrial restraint; (4) a statement of any action the convening authority is obligated to take under a pretrial agreement, if any, or the reason why there is no such obligation; and (5) a specific recommendation concerning what action the convening authority should take. If an allegation of legal error is raised, the SJA should state whether corrective action on the findings or sentence should be taken. Additionally, the SJA may include any other matters deemed appropriate. RCM 1106(d).

The SJA review must be supplied to defense counsel for examination and rebuttal. RCM 1106(f); following receipt of the SJA review, the convening authority is required to state his reasons if he takes action different from that recommended by the SJA. These reasons, if any, are then transmitted along with the record to the Judge Advocate General. *United States v. Keller*, 1 M.J. 159 (C.M.A. 1975).

Regardless of whether there has been an SJA review, the convening authority is required to forward the entire record, complete with disposition and the SJA's opinion, to the Judge Advocate General of the appropriate branch of the service. Articles 64(b), 65(a), and 69(a), UCMJ, 10 U.S.C. §§ 864(b), 865(a) and 869(a); RCM 1111 and 1112. TJAG's review is administrative rather than judicial; the record may be examined to determine if the findings and sentence are supported in law. RCM 1112. If any questions arise concerning the legality of any aspect of the court-martial or the convening authority's action, TJAG may modify or set aside the findings and/or sentence and then must forward the record to the Court of Criminal Appeals. Articles 66(b) and 69(a), UCMJ, 10 U.S.C. §§ 866(b) and 869(a); RCM 1201(a) and (b)(1).

C. COURT OF CRIMINAL APPEALS

The TJAG of each service branch appoints the members of that branch's Court of Criminal Appeals. Article 66(a), UCMJ, 10 U.S.C. § 866(a). The C.C.A. is composed of not less than three members, usually selected from among senior active or retired JAG officers who have previously been appointed as military judges. C.C.A. jurisdiction is mandatory and automatic for all courts-martial where (1) there is a sentence of death, dismissal of an officer, cadet, or midshipman, dishonorable or bad-conduct discharge of any servicemember, or imprisonment of a servicemember for one year or more and (2) the right to appellate review has not been waived or an appeal has not been withdrawn. Articles 66(b), 67(a), 71(c) and 72(c), UCMJ, 10 U.S.C. §§ 866(b), 867(a), 871(c) and 872(c). Additionally, a C.C.A. has jurisdiction to review cases referred to it by TJAG. Article 69(d), UCMJ, 10 U.S.C. § 869(d).

The scope of review exercised by a C.C.A. is unusually broad. The court is permitted to "weigh the evidence, judge the credibility of witnesses, and determine controverted questions of fact." Article 66(c), UCMJ, 10 U.S.C. § 866(c); *United States v. Turner*, 25 M.J. 324 (C.M.A. 1987). It also may decide any questions of law raised by the record. A C.C.A. may affirm a court-martial decision, set aside its findings, order a rehearing, or dismiss charges against the accused. Article 66(c) and (d), UCMJ, 10 U.S.C. § 866(c) and (d). When the C.C.A. finds an error of law in the court-martial, it will hold the findings or sentence incorrect only if the error "materially prejudices the substantial rights of the accused." Article 59(a), UCMJ, 10 U.S.C. § 859(a).

The C.C.A. judges have neither tenure nor fixed terms of appointment but serve, as do court-martial judges, at the pleasure of TJAG. This method of "detailing" judges has been attacked for failure to satisfy requirements of the United States Constitution. In. *United States v. Graf*, 35 M.J. 450 (1992), cert den. 510 U.S. 1085 (1994), the accused argued that the lack of a fixed term of office violated the necessary independence for the judiciary under the Fifth Amendment. In *Weiss v. U.S.*, 510 U.S. 163 (1994), the defendants contended that, because military judges are not confirmed by the Senate, their appointments violated the Appointments Clause of the Constitution. The Supreme Court held that duties of military judges were not significantly different than those of other servicemembers: initial appointment as a commissioned officer of one later detailed to serve as a judge was sufficient to satisfy the Appointments Clause and in a military context, fixed judicial terms were not required since

"Congress has achieved an acceptable balance between independence and accountability."

One year later, the Supreme Court decided another Appointments Clause issue that casts much doubt on the legitimacy of many decisions of the former Coast Guard Court of Military Appeals. *Ryder v. United States*, 515 U.S. 177 (1995), was premised on the underlying illegality of civilians having no proper appointment serving on this court. The Secretary of Transportation exercised his constitutional authority to appoint these judges, but Ryder involved convictions upheld by the C.M.A. prior to proper appointment. The Supreme Court unanimously held that the conviction was unlawful, refusing to find that decisions of improperly appointed judges were "de facto valid." The Court said that its decision would directly affect no more than ten cases raising this issue on direct appeals.

Because a court-martial is not an Art. III court, critics have continued to question the judicial independence of military judges, e.g., Major Fansu Ku, "From Law Member to Military Judge: The Continuing Evolution of an Independent Trial Judiciary in the Twenty-First Century," 199 *Mil. L. Rev.* 49 (2009) and Frederic Lederer & Barbara S., "An Independent Military Judiciary—A Proposal to Amend the UCMJ," 3 *Wm. & Mary Bill of Rts. L. J.* 629 (1994).

D. COURT OF APPEALS FOR THE ARMED FORCES

The C.A.A.F. (formerly the C.M.A.) is the highest civilian court specializing in appeals from military tribunals. It consists of five civilian judges appointed by the President and confirmed by the Senate for staggered 15-year terms. In their capacity at the C.A.A.F., they are not Article III judges. These judges may be removed by the President only for neglect of duty, malfeasance in office, or for mental or physical disability.

C.A.A.F. jurisdiction extends to (1) all cases in which the death sentence is imposed; (2) all cases sent by TJAG for review after C.C.A. review; and (3) those cases reviewed by C.C.A. which, upon petition of the accused and on good cause shown, the C.A.A.F. agrees to review. Art. 67(a), UCMJ; RCM 1204(a).

The review functions of this court are very similar to those of other civilian appeals courts. First, review extends only to questions of law:

> When Congress exercised its power to govern and regulate the Armed Forces by establishing the CAAF [citations omitted], it confined the court's jurisdiction to the review of specified sentences imposed by courts-martial: the CAAF has the power to act "only with respect to the findings and sentence as approved by the [court-martial's] convening authority and as affirmed or set aside as incorrect in law by the Court of Criminal Appeals." 10 U.S.C. § 867(c).

Clinton v. Goldsmith, 526 U.S. 529, 533–34 (1999).

Second, the court's authority includes the power to supervise the administration of the military criminal justice system. The court has taken the position that any accused person deprived of a fundamental right under the UCMJ "need not go outside the military justice system to find relief in the civilian courts of the Federal judiciary." *United States v. Bevilacqua*, 39 C.M.R. 10 (C.M.A. 1968). Thus, acting pursuant to the All Writs Act, 28 U.S.C.A. § 1651(a), the court has issued writs of habeas corpus, prohibition, and coram nobis. However, the broad supervisory power suggested in *Bevilacqua* has subsequently been questioned in *Center for Constitutional Rights v. United States*, 72 M.J. 126 (C.A.A.F. 2013) which adopted the narrower view set forth in *Goldsmith*.

E. PETITION FOR A NEW TRIAL

Any time within two years following approval of sentence by the convening authority, the accused or defense counsel may petition TJAG in writing for a new trial. Such a petition may be grounded upon either newly discovered evidence or fraud upon the initial court-martial. Article 73, UCMJ, 10 U.S.C. § 873; RCM 1210(a). Military regulations require further that the petitioner establish that a new trial "would probably produce a substantially more favorable result for the accused." RCM 1210(f)(2)(C).

When the petition is based on newly discovered evidence, the petitioner is limited to post-trial evidence which could not have been discovered with due diligence before trial. When fraud is the basis for the petition, the fraud must have had a "substantial contributing effect" upon the determination of guilt or the sentence. RCM 1210(f). For example, perjury by witnesses, forgery of documents, and willful prosecutorial concealment of evidence will be construed as fraud upon the court if the outcome probably would have been different absent those actions. RCM 1210.

If an appeal is pending before a military appellate court, TJAG refers the petition to the appropriate court for action. RCM 1210(e). When no such appeal is pending, TJAG is empowered to "vacate or modify, in whole or in part," the court-martial findings, sentence, or both. RCM 1201(b)(2).

When a new trial is ordered by a military appellate court or TJAG, the latter designates a new convening authority. RCM 1210(h)(1). The new convening authority sets the time, place, and personnel for the retrial. RCM 1210(h)(3). The military judge may be the same judge who presided over the original trial, but all members of the court must be different from those who first heard the case. RCM 810(b)(1). Upon retrial, the accused may not be tried for any offense of which he or she was acquitted or not tried at the earlier court-martial. RCM 1210(h)(2). Furthermore, the sentence imposed at retrial may not be more severe than the original sentence. RCM 810(d)(1).

F. CIVILIAN REVIEW OF COURTS-MARTIAL

The UCMJ provides that military review of court-martial convictions is "final and conclusive" and "binding upon all . . . courts . . . of the United States"

(Article 76, UCMJ, 10 U.S.C. § 876) except that decisions may be reviewed by the Supreme Court by writ of certiorari. Article 67(a), UCMJ, 10 U.S.C. § 867(a); 28 U.S.C.A. § 1259. Despite this language, indicating that no collateral review by civilian courts is appropriate, some limited review of courts-martial decisions in the federal courts has always been permitted.

Burns v. Wilson, 346 U.S. 844 (1953), is both the seminal case on civilian review and the source of most of the confusion in this field. In *Burns*, a plurality of the Court found it appropriate to review whether the military courts had "dealt fully and fairly with an allegation raised" in the habeas corpus petition. It was inappropriate, said the plurality, for civilian courts to reexamine and weigh the evidence in a court-martial. In dicta, the Court noted that "in military habeas corpus the inquiry . . . has always been more narrow than in civil cases" and that "this court has played no role in [military law's] development; we have exerted no supervisory power over the courts which enforce it." In *Burns*, various concurring or dissenting members of the Court argued (1) that the federal courts have only the more limited function of seeing whether the military court had jurisdiction, (2) that the case should be reargued; and (3) that federal courts should review the decisions of courts-martial for constitutional errors like the decisions of federal agencies.

Several problems are raised by *Burns*. First, may the federal courts collaterally review military court decisions only in habeas corpus cases? Various other avenues of review accepted in courts of appeals after Burns are (1) Court of Claims suits for back pay, (2) mandamus to compel performance of duties, (3) declaratory judgments under 28 U.S.C.A. § 2201, and (4) injunctive relief under Fed.R.Crim.P. 65. In *Schlesinger v. Councilman*, 420 U.S. 738 (1975), where an injunction was sought, the Supreme Court held that habeas corpus was not the sole vehicle for attacking military court decisions. However, the Court did not address the appropriateness of each of the avenues listed above; moreover, it held that civilian review was inappropriate in *Schlesinger* itself.

Second, what is the scope of civilian court review over military court decisions? As one court noted: "The Supreme Court has never clarified the [Burns] standard of full and fair consideration, and it has meant many things to many courts." *Kauffman v. Secretary of Air Force*, 415 F.2d 991 (D.C.Cir.1969). Some civilian courts have been satisfied to review only whether the military courts considered the petitioner's allegations, while others have stressed the "fullness" and "fairness" of the military court deliberations over the allegations. To date, this divergence of opinion has not been resolved by the Supreme Court.

Third, what prerequisites to and bars from review limit the availability of civilian court review of military court decisions? The most important prerequisite to civilian review is that the accused first exhaust his military appeals. *Parisi v. Davidson*, 405 U.S. 34 (1972). If the attack is upon conviction, the general rule is that all forms of direct military appellate review, automatic and discretionary, must be exhausted. If the attack is upon confinement (e.g., habeas corpus), the accused should (1) petition the C.A.A.F. for extraordinary relief or (2) request administrative relief from his commanding officer under Article 138, UCMJ, 10 U.S.C. § 938.

Finally, considerations of comity will preclude civilian courts from granting injunctive relief for an accused while a court-martial or the military appellate processes are in progress. The comity doctrine of *Younger v. Harris*, 401 U.S. 37 (1971), premised upon federal non-intervention in ongoing state criminal proceedings, was applied in *Schlesinger* even though the Court stated that "the peculiar demands of federalism are not implicated." The *Schlesinger* Court noted that this deficiency was supplied by equally compelling factors: the separateness of military and civilian societies and the mission of the military to fight or be ready to fight wars. Congress, noted the Court, attempted to balance military necessities and demands for fairness by placing a court comprised of civilian judges with lengthy tenure at the apex of the military court hierarchy.

Confusion over the application of *Burns* has resulted in an array of approaches taken by the federal courts. Several of the early decisions avoided reaching the issue of the scope of review under *Burns* entirely. Others refused to review any claims unless the military court "manifestly refused" to consider the accused's constitutional claims. Most courts are conducting de novo reviews of constitutional claims in collateral proceedings, disregarding the military court's determination. Thus, courts either ignore *Burns* or expressly refuse to follow it. Rosen, "Civilian Courts and the Military Justice System: Collateral Review of Courts-Martial," 108 MILITARY L. REV. 5, 56–61 (Spring 1985); Annotation, Review by Federal Civil Courts of Court-Martial Convictions—Modern Status, 95 A.L.R. FED. 472 (1989).

CHAPTER 6

MILITARY CRIMINAL JUSTICE SYSTEM CONSTITUTIONAL SAFEGUARDS

It has long been assumed that members of the Armed Services enjoy constitutional safeguards. *Burns v. Wilson*, 346 U.S. 137, 142 (1953) ("The military courts, like the state courts, have the same responsibilities as do the federal courts to protect a person from a violation of his constitutional rights.") (plurality opinion). The only explicit textual difference between civilian and military criminal defendants' rights in the Bill of Rights is the Fifth Amendment's exception of the requirement for grand jury indictment "in cases arising in the land or naval forces or in the Militia when in actual service in time of War or public danger. . . ." U.S. Const., Amend. V. Yet the scope of constitutional protections for servicemembers has never been fully defined by the Supreme Court. However, military appellate courts have held that servicemembers enjoy extensive Bill of Rights protections: "It is now settled that the protections of . . . the entire Bill of Rights, are applicable to the men and women serving in the military services of the United States unless expressly or by necessary implication they are made inapplicable." *United States v. Ezell*, 6 M.J. 307, 313 (C.M.A. 1979). And the presumption is in favor of the applicability of the Bill of Rights: "the burden of showing that military conditions require a different rule than that prevailing in the civilian community is upon the party arguing for a different rule." *Courtney v. Williams*, 1 M.J. 267 (C.M.A. 1976). A leading treatise on military law notes that "Although the Supreme Court has *assumed* that most of the Bill of Rights does apply, it has yet to squarely hold it applicable." F. Gilligan and F. Lederer, *Court-Martial Procedure* § 1–52.00 at 26 (1991). For example, the Supreme Court only implicitly acknowledged the applicability of the Bill of Rights to servicemembers in *United States v. Davis*, 512 U.S. 452 (1994) where the Court assumed that the Fifth Amendment right against compulsory self incrimination and *Miranda*'s procedural safeguard for a suspect subject to custodial interrogation applied to a sailor questioned my member of the Naval Investigative Service.

Three aspects of the Bill of Rights that deserve careful study in connection with the military criminal law system are search and seizure, self-incrimination, and the right to counsel.

A. SEARCH AND SEIZURE

1. BASIC PRINCIPLES

The Fourth Amendment's prohibition against "unreasonable searches and seizures" applies to searches of military personnel. Probable cause also is required to conduct most searches, within certain exceptions paralleling those in civilian law. MRE 314, 315; *United States v. Stuckey,* 10 M.J. 347 (C.M.A. 1981) ("[O]ur premise must be 'that the Bill of Rights applies with full force to men and women in the military service unless any given protection is, expressly or by necessary implication, inapplicable' and, therefore, that the Fourth Amendment does shield the American serviceperson.").

The warrant must be issued by a neutral and detached official acting in a judicial or quasi-judicial capacity. See *United States v. Sloan,* 30 M.J. 741 (A.F.C.M.R.1990) (neutrality and detachment of a commander). The warrant must be based upon probable cause and be limited at least as to the place to be searched and the things to be seized. However, military officials generally do not obtain civilian search warrants because military law also recognizes as reasonable a search conducted pursuant to a military commander's properly granted authority.

MRE 315(d) allows the issuance of an "authorization to search" by an impartial commander or other officer in a position of command or by a military judge or magistrate. The search authorization, which must be based upon probable cause, grants permission to search a person or area for specified property or evidence or for a specific person. MRE 315(b), (f). A search authorization may be issued for a search of persons subject to military law, military property, persons and property within military control, and non-military property in a foreign country. MRE 315(c).

Application of the Fourth Amendment is evident in recent decisions by the C.A.A.F. For example, a defendant accused of cocaine possession has been held to have a privacy interest in his urine sample and could withdraw consent prior to the testing of his urine sample. *United States v. Dease*, 71 M.J. 116

(C.A.A.F. 2012). The inevitable discovery doctrine did not apply to warrantless analysis of accused's urine sample, and the accused's consent to search his dormitory room and his subsequent statement to investigators were not sufficiently attenuated from the illegal testing of his urine sample. The "exclusionary rule" (evidence illegally obtained may not be used to convict) of *Mapp v. Ohio*, 367 U.S. 643 (1961), is applied in court-martial proceedings through MRE 311:

> Evidence obtained as a result of an unlawful search or seizure made by a person acting in a governmental capacity is inadmissible against the accused if:
>
> (1) *Objection*. The accused makes a timely motion to suppress or an objection to the evidence under this rule; and
>
> (2) *Adequate interest*. The accused had a reasonable expectation of privacy in the person, place or property searched; the accused had a legitimate interest in the property or evidence seized when challenging a seizure; or the accused would otherwise have grounds to object to the search or seizure under the Constitution of the United States as applied to members of the armed forces.

MRE 311(a).

Evidence is admissible if the search resulted from a search authorization where (1) the issuer had a substantial basis for determining the existence of probable cause and (2) the officials executing the authorization or warrant acted reasonably and in good faith relied on its issuance. MRE 311(b); *United States v. Lopez*, 35 M.J. 35 (C.M.A. 1992) (affirming the "good faith" exception for search and seizure).

Increased reliance on computers has raised the applicability of the Fourth Amendment's warrant requirement to computer searches involving servicemembers' e-mail. A person who has an e-mail account through a private company has a reasonable expectation of privacy regarding any messages stored in a computer to which he alone can gain access through the use of a password. A person also has an expectation of privacy for any messages to other subscribers of an e-mail service who have passwords. Probable cause to search an e-mail account does not attach to other user names held by the same individual. There must be probable cause to search each user name. *United States v. Maxwell*, 45 M.J. 406 (C.A.A.F. 1997). However, an accused does not have a reasonable expectation of privacy for e-mail stored in a government computer, which serves as the base's electronic mail host, when all personal mailboxes are issued for official business only, and all users of the system receive notice that the system is subject to monitoring whenever they log on. *United States v. Monroe*, 52 M.J. 326 (C.A.A.F. 1997). Two cases explore the extent of servicemembers' computer privacy. In *United States v. Larson*, 66 M.J. 212 (C.A.A.F. 2008) a warrantless search of accused's government computer disclosed that accused stored pornographic material and used the computer to engage in sexually explicit chat sessions with someone he believed to be a fourteen-year-old girl.

Although the computer was in accused's private office, the computer was accessible to his commander and no evidence was presented that showed any evidence recovered from the computer was password protected. The C.A.A.F. held that the accused had no reasonable expectation of privacy in information contained on the government computer. By contrast, *United States v. Long*, 64 M.J. 57 (C.A.A.F. 2006), which the *Larson* court held to be factually distinguishable, involved testimony by the network administrator to the effect that computer users, including the accused, had a privacy interest in their e-mail. This testimony was "compelling evidence supporting the notion that [the accused] had a subjective expectation of privacy." The *Larson* court emphasized that the decision in *Long* rested on the "particular facts of that case."

2. MILITARY EXCEPTIONS

Military law distinguishes between "inspections" and "searches." Under MRE 313, inspections are lawful only if (1) they are not conducted primarily to obtain evidence to use in a court-martial or disciplinary proceeding and (2) they are ordered and conducted primarily to ensure the security, fitness, or good order and discipline of the military unit. In *United States v. Roberts*, 2 M.J. 31 (C.M.A. 1976), the court said that the "traditional military inspection which looks at the overall fitness of a unit to perform its military mission is a permissible deviation from what may be tolerated in civilian society generally." However, "shakedown inspections" instituted "in search specifically of criminal goods or evidence is not such a permissible intrusion into a person's reasonable expectation of privacy, even in the military setting." Thus, the commander who tailors a barracks or field area inspection for legitimate military reasons can search entire group without probable cause. But, a commander who expressly searches for criminal evidence or contraband among a group, one of whose members is a suspect, is conducting an illegal search. Indeed, MRE 313(b) allows inspections to locate and confiscate weapons or contraband. However, if 1) the inspection was ordered immediately after a reported offense and was not previously scheduled; or if 2) specific persons are selected for examination; or if 3) those examined are subjected to substantially different intrusions during the same inspection, then the prosecution must prove by clear and convincing evidence that the examination was an "inspection" under the rule and not a subterfuge.

Members of the Armed Services have no expectation of privacy with regard to administrative inspections or inventories. MRE 313(b) which can utilize such things as trained dogs to facilitate the inspection. Thus, military commanders may undertake a health and welfare inspection that can include the use of a drug-detection dog as a proper incident of the inspection. Should the dog alert on drugs during the inspection, the commander would have probable cause to authorize a search for contraband. The primary purpose of the inspection would not be defeated by the incidental detection of the contraband subsequently confirmed by a search based on probable cause. *United States v. Middleton*,

10 M.J. 123 (C.M.A. 1981). This situation contrasts sharply with a purported "inspection" based on nothing else but a suspicion of criminal activity. *United States v. Campbell*, 41 M.J. 177 (C.M.A. 1994). Evidence produced by subterfuge inspections is inadmissible. For example, as was stated in *United States v. Bickel*, 30 M.J. 277 (C.M.A. 1990):

> [N]either Mil. R. Evid. 313 nor the Fourth Amendment permits a military commander to pick and choose the members of his unit who will be test for drugs and then to use the resulting evidence to obtain a criminal conviction. Instead, the testing must be performed on a nondiscriminatory basis pursuant to an established policy or guideline that will eliminate the opportunity for arbitrariness by the person performing the tests.

MRE 314 sets forth a list of presumptively "reasonable searches not requiring probable cause." For searches requiring probable cause, MRE 315 delineates the procedures for obtaining a search authorization or warrant and also lists certain "exigencies" for which an authorization or warrant is unnecessary. Searches of a type not otherwise included in MRE 314 and not requiring probable cause may be conducted if allowed under the Constitution as applied to members of the military. MRE 314(k).

These broad exceptions to civilian "lawful search" principles are based on the fact that military missions and expectations of military personnel may make otherwise unjustified searches reasonable.

This explanation is buttressed by the limitation of these searches to military property and persons. "An otherwise impartial authorizing official does not lose that character" merely because that official is present at a search or available to those seeking the issuance of an authorization or because the official previously authorized investigative activities. MRE 315(d)(2).

Courts have held that the protection of the nation's military installations from acts of domestic or international terrorism is a unique circumstance, justifying a greater degree of intrusiveness. *United States v. Green*, 293 F.3d 855 (5th. Cir.2002) (suspicionless roadblock checkpoint on military installation did not violate the Fourth Amendment). *United States v. Stringer*, 37 M.J. 120 (C.M.A. 1993) (warrantless gate search functionally equivalent to a border inspection for purposes of the Fourth Amendment); *United States v. Poundstone*, 46 C.M.R. 277 (C.M.A. 1973) (security concerns may justify random searches of vehicles upon entry to or exit from military installations).

Under MRE 314(g)(2), a search may be made of the passenger compartment of an automobile and containers within that compartment as a contemporaneous incident of apprehending the automobile's occupant, regardless of whether he or she has been removed from the vehicle. That rule was based on a line of cases reversed by *Arizona v. Gant*, 556 U.S. 332 (2009) (warrantless search of an automobile incident to arrest only allowed if either a continuous and present demonstrated threat to officers, or need to preserve evidence from tampering). A new discussion would bring the application of MRE 314(g)(2) in line with the holding of *Gant*. 77 FR 15053-01 (March 14, 2012).

B. SELF-INCRIMINATION

The Fifth Amendment prohibits compelling any person to incriminate himself in a criminal case. Article 31, UCMJ, 10 U.S.C. § 831, which generally conforms to this prohibition, has been construed to grant broader protection in some respects than does the Constitution. There are four parts to Art. 31:

(A) No person subject to the UCMJ may compel any person to incriminate himself or to answer any question, the answer to which might tend to incriminate him.

(B) No person subject to the UCMJ may interrogate an accused or a suspect without first informing him of (a) the nature of the accusation; (b) that he does not have to make a statement; and (c) that any statement made may be used against him.

(C) No person subject to the UCMJ may compel any person to make a statement or produce evidence before any military tribunal which is not material and which may degrade him.

(D) Any statement received in violation of Art. 31 is inadmissible at trial by court-martial.

MRE 301(a) states that a servicemember has the protections of both the Fifth Amendment and Art. 31 and can assert the privilege most beneficial to him or her. In *United States v. Tempia*, 37 C.M.R. 249 (C.M.A. 1967), the Court of Military Appeals held that Art. 31 custodial interrogations of suspects did not fully comply with *Miranda v. Arizona*, 384 U.S. 436 (1966). Prospectively, it required that warnings also include telling the accused that he is entitled to the presence of an attorney, either retained or appointed. After *Tempia*, the MCM was revised to require full *Miranda* warnings when evidence of a testimonial or communicative nature with the meaning of the Fifth Amendment is sought. MRE 305(d). Moreover, unlike civilian *Miranda* warnings, Article 31 warnings are required even when the accused is not in custody. However, no indication was given as to whether these regulations were intended merely to reaffirm then-existing law or were supposed to set forth an independent standard for military practice. This became important when the Supreme Court, in *Harris v. New York*, 401 U.S. 222 (1971), withdrew from its reasoning in *Miranda* somewhat and permitted use of statements obtained after a defective warning to impeach the accused's credibility. MRE 304(b)(1) adopts *Harris*, permitting impeachment when "the accused first introduces into evidence such [privileged] statement or derivative evidence." However, introducing demeanor evidence, such as a defendant lowering his head and slumping his shoulders during an interrogation, violates a defendant's Fifth Amendment rights. *United States v. Clark*, 69 M.J. 438 (C.A.A.F. 2011).

Military law permits taking handwriting exemplars, urine samples, blood samples, and statements for voice identifications. Because such body evidence and exemplars are not protected by the privilege against self-incrimination, their production may be compelled. See MRE 301.

C. RIGHT TO COUNSEL

Whether the Sixth Amendment right to counsel applies fully in courts-martial is a question over which commentators disagree and which the courts have never squarely faced. UCMJ provisions, MCM regulations, and case law developments have diminished the practical significance of this question. However, the Sixth Amendment backdrop has substantially influenced statutory, regulatory, and judicial approaches to the right to counsel in the military.

1. COUNSEL IN DIFFERENT TYPES OF COURT-MARTIAL

Military law gives the accused the right to counsel before a general or special court-martial or at an Art. 32 investigation. Article 38(b), UCMJ, 10 U.S.C. § 838(b). Military regulations do not extend this right to summary courts-martial, RCM 1301(e), and in *Middendorf v. Henry*, 425 U.S. 25 (1976), the Supreme Court held that there was no constitutional right to counsel in summary courts-martial. The Court avoided the issue of the Sixth Amendment's general applicability to the military by deciding that summary courts-martial are not "criminal proceedings" because of the limits on penalties imposable, the procedural distinctions present between summary and other courts-martial, and the historical differences between the military and civilian communities. At the same time that it found no Sixth Amendment right to counsel in summary courts-martial, the Court declined to find any deprivation of due process under the Fifth Amendment. Thus, summary courts-martial may be held without any involvement of counsel. However, when the accused is convicted in such a counsel-free disciplinary proceeding, the "conviction" may not be used later (1) to increase punishment under the "escalator clause" of Section B of RCM 1003(d), (2) to upgrade an offense under RCM 1001 or (3) to impeach a witness under MRE 609(a) absent a valid personal waiver by the accused of counsel prior to the earlier disciplinary hearing. *U.S. v. Booker*, 5 M.J. 238 (C.M.A. 1977).

Generally in special courts-martial, the accused has the right to (1) civilian counsel of his own choosing, (2) military counsel of his own selection at government expense if such counsel is reasonably available, or (3) appointed military counsel at government expense. Article 38(b), UCMJ, 10 U.S.C. § 838(b). In multiple defendant cases, separate counsel normally should be appointed for each defendant to avoid any problem of conflict of interest. *United States v. Blakey,* 1 M.J. 247 (C.M.A. 1976). The accused who chooses a civilian counsel is still entitled to appointed military associate counsel. Article 38(b)(4), 10 U.S.C. § 838(b)(4). Moreover, the accused may refuse counsel altogether and proceed pro se if he effectively waives his right to counsel and satisfies the court of his mental competence.

For all general courts-martial, at a minimum, counsel must be admitted to a federal bar or the highest court of a state and military counsel must be certified as competent to perform such duties by the Judge Advocate General of the applicable armed force. Article 27(b), UCMJ, 10 U.S.C. § 827(b); RCM 502(d). In special courts-martial, similar requirements apply "unless counsel having such qualifications cannot be obtained on account of physical conditions or military exigencies." Article 27(c)(1), UCMJ, 10 U.S.C. § 827(c)(1). Only if it is impossible or impracticable to obtain such qualified counsel will someone with lesser qualifications be acceptable in special courts-martial. RCM 502(d)(2). Persons chosen as counsel by the accused must meet the same general standards that are applied for assigned counsel. RCM 502(d)(3). However, if the military counsel selected by the accused is not "reasonably available," the defendant must select another counsel. Article 38(b)(3)(B), UCMJ, U.S.C. § 838(b)(93)(B). The decision concerning availability is made by counsel's commanding officer but is subject to the convening authority's review.

Once an attorney-client relationship has attached, the "reasonably available" standard ceases to apply; once appointed, counsel may be severed from the case only if the accused so demands or "good cause" is shown for severance based on extraordinary problems. *United States v. Taylor*, 3 M.J. 947 (N.C.M.R. 1977). Routine transfers, financial, logistical, or administrative burdens are not sufficient "good cause." The test is met, however, when original counsel leaves the service or becomes ill.

2. COUNSEL AT DIFFERENT STAGES OF PROCEEDINGS

The right to counsel attaches not only at trial, but also at pretrial investigations, Article 32 investigations, pretrial lineups (more broadly than in civilian practice), depositions, and upon appeal. The warning requirement of *Tempia*, supra, ensures that counsel often will be brought into criminal matters quickly and the Article 70 practice of appointing new counsel upon appeal helps insure a fresh look at trial errors and competency of trial defense counsel.

There are, however, problems which may arise in the transition from trial counsel to appellate counsel. For example, in *United States v. Palenius*, 2 M.J. 86 (C.M.A. 1977), trial counsel persuaded the accused not to request appellate counsel for his automatic appeal to the C.M.R. on the erroneous theory that waiver of counsel would speed reversal on appeal of the court-martial conviction. When such relief was denied, the accused raised the issue of inadequate post-conviction representation of counsel. The court agreed with the accused, citing the right to appellate defense counsel. Furthermore, it outlined the responsibilities of trial defense counsel after conviction so that effective representation will not fall in the cracks during the transition from trial to appeal. The court said that, to avoid "fragmented, noncontinuous representation," trial defense counsel should (1) advise his client concerning the appeal process, taking action as necessary during such intermediate stages as the SJA review and presentation of pleas to the convening authority for modification or reduction of sentence; (2) familiarize himself with any issues that should be argued on appeal and discuss these with both the accused and appellate defense counsel; (3) remain attentive to his client's needs for advice on such matters as the possibility of an Article 57(b) deferment of sentence; and (4) maintain the attorney-client relationship until substitute defense counsel or appellate counsel have been properly designated and have commenced the performance of their duties.

3. COMPETENCY AND INTEGRITY OF COUNSEL

The general test of competency of counsel, whether appointed or selected, was explored in depth by the C.M.A. in *United States v. Rivas*, 3 M.J. 282 (C.M.A. 1977). The *Rivas* court rejected the low standard that incompetency will be found only when the "attorney's efforts [were] so poor as to have rendered the trial a farce or mockery." Rather, a two-pronged standard of average competency was adopted: (1) counsel must be of average competency in recognizing legal issues and defenses in the military criminal law field and (2) counsel must exercise that competence "without omission throughout the trial." While it is inappropriate for appellate courts to "second-guess the strategic or tactical decisions made at trial by defense counsel," inaction where there is no "realistic strategic or tactical decision" behind counsel's silence constitutes incompetency.

Finally, defense counsel must be careful to avoid command pressures which might weaken the professional and moral obligation to provide the best possible defense of the client. For example, a conviction was reversed when defense counsel, after repeated requests for a witness he felt was essential to his client's case, caved in and withdrew his request following the military judge's stern and intimidating lecture. *United States v. Giermek*, 3 M.J. 1013 (C.G.C.M.R. 1977). In another instance, the appeals court noted that defense counsel was obligated to present at the court-martial level any evidence of command pressure or improper SJA remarks to court members which might taint the fairness of the trial. *United States v. Borner*, 12 C.M.R. 62 (C.M.A. 1953).

CHAPTER 7

MILITARY LAW: CRIMES, DEFENSES, AND PUNISHMENTS

Articles 77–134, UCMJ, 10 U.S.C. §§ 877–934, known as the Punitive Articles, contain the substantive offenses for which one subject to the UCMJ may be held accountable. The offenses are briefly summarized to provide an overview and finding aid. For a detailed discussion of the elements of an offense, explanatory information, information on maximum punishments and sample specifications, please consult the discussion after each article in the MCM. This chapter is intended for general reference only.

A. PUNITIVE ARTICLES

Article 77 (10 U.S.C. § 877) defines as a "principal" a person, punishable under the UCMJ, who perpetrates or commits an offense and as aiders or abettors those who assist, advise or encourage the commission of the offense.

Article 78 (10 U.S.C. § 878) defines as an "accessory" a person, punishable under the UCMJ, who is aware of the commission of an offense and assists and offender or prevents the offender's apprehension.

Article 79 (10 U.S.C. § 879) deals with lesser included offenses and attempts. A lesser included offense is an offense that is "necessarily included" in the offense charged or one in which the elements of the lesser offense are a subset of the elements of the charged offense. The purpose of requiring that the offense be "necessarily included" is to put an accused on notice of the necessity of defending against the offense specifically charged as well as the lesser included offense. For example, "wrongful appropriation" is a lesser included offense of "larceny." Article 79(b)(2) (10 U.S.C. § 879(b)(2)) authorizes the President to prescribe "lesser included offenses" in a non-exhaustive (but obviously helpful) list, which is found in Appendix 12A of the MCM. A court may also identify an offense as a "Necessarily included" offense. RCM 307(c)(3) includes examples of offenses that may or may not be lesser included offenses.

Article 80 (10 U.S.C. § 880) defines attempt as an overt act, beyond mere preparation, with specific intent to commit an offense that fails or falls short of its intended objective. For example, purchase of matches with intent to commit arson is not an attempt. If however, the perpetrator sets fire to the wooden building that is wet and will not ignite, that would be attempt. Note the failure to complete the offense is not a defense. Attempts that are specifically addressed under other articles such as desertion (Article 85), mutiny or sedition (Article 94), subordinate compelling surrender (Article 100), espionage (Article 103a), aiding the enemy (Article 103b), death or injury of an unborn child (Article 119a), and assault (Article 128) should be charged under the specific article and not under Article 80. Generally, a person found guilty of attempt under

Article 80 is subject to the same maximum punishment as if the offense attempted succeeded.

Article 81 (10 U.S.C. § 881) defines the offense of conspiracy. Conspiracy an agreement with one or more persons to commit an offense under the UCMJ. The accused must be subject to the UCMJ although other co-conspirators need not be. There must be an agreement among the parties although it need not take a particular form so long as it reflects a common understanding reflected in the conduct of the parties. An overt act is required independent of the agreement of manifest execution of the offense. A party to a conspiracy may withdraw, but the withdrawal must be evident from affirmative conduct that is wholly inconsistent with the agreement.

Article 82 (10 U.S.C. § 882) defines soliciting the commission of an offense. The accused must intend the actual commission of the solicited offense. Soliciting desertion in violation of article 85, mutiny or sedition in violation of article 94, or misbehavior before the enemy in violation of article 99 is subject to punishment as defined in Article 82(b). For additional information on the offense of solicitation see Article 134, MCM, Part IV, ¶ 105.

Article 83 (10 U.S.C. § 883) defines the offense of malingering. Malingering is the avoidance of assigned work, duty or service for which one is otherwise available by feigning illness or disability or intentionally injury one's self. If committed in time of war or in a hostile fire pay zone, the offense is more serious.

Article 84 (10 U.S.C. § 884) defines the offense of breach of medical quarantine. Any person subject to the UCMJ who is ordered into medical quarantine by a person authorized to issue such an order and goes beyond the limits imposed by the quarantine commits the offense. The maximum punishment for a breach of medical quarantine involving a communicable disease defined by 42 C.F.R. § 70.1 is dishonorable discharge, forfeiture of all pay and allowances, and confinement for 1 year. For additional information on the offense of breach of medical quarantine see Article 134, MCM, Part IV, ¶ 100.

Article 85 (10 U.S.C. § 885) defines the offense of desertion. Any member of the armed forces who without authority goes or remains absent from his unit or duty station with intent to remain away permanently or does so to avoid hazardous duty or shirk important service or accepts appointment in the same or another armed service without having been separated from the former armed force or enters any foreign armed service without authorization form the United States commits the offense of desertion. More serious punishment is directed if the desertion is in time of war.

Article 86 (10 U.S.C. § 886) defines the offense of absence without leave (AWOL). A member of the armed forces who without authority fails to go to that member's appointed place of duty at the prescribed time, departs or remains absent is AWOL. This includes abandoning a watch or guard duty. Surrender to military authority terminates unauthorized absence. This is true, whether or not the servicemember is a member of that branch of military service.

Article 87 (10 U.S.C. § 887) defines the offense of missing movement or jumping for a vessel into the water. A person subject to the UCMJ who through neglect or design misses the movement of a ship, aircraft, or unity to which he or she is assigned and required to move commits the offense. The accused must know of the prospective movement, and knowledge may be proved by circumstantial evidence. A person who wrongfully or intentionally jumps into the water from a vessel in use by the armed forces similarly offends. This offense may be committed at sea, at anchor, or in port. For additional information on the offense of jumping from a vessel see Article 134, MCM, Part IV, ¶ 91.

Article 87a (10 U.S.C. § 887a) defines the offense of resistance, flight, breach of arrest, and escape. A person subject to the UCMJ who resists or flees apprehension, breaks arrest, or escapes from custody or confinement commits the offense. Apprehension is taking a person into custody. RCM 302. As discussed elsewhere, arrest is a term of art in military law referring to an order by a competent authority to direct an accused to remain within specified limits. RCM 304.

Article 87b (10 U.S.C. § 887b) defines offenses against correctional custody including escape from correctional custody, breach of correctional custody, and breach of restriction. The maximum punishment for escape from correctional custody is dishonorable discharge, forfeiture of all pay and allowances, and confinement for 1 year. For breach of correctional custody, bad-conduct discharge, forfeiture of all pay and allowances, and confinement for 6 months; for breach of restriction, confinement for 1 month and forfeiture of two-thirds pay per month for 1 month.

Article 88 (10 U.S.C. § 888) defines the offense of contempt toward officials. It applies to commissioned officers of the armed forces and not to enlisted personnel. Any commissioned officer who uses contemptuous words against the President, the Vice President, Congress, the Secretary of Defense, the Secretary of a military department, the Secretary of Homeland Security, or the Governor or legislature of any State, Commonwealth, or possession in which he or she is on duty or present shall be punished as a court-martial may direct. As a speech restriction, this article is narrowly construed. The focus is on personally contemptuous language. If the language is not personally contemptuous, but merely adverse criticism, even emphatically expressed is not chargeable as a violation of the article, nor or expressions of expressions of opinion in a purely private conversation. However, broad circulation in writing of contemptuous words or their utterance particularly in the presence of military subordinates would be chargeable.

Article 89 (10 U.S.C. § 889) defines the offense of disrespect toward a superior commissioned officer, which consists of behaving with disrespect toward own's superior officer, and of assault of one's superior officer either by drawing or lifting up a weapon or by offering violence toward one's superior officer. The maximum punishment if committed in time of war is death, but if committed at any other time, less than death. A victim who, for example, initiated an unlawful attack on an accused causing him or her to act in self-defense would lose the protection provided by this article.

Article 90 (10 U.S.C. § 890) defines the offense of willfully disobeying a superior commissioned officer. The order to which the accused is subject must require performance of a military act and must be lawful. When contested, the lawfulness of an order is ultimately a question of law for a military judge. The commissioned officer issuing the order must have authority to issue the order. Military duty includes all activities reasonably necessary to accomplish a military mission or to safeguard or promote the morale, discipline, and usefulness of servicemembers subject to the officer's command and be directly connected with the good order and discipline of the Service. If committed during time of war, it may be punishable by death.

Article 91 (10 U.S.C. § 891) defines the offense of insubordinate conduct toward a warrant officer, noncommissioned officer, or petty officer. The conduct covered by the offense includes striking or assaulting, willfully disobeying a lawful order, or treating the officer with contempt or acting disrespectfully in language or deportment while the officer is in the execution of his or her office. Article 91 has the same general objects with respect to warrant, noncommissioned, and petty officers as articles 89 and 90 have with respect to commissioned officers. However, article 91 does not require a superior-subordinate relationship as an element of the offense.

Article 92 (10 U.S.C. § 892) defines the offense of failure to obey an order or regulation. This offense takes three forms. It consists of (1) a failure to obey any lawful general order or regulation of which is an order that is generally applicable to an armed force or a command. The accused must have a duty to obey. (2) A failure to obey any other lawful orders by one superior in rank or one not superior in rank that the accused has a duty to obey, e.g., a sentinel or a member of the armed forces police. (3) An accused who is derelict in the performance of duties. A duty may be imposed by a treaty, statute, regulation, lawful order, standard operating procedure, or custom of the service. An accused must have actual knowledge of the duties imposed. The dereliction must be the result of willfulness, negligence, or culpable inefficiency, i.e., inefficiency for which there is not reasonable excuse. A person may not be considered derelict if the failure to perform is caused by ineptitude. For example, a recruit who fails to qualify with a weapon after earnestly trying to do so is inept and not derelict under the article. Punishments for dereliction in the performance of duties varies depending on the consequences of the dereliction. For example, dereliction resulting in death or grievous bodily harm merit more serious consequences.

Article 93 (10 U.S.C. § 893) defines the crime of cruelty and maltreatment of a person subject to the orders of another. The article applies to all persons, subject to the UCMJ who are required to obey lawful orders of the accused irrespective of whether the accused is in the direct chain of command over the victim. It includes assaults, improper punishment, and sexual harassment. Sexual harassment includes influencing, offering to influence, or threatening career, pay, etc. in exchange for sexual favors, or deliberate or repeated comments or gestures of a sexual nature.

Article 93a (10 U.S.C. § 893a) prohibits activities with a military recruit or trainee by a person in a position of special trust. This can involve abuse of a training leadership position by an officer, noncommissioned officer or petty officer who, in a training leadership position, engages in prohibited sexual activity with a specially protected junior member of the armed forces, e.g., a member of the armed forces awaiting assignment to basic training or initial active duty for training, or enlisted under a delayed entry program, or a cadet or midshipman. Training leadership positions include drill instructors, military academy faculty and staff, etc. Consent is no defense.

Article 94 (10 U.S.C. § 894) defines the offense of mutiny or sedition by one subject to the UCMJ. There are two types of mutiny. The first involves the intentional usurpation or overriding of lawful military authority and creating violence or disturbance. The second offense consists of acting in concert with any other person to resist lawful military authority by refusing to obey orders or do assigned duty. It is concerted insubordination by two or more persons. It need not be violent or result in disturbance. Sedition involves intentional action in concert with another person to cause the overthrow or destruction of lawful civil authority that causes revolt, violence or other disturbance against that authority. A person who has reason to believe mutiny or sedition is taking place who fails to prevent, suppress or report it is guilty of the separate offense of "failure to suppress or report a mutiny or sedition." The report must be made to a superior commissioned officer in the chain of command. Attempted mutiny or sedition is a separate offense under this article.

Article 95 (10 U.S.C. § 895) defines offenses by a sentinel or lookout. They include being drunk or sleeping on post, or leaving a post before being regularly relieved, and loitering or wrongfully sitting on post. "Post" is the area where a sentinel or lookout is required to be for the performance of assigned duties. These include observation to guard against threats or danger as well as an order to guard stores or prisoners.

Article 95a (10 U.S.C. § 895a) defines the offense of disrespect toward a sentinel or lookout. It can take the form of disrespectful *language* directed toward a sentinel or lookout or disrespectful *behavior* toward a sentinel or lookout.

Article 96 (10 U.S.C. § 896) defines two prisoner-related offenses. The first comprises releasing a prisoner without authority, or, through neglect or design, allowing a prisoner to escape. The second involves drinking any alcoholic beverage with a prisoner.

Article 97 (10 U.S.C. § 897) defines the offense of unlawful detention. It consists of apprehending, arresting, or confining a person without lawful authority to do so.

Article 98 (10 U.S.C. § 898) defines the offense of misconduct as a prisoner while in the hands of an enemy in time of war. The proscribed conduct includes acting without proper authority for the purpose of securing more favorable treatment to the detriment of others. "Others" include persons of whatever nationality held by the enemy as civilian or military prisoners. It can also entail maltreatment of other prisoners while in a position of authority. Escape from enemy custody or confinement is authorized by custom. Escape or attempted escape which results in detriment to others, e.g., closer confinement, or reduced rations, for fellow prisoners is not an offense under this article. With respect to maltreatment of others while in "authority," authority may be conferred by a spectrum of sources, e.g., by rank, by designation of captor authorities, or by election or selection by fellow prisoners. The source of authority for the purposes of this article is immaterial.

Article 99 (10 U.S.C. § 899) defines the offense of misbehavior before the enemy. It comprises nine specific offences. Any member of the armed forces who before or in the presence of the enemy (1) runs away, (2) shamefully abandons, surrenders or delivers up any command, unit, place or military property he or she is under a duty to defend violates this article. The article also covers (3) endangering the safety of a command, unit, place, or military property through disobedience, neglect, or intentional misconduct. It also includes (4) casting away one's arms or ammunition; (5) engaging in cowardly conduct; (6) quitting ones place of duty to plunder or pillage; (7) causing false alarms in any command, unit, or place of control of the armed forces; (8) willfully failing to encounter, engage, capture, or destroy and enemy troops, combatants, vessels, aircraft, or other thing for which there is a duty to encounter, engage, capture, or destroy to one's utmost; (9) fail to afford all practicable relief and assistance to any United States or allied armed forces (including troops, combatants, vessels, or aircraft) when engaged in battle.

Article 100 (10 U.S.C. § 900) defines the offense of a subordinate compelling surrender. An accused violates this article by compelling or attempting to compel a commander to surrender or give up, abandon, or strike the colors or flag to an enemy without proper authority to do so. The offense is similar to mutiny or attempted mutiny, but differs in that concert of action is not an essential element of the offenses under this article. The offense is not complete until surrender or abandonment to an enemy has taken place.

Article 101 (10 U.S.C. § 901) defines the offense of improper use of a countersign. Any person subject to the UCMJ who in time of war discloses a "parole" (a word used as a check on a countersign) or a "countersign" (a word or signal, or procedure to aid guards and sentinels in scrutinizing persons who apply to pass the lines) to any person not entitled to receive it or gives a different parole or countersign than one authorized to another person violates this article. A countersign consists of a secret challenge and a password, signal, or procedure.

Article 102 (10 U.S.C. § 902) defines the offense of forcing a safeguard. A safeguard is a detachment, guard, or detail posted by a commander for the protection of persons, places, or property of the enemy, or of a neutral affected by the relationship of belligerent forces in their prosecution of war or during a state of belligerency. A safeguard is a pledge of national honor that the person or property secured by the safeguard will be respected by the armed forces of the nation extending the safeguard. An accused forces a safeguard by violating its protection by overwhelming the guard posted for its protection.

Article 103 (10 U.S.C. § 903) defines the offense of spying. A spy is any person who in time of war is found lurking or acting as a spy in or about any military facility or manufacturing or industrial plant engaged in or working in aid of the prosecution of war by the United States. This section does not apply to a trial by military commission. Because the offense of spying under this article applies to "any person," it brings an accused within the jurisdiction of general courts-martial and military commissions irrespective of military status or status under the UCMJ. The offense consists of acting clandestinely or under false pretenses to obtain information with the intention of conveying it to a hostile party. Members of a military organization who carry out their mission openly even behind enemy lines and are not wearing a disguise or acting under false pretenses are not considered to be spies. A person who without lurking, acting clandestinely, or under false pretenses merely reports what is seen or heard through agents to an enemy may not be charged as a spy, but can be charged with espionage under Article 103a.

Article 103a (10 U.S.C. § 903a) defines the offense of espionage. This article applies to persons subject to the UCMJ. An accused who, intending to injure the United States or to advantage of a foreign nation and who acts in the belief that his or her act will cause such injury or advantage transmits a document, writing or any similar form of information relating to national defense commits the offense of espionage. The article distinguishes four categories of disclosures of varying degrees of seriousness and punishments. (A) Communicating information about means of defense or retaliation against large-scale attack, e.g., nuclear weaponry, military spacecraft or satellites or early warning systems; (B) war plans; (C) communications intelligence or cryptographic information; or (D) any other major weapons system or element of defense strategy.

Article 103b (10 U.S.C. § 903b) defines the offense of aiding the enemy. This article applies to any person, whether they are otherwise subject to military law or not. An accused who aids or attempts to aid an enemy with arms, ammunition, supplies, money or any other thing, or without authority harbors, protects, shares intelligence with or communicates or corresponds with the enemy either directly or indirectly commits the offense. Offenders may be tried by court-martial or by military commission.

Article 104 (10 U.S.C. § 904) defines various public records offenses. It applies to persons subject to the UCMJ. It includes an accused who willfully and unlawfully alters, conceals, removes. mutilates or destroys a public record or takes a public record with the intent to alter, conceal, etc. it.

Article 104a (10 U.S.C. § 904a) defines the offense of fraudulent enlistment, appointment, or separation. Fraudulent enlistment, appointment, or separation can be procured either by knowingly false representation of qualifications for the enlistment, appointment, or separation or by deliberate concealment of a disqualification. The maximum punishment for fraudulent enlistment or appointment is dishonorable discharge, forfeiture or all pay and allowances, and confinement for 2 years. The maximum punishment for fraudulent separation is dishonorable discharge, forfeiture of all pay and allowances, and confinement for 5 years.

Article 104b (10 U.S.C. § 904b) defines the offense of unlawful enlistment, appointment, or separation. This offense applies to persons subject to the UCMJ who effects an enlistment, appointment, or separation from the armed forces who knows of his or her ineligibility for enlistment, appointment, or separation because it is prohibited by law, regulation, or order.

Article 105 (10 U.S.C. § 905) defines the offense of forgery. The offense applies to any person subject to the UCMJ who falsely makes or alters a signature to any writing, which if genuine would impose legal liability on another or legally prejudice another. It includes any person who knowingly utters or transfers a forged writing. The elements of forgery are complex and should be reviewed to conform the facts to the offense charged.

Article 105a (10 U.S.C. § 905a) defines three false or unauthorized pass offenses. They apply to persons subject to the UCMJ. The first makes it an offense to wrongfully and falsely make, alter, counterfeit or tamper with a military or official pass, permit, discharge certificate or identification card. The second makes it an offense to wrongfully sell, give, lend, or disposes of a false or unauthorized military or official pass, permit, discharge certificate or identification card knowing of its falsity or unauthorized character. The third makes it an offense to use or possess a false or unauthorized military or official pass, permit, discharge certificate or identification card knowing of its falsity or unauthorized character.

Article 106 (10 U.S.C. § 906) defines the offense of impersonating an officer, noncommissioned or petty officer, or agent or official. It applies to persons subject to the UCMJ. It takes two forms, impersonation with intent to defraud and impersonation without intent to defraud.

Article 106a (10 U.S.C. § 906a) defines the offense of wearing an unauthorized insignia, decoration, badge, ribbon, device, or lapel button. It applies to persons subject to the UCMJ who wear an unauthorized insignia, decoration, badge, ribbon, device, or lapel button or who wrongfully wear an unauthorized insignia, decoration, badge, ribbon, device, or lapel button on their uniform or civilian clothing. The wrongful wearing of the Medal of Honor, Distinguished Service Cross, Navy Cross, Air Force Cross, Silver Star, Purple Heart or valor device on any personal award carries a more serious penalty.

Article 107 (10 U.S.C. § 907) defines the offenses of false official statements and false swearing. The article applies to persons subject to the UCMJ. The first offense describes any person who with an intent to deceive signs any false record, return, regulation, order, or other official document, knowing it to be false. The second offense describes any person who takes an oath in which the accused makes or subscribes to a statement known at the time to be false or which the accused believes to be untrue.

Article 107a (10 U.S.C. § 907a) defines the offense of parole violation. A person subject to the UCMJ who, having been a prisoner as a result of a court-martial conviction or other criminal proceeding is on parole and violates the conditions of parole violates this article. A person on parole or parolee agrees to adhere to a parole plan which defines acts and activities which the parolee is obligated to observe. An accused offends by failing to adhere to the plan.

Article 108 (10 U.S.C. § 908) defines offenses relating to military property of the United States. These include selling or otherwise disposing of military without proper authority, willfully or through neglect damages, destroys or loses military property, or who willfully or through neglect causes the loss, damage, destruction, sale, or wrongful disposition of military property. Military property is a term of art referring to all property real or personal owned, held, or used by one of the armed forces of the United States. Government property should not be conflated with military property. All military property is Government property, but not all government property is military property. The only property that meets the definition of military property is that which meets the definition above.

Article 108a (10 U.S.C. § 908a) defines offenses related to captured or abandoned property. All persons subject to the UCMJ are obligated to secure all public property taken from the enemy for the service of the United States, and shall without delay turn over to proper authority without delay all captured or abandoned property in their possession, custody, or control. Any such person who fails to carry out the duty imposed by this article, or buys, sells, trades, or deals in or disposes of captured or abandoned property for profit, benefit or advantage for himself or herself or another with whom there is a connection violates this article. A person who engages in looting or pillaging, i.e., unlawfully seizing or appropriating property located in enemy or occupied territory, violates this article.

Article 109 (10 U.S.C. § 909) defines the offense of willfully or recklessly wasting, spoiling, or otherwise destroying non-military property of the United States.

Article 109a (10 U.S.C. § 909a) defines offenses related to "mail matter" or any matter deposited in a postal system of any government or any authorized depository thereof or in official mail channels of the United States or agency thereof including the armed forces. It includes taking any mail matter or opening, secreting, destroying, or stealing it before the mail matter is delivered or received by the addressee.

Article 110 (10 U.S.C. § 910) defines the offense of improper hazarding of a vessel or aircraft. Hazarding means putting in danger of loss or injury a vessel or aircraft of the armed forces by collision, stranding, running upon a shoal or a rock. Hazarding can be willful and wrongful or the product of negligence such as the failure to exercise requisite care, caution, or attention to duties.

Article 111 (10 U.S.C. § 911) defines the offense of leaving the scene of a vehicle accident. It applies to persons subject to the UCMJ. A driver of a vehicle involved in an accident that results in personal injury or property damage who wrongfully leaves the scene of the accident without providing assistance to an injured person or without providing personal identification to others involved in the accident or to appropriate authorities violates this article. A senior commissioned or noncommissioned officer who is a passenger of the driver in an accident resulting in personal injury or property damage who wrongfully causes or permits the driver to leave the scene of the accident also violates this article.

Article 112 (10 U.S.C. § 912) defines offenses related to drunkenness and incapacitation. This article includes being drunk on duty, incapacitation for duty from drunkenness or drug use. Being a drunk prisoner is also an offense.

Article 112a (10 U.S.C. § 912a) defines offenses related to the wrongful use, possession, etc. of controlled substances. Any person subject to the UCMJ who wrongfully uses, possess, manufactures, distributes, imports into the customs territory of the United States, i.e., the States, the District of Columbia, and Puerto Rico, exports from the United States, or introduces into an installation, vessel, vehicle, or aircraft used by or under the control of the armed forces any controlled substance violates this article. Controlled substances include opium, heroin, cocaine, amphetamine, lysergic acid diethylamide, methamphetamine, phencyclidine, barbituric acid, and marijuana and any compound or derivative of any such substance as well as any not otherwise specified that are listed on a schedule of controlled substances prescribed by the President for the purposes of this article or listed in schedules I through V or section 202 of the Controlled Substances Act (21 U.S.C. § 812).

Article 113 (10 U.S.C. § 913) defines the offense of drunken or reckless operation of a vehicle, aircraft or vessel. The article proscribes operating or physically controlling any vehicle, aircraft, or vessel in a reckless or wanton manner or while impaired by a substance described in Article 112a or does so when the alcohol concentration in a person's blood or breath is equal to or exceeds the limits set forth in this article. The limits vary by the location where the offense occurred. Consult the standards set forth in this article.

Article 114 (10 U.S.C. § 914) defines four endangerment offenses applicable to persons subject to the UCMJ. They are (1) reckless endangerment, i.e., wrongful and reckless or wanton conduct that is likely to produce death or grievous bodily harm to another person; (2) dueling, i.e., combat with another with deadly weapons for private reasons by prior agreement; (3) the willful and wrongful discharge of a firearm under circumstances likely to endanger human life; and (4) unlawfully carrying a dangerous weapon concealed on or about one's person.

Article 115 (10 U.S.C. § 915) defines the offense of communicating threats by persons subject to the UCMJ. The article specifies three types of threats are specified: The first covers any person who wrongfully communicates a threat to injure the person, property or reputation of another, a general threat. The second, adds to the first a threat to carry it out by use of (1) an explosive, (2) a weapon of mass destruction, (3) a biological or chemical agent, substance, or weapon, or (4) a hazardous material. The third proscribes falsely communicating a threat of the second sort. A false threat is one that is known by the person communicating the threat at the time it is communicated to be false. An element of the threat is that it must be malicious, that is believed by an accused that is would probably interfere with the peaceful use of the building, vehicle, aircraft or other property concerned, or would cause fear or concern to one or more persons.

Article 116 (10 U.S.C. § 916) defines the offense or riot or breach of the peace. Any person subject to the UCMJ who causes of participates in any riot or breach of the peace is guilty of this offense. To violate this article, an accused must be a member of an assembly of three or more persons, they must unlawfully commit a tumultuous disturbance of the peace in a violent or turbulent manner, and these acts must terrorize the public in general by causing public alarm or terror. A breach of the peace is an unlawful disturbance of the peace, for example, by engaging in an affray and unlawful discharge of firearms. Loud speech and unruly conduct may constitute a breach of the peace if the speaker uses language which can reasonably be expected to produce a violent or turbulent response and produces a breach.

Article 117 (10 U.S.C. § 917) defines the offense of provoking speech or gestures. any person subject to the UCMJ who uses provoking or reproachful words or gestures towards another person also subject to the UCMJ is guilty of this offense. The conduct proscribed must be used in the presence of the person toward whom they are directed and must be ones which a reasonable person would expect to induce a breach of the peace. Not proscribed by this article are reprimands, censures, reproofs administered in the interests of training, efficiency, or discipline of the armed forces.

Article 117a (10 U.S.C. § 917a) prohibits the knowing and wrongful broadcasting or distribution of an intimate visual image of another person or of sexually explicit conduct involving a person who was at least 18 years of age at the time the image was created, who is identifiable, and has not consented to the broadcast of distribution; or of another person who reasonably retained a reasonable expectation of privacy in the image; or who know or reasonably should have known that the broadcast or distribution of the image is likely to cause harm, harassment, intimidation, emotional distress, or financial loss; and whose conduct, under the circumstances, had a reasonably direct and palpable connection to a military mission or military environment.

Article 118 (10 U.S.C. § 918) defines the offense of murder. A person subject to the UCMJ commits murder when without justification or excuse, unlawfully kills a human being when he or she (1) has a premeditated design to kill; (2) intends to kill or inflict great bodily harm; (3) engages in an act which is inherently dangerous to another and evinces a wanton disregard of human life; or (4) engages in the perpetration or attempted perpetration of burglary, rape, rape of a child, sexual assault, sexual assault of a child, aggravated sexual contact, sexual abuse of a child, robbery, or aggravated arson.

Article 119 (10 U.S.C. § 919) defines the offenses of voluntary and involuntary manslaughter. A person subject to the UCMJ commits manslaughter when with an intent to kill or inflict great bodily harm he or she unlawfully kills a human being in the heat of sudden passion caused by adequate provocation. If there is not intent to kill or inflict great bodily harm, the killing instead results from culpable negligence or occurs in the course of perpetrating an offense listed in Article 118, the accused is guilty of involuntary manslaughter.

Article 119a (10 U.S.C. § 919a) defines the offenses of causing the death or injury of an unborn child. The article proscribes conduct that causes the death or a child in utero at the time of the conduct. The conduct if that proscribed in Articles 118, 119a, 119(b)(2), 120(a), 122, 126, 128, and 128a. An accused need not know that the victim of the underlying offense was pregnant nor need he or she have intent to cause the death of or bodily injury to the unborn child. This article does not permit the prosecution of any person for (1) conduct relating to an abortion for which the consent of the pregnant woman, or person authorized by law to act on her behalf has been obtained or for which such consent is implied by law; or (2) for any medical treatment of a pregnant woman or her unborn child; (3) or of any woman with respect to her unborn child. An unborn child under this article refers to a human child "at any stage of development, who is carried in the womb."

Article 119b (10 U.S.C. § 919b) defines the offense of child endangerment. The article applies to any person subject to the UCMJ who has a duty of the care of a child under the age of 16 years who intentionally or by design, or culpable negligence endangers a child's mental, physical health, safety, or welfare.

Article 120 (10 U.S.C. § 920) defines the offense of rape and sexual assault. (This statute applies to offenses committed on or after 1 January 2019. For earlier offenses, see the Note in the MCM.) The article applies to any person subject to the UCMJ. A person commits rape who commits a sexual act upon another person by the use of unlawful force that is likely to cause death or grievous bodily harm to the person, or who threatens to cause such harm, by first rendering the person unconscious, or by administering either by force or without the knowledge or consent of the person a drug, intoxicant or similar substance that substantially impairs the ability of that person to appraise or control their conduct. A sexual assault is a sexual act perpetrated on another person by threat, fraudulent representation, false representation, or without consent because the person is unconscious, asleep, or otherwise unaware that the sexual act is occurring, or by impairment caused by a drug or alcohol. A sexual act refers to acts involving the penetration, however slight, of the penis into the vulva, anus or mouth or contact between the mouth and the penis, vulva, scrotum or anus.

An important factor with respect to crimes involving this article is consent. Consent means agreement freely given for the conduct at issue by a competent person. Indication of a lack of consent either through words or conduct means there is no consent. And lack of resistance to the conduct at issue does not constitute consent. Sleeping, unconscious, or incompetent persons cannot consent.

Article 120a (10 U.S.C. § 920a) defines the crime of mailing obscene matter. Whether matter is obscene is a question of fact. Under ¶ 104.a. "Obscene" has the same meaning as "indecent." Indecent refers to a form of immorality relating to sexual impurity which is grossly vulgar, and repugnant to common propriety that "tends to excite sexual desire or deprave morals with respect to sexual relations."

Article 120b (10 U.S.C. § 920b) defines the crime of rape and sexual assault of a child. (This statute applies to offenses committed on or after 1 January 2019. For earlier offenses, see the Note in the MCM.) The article applies to any person subject to the UCMJ. A person commits the crime of rape or sexual act on a child by commission of the conduct described in Article 120 if the victim is child under the age of 12 years or under the age of 16 years. It is a defense under this article if the accused can proved by a preponderance of the evidence that at the time of the alleged offense the parties were married to each other. This crime includes performing a lewd act with a child, which includes sexual contact with a child, exposing one's genitalia or female areola or nipple to a child for the purpose of abusing humiliating, degrading, or arousing the sexual desire of any person, or for an indecent purpose.

Article 120c (10 U.S.C. § 920c) defines other offenses related to sexual misconduct. These offenses apply to persons subject to the UCMJ. They include (1) viewing, visually recording, or broadcasting the "private area" of another person without their consent or under circumstances when the person viewed had a reasonable expectation of privacy; (2) forcible pandering, i.e., compelling another person to engage in prostitution; (3) indecent exposure. "Private area" means the naked or underwear-clad genitalia, anus, buttocks, or female areola or nipple of a person.

Article 121 (10 U.S.C. § 921) defines the offenses of larceny and wrongful appropriation. Whoever, subject to the UCMJ wrongfully takes, obtains, or withholds money, personal property or any article of value from its owner with the intent of permanently depriving the owner is guilty of larceny. If the deprivation is intended to be temporary, the crime is wrongful appropriation. Intent to pay for or replace stolen property is not a defense nor is return of the property.

Article 121a (10 U.S.C. § 921a) defines the offense of fraudulent use of credit cards, debit cards, or access devices. An "access device" is defined in 18 U.S.C. § 1029 as "any card, plate, code, account number, electronic serial number, mobile identification number, personal identification number, or other telecommunications service, equipment, or instrument identifier, or other means of account access, that can be used alone or in conjunction with another access device, to obtain money, goods, services, or any other thing of value, or that can be used to initiate a transfer of funds (other than a transfer originated solely by paper instrument)." The offense includes knowingly and with fraudulent intent using stolen, revoked, cancelled or invalid cards or similar devices.

Article 121b (10 U.S.C. § 921b) defines the offense of false pretenses to obtain services. Although similar to the offenses of larceny and wrongful appropriation, this offense applies to services, like telephone, or internet services, rather than property like money or property. More serious punishment is imposed for services of value greater than $1,000.

Article 122 (10 U.S.C. § 922) defines the offense of robbery. Robbery consists of taking anything of value from a person or in the presence of another against his or her will, by means of force or violence of fear of immediate or future injury to the person's property or of a relative or family member or someone in his or her company at the time of the robbery.

Article 122a (10 U.S.C. § 922a) defines the offense of receiving stolen property. Any person subject to the UCMJ who wrongfully receives, buys or conceals stolen property, knowing that the property was stolen is guilty of the offense of receiving stolen property. Although actual knowledge that the property was stolen is required, such knowledge may be proved by circumstantial evidence. More serious punishment is imposed for property of value greater than $1,000.

Article 123 (10 U.S.C. § 923) defines offenses related to government computers. There are three forms of this offense all of which apply to any person subject to the UCMJ. The first offense applies to a person who knowingly accesses a government computer with an unauthorized purpose. If that person by so doing obtains classified information, having reason to believe such information could be used to the injury of the United States or the advantage of any foreign nation, intentionally communicates, delivers, transmits, or causes to be communicated, delivered, or transmitted such information to any person not entitled to receive it, he or she is guilty of this offense. The second offense applies to a person who either 1) intentionally accesses a government computer with an unauthorized purpose and thereby obtains classified or other protected information or 2) causes the transmission of a program, information, code, or command that intentionally causes damage without authorization to a government computer. A "government computer" is one owned or operated by or on behalf of the United States government. Classified information is defined in 10 U.S.C. § 801(15). The definition of "damage" and "computer" is supplied by 18 U.S.C. § 1030. Damage is any impairment to the integrity or availability of data, a program, a system, or information. A smartphone is a type of computer.

Article 123a (10 U.S.C. § 923a) defines the offense of making, drawing, or uttering a check, draft, or order without sufficient funds. The offense applies to a person subject to the UCMJ who procures and article or thing of value with intent to defraud or offers in payment of a past due obligation knowing that there are insufficient funds for the payment of the check, draft, or order. To utter or deliver both refer to transferring an instrument to another person. The perpetrator of this offense need not be the check's drawer or maker. Thus, if a check drawn by someone else is known to be worthless and is transferred it to another, this article would apply.

Article 124 (10 U.S.C. § 924) defines the offense frauds against the United States. The offense applies to a person subject to the UCMJ who knowingly makes a false claim, or in making a false claim made or used a false writing, or included material statements that were false or fraudulent, or a forged or false signature.

Article 124a (10 U.S.C. § 924a) defines the offense of bribery. The offense applies to a person subject to the UCMJ, who occupies an official position or who has official duties, wrongfully asks for, accepts, or receives a thing of value with the intent that his or her decision or action will be influenced with respect to an official matter of interest to the United States. It also applies to a person who offers a bribe.

Article 124b (10 U.S.C. § 924b) defines the offense of graft. The offense applies to a person subject to the UCMJ who wrongfully asks for, accepts, or receives a thing of value as compensation for or in recognition of services rendered or to be rendered in an official matter of interest to the

United States. It also applies to a person who promises or offers graft.

Article 125 (10 U.S.C. § 925) defines the offense of kidnapping. The offense applies to a person subject to the UCMJ, who wrongfully seizes, confines, inveigles, decoys, or carries away another person; and holds that person against his or her will. "Inveigle" means to lure, lead astray, or entice another by false representations or other deceitful means. Confinement or detention must be more than momentary to constitute kidnapping.

Article 126 (10 U.S.C. § 926) defines the offense of arson. The offense applies to a person subject to the UCMJ who burns property. There are three forms of arson under the article. 1) Aggravated arson consists of willfully and maliciously burning or setting on fire an inhabited building or structure (movable or immovable) with knowledge that there is a person in the building or structure. 2) Simple arson consists of willfully and maliciously burning the property of another. 3) Willfully and maliciously burning or setting fire to property with the intent to defraud is a form of arson.

Article 127 (10 U.S.C. § 927) defines the offense of extortion. The offense applies to a person subject to the UCMJ who communicates threats to another person intending to obtain anything of value or any acquittance, advantage or immunity. An "acquittance" is a release or a discharge from an obligation.

Article 128 (10 U.S.C. § 928) defines the offense of assault. The offense applies to a person subject to the UCMJ who attempts or offers to do harm to another person by means of unlawful force or violence. The crime is complete whether or not the offer of attempt is consummated. The elements of simple assault are as described. The more serious crime, assault committed by battery occurs when the assault when the offer or attempted is consummated. Increased punishment is permitted when, for example, the victim is a commissioned, warrant, noncommissioned or petty officer, or a sentinel or person executing law enforcement duties. An assault committed by battery on a child under 16 years of age permits increased punishment as does an assault that results from the intentional infliction of grievous bodily harm.

Article 128a (10 U.S.C. § 928a) defines the offense of maiming. The offense applies to a person subject to the UCMJ who inflicts upon another person with the intent to injure or disfigure an injury which disfigures the person by mutilation, by disabling a member or organ of his or her body or disables or diminishes the vigor of a member or organ. Nonexclusive examples of this offense include eye gouging, cutting off a hand, foot or finger. Disfigurement examples include facial scarring or cutting off someone's ear. The completion of the offense is unaffected by the possibility of recovery of the use of a member or organ or restoration by means of surgical correction.

Article 128b (10 U.S.C. § 928b) defines the offense of domestic violence. The offense applies to a person subject to the UCMJ who commits a violent offense against a spouse, intimate partner or immediate family member with intent to threaten or intimidate them. This offense applies as well to any person who commits such an offense against any property, including an animal. It also includes commission of a violent offense against or assault by strangling or suffocating with intent to intimidate.

Article 129 (10 U.S.C. § 929) defines the offenses of burglary and unlawful entry. Both offenses apply to a person subject to the UCMJ who acts with the intent to commit an offense punishable under the UCMJ. Burglary entails breaking and entering a building or structure of another. Unlawful entry entails unlawfully entering either the real property of another or the personal property of another which amounts to a structure usually used for habitation or storage such as a tent or trailer.

Article 130 (10 U.S.C. § 930) defines the offense of stalking. The offense applies to a person subject to the UCMJ who wrongfully engages in a course of conduct directed at a specific person that would case a reasonable person to fear death or bodily harm including sexual assault to himself or herself, a member of his or her immediate family, or to an intimate partner, or who has or should have knowledge that such conduct will induce reasonable fear of such harms.

Article 131 (10 U.S.C. § 931) defines the offense of perjury. The offense applies to a person subject to the UCMJ who gives any false testimony material to an issue or matter of inquiry in a judicial proceeding or in a course of justice. A judicial proceeding includes a trial by court-martial, and a "course of justice" includes an Article 32 investigation. A false statement in a declaration, certificate, verification or statement material to an issue or matter of inquiry where the document provides for subscribing to its truth by signing is subject to the Article under 28 U.S.C. § 1746. For example, a witness who signs summarized testimony in an Article 32 investigation does so under penalty of perjury.

Article 131a (10 U.S.C. § 931) defines the offense of subornation of perjury. The offense applies to a person subject to the UCMJ who induces and procures another person to take an oath and falsely testify or depose under oath.

Article 131b (10 U.S.C. § 931b) defines the offense of obstructing justice. The offense applies to a person subject to the UCMJ who engages in conduct in the case of a certain person against whom the accused had reason to believe there would be criminal or disciplinary proceedings pending with intent to influence, impede, or otherwise obstruct due administration of justice.

Article 131c (10 U.S.C. § 931c) defines the offense of misprision of serious offense. The offense applies to a person subject to the UCMJ who knows another person has committed a serious offense and wrongfully conceals the offense and fails to make it known to civilian or military authorities as soon as possible.

Article 131d (10 U.S.C. § 931d) defines the offense of wrongful refusal to testify. The offense applies to a person subject to the UCMJ who wrongfully refuses to qualify as a witness or answer questions after having been directed to do so in a court-martial, or by a board of officers, military commission, court of inquiry, preliminary hearing, or officer taking a deposition.

Article 131e (10 U.S.C. § 931e) defines the offense of prevention of authorized seizure of property. The offense applies to a person subject to the UCMJ who knowing that person or persons authorized to make searches and seizures and are about to seize or are endeavoring to seize property destroys, removes, or otherwise disposes of the property to be seized with intent to prevent its seizure violates this article.

Article 131f (10 U.S.C. § 931f) defines the offense of noncompliance with procedural rules. The offense applies to a person subject to the UCMJ who is responsible for the unnecessary delay in the disposition of the case of a person accused of an offense under the UCMJ or knowingly and intentionally fails to enforce or comply with regulations governing proceedings before, during or after the trial of an accused.

Article 131g (10 U.S.C. § 931g) defines the offense of wrongful interference with an adverse administrative proceeding. The offense applies to a person subject to the UCMJ who wrongfully acts to influence, impede, or obstruct the conduct of the proceeding or otherwise obstruct the due administration of justice by taking or threatening adverse personnel action against any person or withholding or threatening to withhold a favorable personnel action.

Article 132 (10 U.S.C. § 932) defines the offense of retaliation. The offense applies to a person subject to the UCMJ who intends to retaliate against any person for reporting or planning to report a criminal offense or make a protected communication. A "protected communication" means a lawful communication to a Member of Congress or an Inspector General (see 10 U.S.C. § 1034(j)), or disclosure of evidence of a violation of a law or regulation including sexual harassment or unlawful discrimination.

B. UNSPECIFIED OFFENSES— THE GENERAL ARTICLES

Article 133 (10 U.S.C. § 933) defines the offense of conduct unbecoming an officer and gentleman. This article applies to any male or female commissioned officer, cadet, or midshipman. The conduct proscribed by this article is any action or behavior in an official capacity which dishonors or disgraces the individual as an officer or in a private that which dishonors or disgraces the individual in a way that compromises that person's standing as an officer. In general terms, this can include acts of dishonesty, unfair dealing, indecency, indecorum, lawlessness, injustice, or cruelty. Specifically, this can include acts punishable by any other article in the MCM. When an offense under the Manual is joined with an offense under Article 133, in addition to the elements of the offense, the prosecution must prove that the acts of the accused were "unbecoming of an officer."

Article 134 (10 U.S.C. § 934), the General Article, makes punishable "all disorders and neglects to the prejudice of good order and discipline in the armed forces, all conduct of a nature to bring discredit upon the armed forces, and crimes and offenses not capital, or which persons subject to the UCMJ may be guilty" and cognizable by a general, special, or summary court-martial which can punish in its discretion. The term "crimes and offenses not capital" includes any conduct engaged in outside the United States, as defined in section 5 of title 18, that would constitute a crime or offense not capital if the conduct had been engaged in within the special maritime and territorial jurisdiction of the United States, as defined in section 7 of title 18.

The Manual for Courts-Martial offers important clarification of acts punishable under Article 134. They comprise three categories of offenses not specifically covered in any other article of the UCMJ identified in three clauses of Article 134. Clause 1 offenses are "all disorders and neglects to the prejudice of good order and discipline in the armed forces." Clause 2 offenses are all conduct of a nature to bring discredit upon the armed forces." Clause 3 offenses are "noncapital crimes or offenses which violate Federal law including law made applicable through the Federal Assimilative Crimes Act [18 U.S.C. § 13]." Part IV, ¶ 90c(2), MCM. To be cognizable under clause 1, an offense must directly prejudice good order and discipline. Although virtually any improper act by a servicemember could be considered prejudicial in an indirect or remote sense, only direct and palpable acts are considered within the scope of Article 134. A breach of a custom of the service may be considered a clause 1 violation if it is a long-established practice which has attained the force of law within the military, but if is set forth in a regulation, it should be charged under Article 92. Clause 2, which deals with service discrediting conduct, made punishable as conduct with a tendency to bring the service into disrepute or lower it in public esteem.

Prosecution of Clause 1 offenses under Article 134 require proof that an accused (1) did or failed to do certain acts; and (2) that, under the circumstances, the accused's conduct was to the prejudice of good order and discipline in the armed forces. Prosecution of Clause 2 offenses under Article 134 require proof that an accused (1) did or failed to do certain acts; and (2) that, under the circumstances, the accused's conduct was of a nature to bring discredit on the armed services. Prosecution of Clause 3 offenses under Article 134 require proof that an accused (1) did or failed to do certain acts that satisfy each element of the federal statute or assimilated state law; and (2) that the offense charged was not capital.

The C.A.A.F. has held that prosecutions under Article 134 must meet certain specificity requirements in charging offenses. Specifically, in an Article 134 prosecution, the government must prove beyond a reasonable doubt that the accused engaged in certain conduct that violated at least one of the three clauses of the article. This is known as the "terminal element" of the offense *United States v. Fosler*, 70 M.J. 225 (C.A.A.F. 2011). *Fosler* followed the holding of *Schmuck v. United States*, 489 U.S. 705, 718 (1989), and concluded that "the historical practice of implying Article 134's terminal element in every enumerated offense was no longer permissible." *Fosler* at 228. (citations omitted). The rationale for this justification is found in the Fifth and Sixth Amendments to the Constitution which prescribe due process before one is deprived of life, liberty, or property, and that an accused be informed "of the nature and cause of the accusation." Because the military is a notice pleading jurisdiction, it is necessary that every element of a charged offense be alleged expressly or by necessary implication in order to assure that a defendant understands what to defend against. R.C.M. 307(c)(3). Prosecutions are limited, however, by the preemption doctrine which prohibits application of Article 134 to conduct covered by Articles 80 through 132 of the UCMJ. MCM, pt. IV, ¶ 91.c.(5)(a). In *United States v. Poynor*, (A.F.Ct.Crim.App. (2018) the U.S. Air Force Court of Criminal Appeals upheld a conviction under Article 134 for reckless endangerment by pointing a firearm. While the appellant sought to argue that a prosecution for reckless endangerment was preempted by Article 128, which defined the crime of aggravated assault, the court noted that "the mens rea requirement for reckless endangerment is fundamentally different from that for aggravated assault by pointing a loaded weapon" and was thus a distinct offense from aggravated assault, one with different elements.

Clause 3 of Article 134 allows military prosecutors to assimilate state criminal statutes for noncapital offenses that take place in areas of concurrent or exclusive federal jurisdiction under the federal Assimilative Crimes Act (ACA)(18 U.S.C. § 13). In *Lewis v. United States*, 523 U.S. 155 (1998) (killing of a 4-year-old child on an Army base), the Supreme Court explained the application of the ACA. It involves two questions: first, whether the crime is made punishable by any federal law including the UCMJ. If not, the ACA would apply unless its application "would interfere with the achievement of a federal policy [citation omitted], because the state law would effectively rewrite an offense definition that Congress carefully considered [citation omitted], or because federal statutes reveal an intent to occupy so much of a field as would exclude use of the particular state statute at issue . . . ." For an example of applications of the ACA see *United States v. Robbins*, 52 M.J. 159 (C.A.A.F. 1999) (upheld conviction of violation of Article 128 and of an Ohio statute proscribing causing "the unlawful termination of another's pregnancy as the proximate result of *offender's* committing or attempting to commit a felony.") Note that since the decision in *Robbins* the UCMJ added Article 119a, Death or Injury to an Unborn Child which would preclude a similar prosecution under the ACA.

Until 1974, most commentators argued that the general articles were constitutionally defective because of vagueness, overbreadth, potential for abuse of prosecutorial discretion, and lack of delineation of punishment. Those who disagreed, including various military courts, relied primarily on court decisions construing the articles, statutory language limiting the possibilities for abuse, a long military custom and history behind the articles, special constitutional standards applicable to military law, and restraint by the military in use of the articles.

In *Parker v. Levy*, 417 U.S. 733 (1974), however, the Supreme Court upheld the general articles against a wide range of constitutional challenges raised by Captain Howard Levy, an army physician on active duty at the Fort Jackson Army Hospital. As part of his duties, Levy was to conduct a clinic for Special Forces troops. Upon discovering that these duties were being neglected, his commander called Levy to his office and handed him a written order to conduct the training. Levy read the order and stated that he would not obey it because of medical ethics. About the same time, Levy made several public statements to enlisted personnel at the post which urged black soldiers to refuse to go to Vietnam because "they are discriminated against and denied their freedom in the United States." He also referred to Special Forces troops as "liars and thieves and killers of peasants and murderers of women and children." Levy was charged and convicted by general court-martial of violating Articles 133 and 134. The conviction was sustained by the military courts of appeal, and habeas corpus relief was denied in federal district court. Reversing a Third Circuit decision holding Articles 133 and 134 void for vagueness, the Supreme Court found the articles to be neither vague nor overbroad.

Much of the majority opinion rested on differences between military and civilian law and the need for immediate obedience and discipline in the military: "Just as military society has been a society apart from civilian society, so military law is a jurisprudence which exists separate and apart from the law which governs in our federal judicial establishment." Additionally, the opinion cited several factors narrowing the broad language of the general articles. Furthermore, the court concluded that numerous examples in the MCM have imparted "accepted meaning to the seemingly imprecise standards of Articles 133 and 134" and that: "[e]ach of these articles has been construed by the [C.M.A.] or by other military authorities in such a manner as to at least partially narrow its otherwise broad scope. . . ."

The effect of these constructions of Articles 133 and 134 by the C.M.A. and by other military authorities has been twofold: It has narrowed the very broad reach of the literal articles, and at the same time has supplied considerable specificity by way of examples of the conduct which they cover.

Finally, the Court conceded that some areas of vagueness remain even after such construction, but that these areas of uncertainty are narrowed further by less formalized custom and usage. Levy's conduct, said the Court, clearly fell within the prohibited range of the article's proscriptions in light of an example in the MCM that squarely covered his statements.

In dissent, Justice Stewart said, "I find it hard to imagine criminal statutes more patently unconstitutional than these vague and uncertain general articles. . . ." Moreover, he found little comfort in the narrowing effects of history, regulations, and court decisions:

> If there be any doubt as to the absence of truly limiting constructions of the general articles, it is swiftly dispelled by even the most cursory review of convictions under them in the military courts. Art. 133 has been recently employed to punish such widely disparate conduct as dishonorable failure to repay debts, selling whiskey at an unconscionable price to an enlisted man, cheating at cards, and having an extramarital affair. Art. 134 has been given an even wider sweep, having been applied to sexual acts with a chicken, window peeping in a trailer park, and cheating while calling bingo numbers.

417 U.S. 733, 777.

As discussed above, since *Parker*, specificity requirements and the preemption doctrine have addressed some of the earlier concerns.

C. DEFENSES TO CRIMINAL LIABILITY

As in the civilian sector, the military criminal law system contains many potential defenses which may be raised by motion or introduced at trial. Motions which may result in dismissal of the charges without reaching the guilt or innocence of the defendant include motions to dismiss for lack of jurisdiction or expiration of the statute of limitations period and motions based on former jeopardy, pardon, former punishment, and denial of speedy trial. RCM 907. Note that RCM 907(b)(2)(E) requires that an accused move for dismissal of a charge or specification for failure to state an offense before the final adjournment of the court-martial. Special or "affirmative" defenses, which deny criminal responsibility wholly or partially while admitting the objective acts charged, include justification or excuse, self-defense, obedience to lawful orders, entrapment, inability, ignorance or mistake of fact, and lack of mental responsibility. RCM 916. Other defenses, such as mistaken identity, alibi, and good character, deny that the accused committed the acts charged. RCM 916(a). Before trial, Defense Counsel must notify Trial Counsel of "intent to offer the defense of alibi, innocent ingestion, or lack of mental responsibility, or its intent to introduce expert testimony as to the accused's mental condition." RCM 701(b)(2).

There is little substantive difference between civilian and military affirmative defenses. Justification is a defense to death, injury, or other acts done in proper performance of a legal duty. Thus, military police engaged in lawful apprehension may use force, if reasonably necessary. When an accident (not negligence) results in death or injury during the performance of a lawful act in a lawful manner, the result is excusable. RCM 916(f).

There are, however, four defenses that are either unique to the military or have particular application to the military. These are (1) "Obedience to Orders," RCM 916(d); (2) duress or coercion, RCM 916(h); (3) lack of mental responsibility, RCM 916(k)(1); and (4) the "good soldier" defense, *United States v. Clemons,* 16 M.J. 44 (C.M.A. 1983); *United States v. Belz,* 20 M.J. 33 (C.M.A. 1985).

(1) Obedience to apparently lawful orders is a defense peculiar to the military. However, this defense is inapplicable where "the accused knew the orders to be unlawful or a person of ordinary sense and understanding would have known the orders to be unlawful." RCM 916(d). For example, in *U.S. v. Calley*, 46 C.M.R. 1131 (A.C.M.R.1973), the superior orders defense was rejected in connection with murder charges relating to the killing of unarmed civilians, including women and children. The court noted that, under the circumstances, the order to kill was so far removed from combat necessities as to be patently illegal. *Calley v. Callaway*, 519 F.2d 184, 190–91 includes a full history of the *Calley* litigation.

(2) Duress or coercion is recognized in the military as a defense.

> It is a defense to any offense except killing an innocent person that the accused's participation in the offense was caused by a reasonable apprehension that the accused or another innocent person would be immediately killed or

> would immediately suffer serious bodily injury if the accused did not commit the act. The apprehension must reasonably continue throughout the commission of the act. If the accused has any reasonable opportunity to avoid committing the act without subjecting the accused or another innocent person to the harm threatened, this defense shall not apply.

RCM 916(h).

In *United States v. Le*, 59 M.J. 859 (A.Ct.Crim.App. 2004) (accused's asserted fear of immediate death or serious bodily injury rendered his guilty plea to desertion improvident), the accused raised a defense of duress, RCM 916(h) which the Army Court of Criminal Appeals accepted as a partial excuse for his absence charge under Article 85, UCMJ, 10 U.S.C. § 885. A duress defense is unavailing for refusal to obey an order to perform dangerous military duty. *United States v. Talty*, 17 M.J. 1127 (N.M.C.J.R. 1984) (accused's belief that entry into reactor compartment of nuclear submarine would expose accused to hazardous levels of radiation did not establish defense of duress to a charge under Article 90, UCMJ, 10 U.S.C. 890, of willfully disobeying an order of a superior commissioned officer. The duress defense is distinct from its civilian counterpart, the defense of necessity (conduct was a choice between the "lesser of two evils"). *United States v. Banks*, 37 M.J. 700 (A.C.M.R. 1993) ("necessity defense" is not part of military law). There have been suggestions that the concepts of duress and necessity have fused. At least the possibility that military law has followed that path was opened by *United States v. Rockwood*, 52 M.J. 98 (C.A.A.F. 1999) ("In our view, a necessity instruction was in fact given, and the military judge formulated the instruction in a manner that comported well with general civilian criminal law." (Cox, Chief Judge).

(3) A third military-related affirmative defense is an accused's lack of mental responsibility. The accused argues that he or she lacked mental responsibility because "at the time of the commission of the criminal acts constituting the offense, as a result of a severe mental disease or defect, the accused was unable to appreciate the nature and quality of the wrongfulness of his or her acts." RCM 916(k)(1). This defense is separable from other mental capacity issues such as whether during the pretrial stages of investigation, the accused's mental condition warrants a mental examination (RCM 706); whether the accused has the capacity to stand trial (RCM 706 and RCM 909); or a post-trial hearing for a person found not guilty only by reason of a lack of mental responsibility of an offense involving bodily injury to another, or involving a substantial risk of such injury or damage. (RCM 1102A).

In military law, one is insane who "lacked mental responsibility" at the time of the offense or who lacks the requisite mental capacity at the time of trial. Art. 50a, UCMJ, 10 U.S.C. 850a; RCM 916(k), 909(a). The test applied for the former type of insanity is based in part on the American Law Institute's Model Penal Code test and *United States v. Frederick*, 3 M.J. 230 (C.M.A. 1977). Under the test, one is not criminally responsible if, (1) at the time of the acts (2) as a result of a severe mental disease or defect, (3) he or she was unable to appreciate the nature and quality or the wrongfulness of the acts. Art. 50a(a), UCMJ, 10 U.S.C. § 850a(a); RCM 916(k).

A finding that the defendant lacks mental capacity at the time of trial does not necessarily exonerate the accused of the offense, but merely suspends the proceedings. The case may be continued or charges withdrawn or dismissed depending upon the nature and potential duration of the accused's incapacity. RCM 909(f).

With respect to Defense Counsel's tactical decisions regarding pursuit or not of an insanity defense, note *United States v. Morgan*, 37 M.J. 407 (C.M.A. 1993) (defense counsel's failure to investigate or to present potentially viable insanity defense or evidence of appellant's personality disorder in mitigation was tactical decision and not ineffective assistance of counsel).

(4) The "good soldier" defense is the final peculiarly military defense. The "good soldier" defense allows an accused to offer evidence of his or her general good military character and lawful disposition in order to raise a reasonable doubt as to guilt. Evidence of such a pertinent trait of accused's character is admissible under MRE 404(a)(1). In *United States v. Clemons*, 16 M.J. 44 (C.M.A. 1983), the Court of Military Appeals held that it was prejudicial for the trial judge to refuse admission of evidence of accused's good military character and character from lawfulness. As Chief Judge Everett

noted in his concurring opinion, "As we noted in *United States v. Browning* (citation omitted), "Wigmore goes so far as to say that evidence of good soldierly character is even stronger than the customary evidence of good general character." It should be noted that the "good soldier" defense is not without critics, e.g., Elizabeth Lutes Hillman, Note, "The 'Good soldier' Defense: Character Evidence and Military Rank at Courts-Martial," 108 Yale L.J. 87 (1999) ("By permitting the introduction of good military character evidence during the guilt phase of a court-martial, the good soldier defense encourages factfinders to focus on the reputation of accused individuals rather than on their alleged criminal acts.")

Entrapment is a defense when "the criminal design or suggestion to commit the offense originated in the Government and the accused had no predisposition to commit the offense." RCM 916(g). The principal aspect of the defense is the accused's lack of predisposition to commit the offense alleged, not the deterrence of government involvement in criminal activity: "The fact that persons acting for the Government merely afford opportunities or facilities for the commission of the offense does not constitute entrapment." RCM 916(g).

Ignorance or mistake of fact is a defense when knowledge of that fact is an element of the offense, or when the mistake negates the mental state required for the offense. RCM 916(j). Thus, in general intent offenses, mistaken belief must be reasonable and must have existed in the accused's mind to serve as a defense, while in specific intent crimes, the mistake need only have existed in the mind of the accused. Even an honest and reasonable mistake of law is generally no defense unless the mistake negates the mental state required for the crime. RCM 916(*l*)(1). The generalization that "ignorance of the law is no defense" refers to the usual offense which requires no actual knowledge by the accused of the law or the legal effects of his actions.

Voluntary drunkenness does not excuse offenses committed while intoxicated, nor can it be used to lower a charge of premeditated murder or unpremeditated murder to manslaughter. However, intoxication may negate actual knowledge, specific intent, or premeditation such that a charge of premeditation may be reduced to unpremeditated. RCM 916(*l*)(2); *United States v. Morgan*, 37 M.J. 407 (C.M.A. 1993) (voluntary intoxication cannot defeat capacity of accused to entertain intent to kill or inflict great bodily harm).

D. PUNISHMENT

Most of the Punitive Articles merely recite that violations will be punished "as a court-martial may direct." While military punishment goals include those of civilian punishment such as deterrence and rehabilitation, military punishment is also imposed to further discipline and maintain order in fulfilling the military's mission. Limitations on the severity of punishments which may be imposed by summary, special, and general courts-martial are set on in the

Maximum Punishment Chart found in Appendix 12, MCM.

Rather than restate the information available in the Maximum Punishments Chart, only a few general comments on the sweep of military punishments will be made here. First, cruel or unusual punishment, such as flogging, branding or tattooing, is prohibited. Article 55, UCMJ, 10 U.S.C. § 855. Congress "intended to grant protection covering even wider limits" than those encompassed by the Eighth Amendment. *United States v. Matthews*, 16 M.J. 354 (C.M.A. 1983). Second, military punishments may take more varied forms than straight imprisonment (called "confinement at hard labor" in the military). Serious offenses may be punished by dishonorable or bad conduct discharges, and most offenses will lead to varying lengths of imprisonment. Differing amounts of pay forfeitures also may be adjudged. Third, as in civilian law, prior convictions may provide grounds for increasing punishment beyond the limits established for first offenders. Finally, RCM 1004 lists specific procedures that must be followed before the death penalty may be imposed.

Inequities in the treatment of offenders based on their rank continue to challenge the asserted fairness of military justice and prompt calls for reform. See Pound, "Unequal Justice," 133 U.S. NEWS & WORLD REPORT 18–30 (Dec. 16, 2002). For example, the notorious case of Army General David Hale, now retired, illustrates how these problems infect the perception, both by those within the military as well as the public at large, of the fairness and impartiality of the military.

General Hale was court-martialed on charges that he carried on affairs with the wives of four subordinate officers and lied to Pentagon investigators about his adultery. He could have been sentenced to 11 years in prison, forfeiture of all retirement pay, and dismissal from the service. Instead, he got a plea bargain, amounting to little more than a slap on the wrist; in return for pleading guilty to eight of the charges, he was reprimanded, fined $10,000, and ordered to forfeit $1,000 monthly pay for a year. He was subsequently demoted from a major general to brigadier general, but nevertheless retired as a general officer. Although it is difficult to conceive of activity more corrosive to morale, good order and discipline than Hale's (cf. 2 Sam. ch. 11, David and Bathsheba), his punishment was mild. A survey of reported appellate cases of adultery prosecutions presenting similar facts shows that enlisted servicemembers and company grade officers receive far harsher punishment. Similar considerations apply to the case of Lt. Gen. Craig A Franklin's decision to dismiss the conviction of Lt. Col James Wilkerson discussed above.

In addition to disparities based on rank, the military is also addressing racial disparities in the military justice system. Years of data show that white servicemembers are subjected to discipline less frequently than servicemembers of color. Congress included a provision in the 2020 National Defense Authorization Act that would require tracking of information on race, ethnicity, and gender in court-martial proceedings. Dan Lamothe, *Military Leaders Promise to Address Systemic Racial Disparities in the Military Justice System*, The Wash. Post (June 16. 2020), https://www.washingtonpost.com/national-security/2020/06/16/military-leaders-promise-address-systemic-racial-disparities-military-justice-system/.

CHAPTER 8

RIGHTS OF SERVICEMEMBERS

As noted elsewhere, the military services are a "society apart" from civilian society by virtue not only of function, but also by virtue of the fact that servicemembers enjoy more limited Constitutional rights than American civilians. As Yale Law Professor Joseph W. Bishop, Jr. observed in *Justice Under Fire: A Study of Military Law*, at 114 (1974), the Supreme Court "has never to this day squarely held that a soldier has any constitutional rights when he is court-martialed, or indeed that he has any constitutional rights of any variety." His appraisal of the state of the law then was as follows: "[n]o matter what the draftsmen of the Constitution intended, and no matter what the Supreme Court may have said and done between 1791 and the Korean War, I think it safe to say that soldiers today have constitutional rights, although it would be most unsafe to dogmatize about the precise extent of those rights." Id. at 122.

Subsequent developments have substantially qualified Bishop's generalization. As Chief Judge Robinson Everett of the C.A.A.F. put it, "The time is long past when scholars disputed the applicability of the Bill of Rights to service personnel. Instead, our premise must be 'that the Bill of Rights applies with full force to men and women in the military service unless any given protection is, expressly or by necessary implication, inapplicable. . . .' *United States v. Stuckey*, 10 M.J. 347 (C.M.A.1981) (Everett, C.J.). Servicemembers also enjoy analogous (and sometimes more generous) rights secured by statute and executive order. See Gilligan, "The Bill of Rights and Service Members," The Army Lawyer, Dec. 1987, 3–11.

A. DUE PROCESS RIGHTS

In marked contrast to the due process rights of those not in the military, the due process rights of members of the armed services begin and often end with the process Congress has provided. In a civilian context, *Mathews v. Eldridge*, 424 U.S. 319 (1976), set the standard that due process "generally requires consideration of three distinct factors: the private interest that will be affected by the official action; the risk of erroneous deprivation and the value of additional or substitute procedural safeguards; and the Government's interest in the fiscal and administrative burdens" such additional process would entail.

In place of *Mathews*, the Supreme Court employs a different standard to determine the due process rights of members of the armed services. In determining what process is due, courts "must give particular deference to the determination of Congress, made under its authority to regulate the land and naval forces [asking] whether the factors militating in favor of the [asserted due process right] are so extraordinarily weighty as to overcome the balance struck by Congress." *Middendorf v. Henry*, 425 U.S. 25 (1976).

With respect to members of the armed services, early cases painted a starker picture: "To those in the military or naval service of the United States, the military law is due process." *Reaves v. Ainsworth*, 219 U.S. 296 (1911). An even earlier case, *Dynes v. Hoover*, 61 U.S. 65 (1857), concluded from Congress' power to regulate the land and naval forces (U.S. Const. Art. I, § 8) and the grand jury exception for "cases arising in the land and naval forces" (U.S. Const. Amend. 5) that Congress has more, and the courts less, constitutional authority than in civilian affairs. *Dynes* held that the power to prescribe rules for those in the armed services "is given without any connection between it and the 3d Article of the Constitution defining the judicial power of the United States; indeed, that the two powers are entirely independent of each other." A member of the armed services is "subject to military law and the principles of that law; as provided by Congress, [constitute] for him due process of law in a constitutional sense." *United States ex rel. French v. Weeks*, 259 U.S. 326 (1922).

Despite strong deference shown in *Dynes* to the power of Congress over military personnel, however, the Supreme Court insisted on careful adherence to the law Congress made. Thus, in *Runkle v. United States*, 122 U.S. 543 (1887), the Court held with regard to a court-martial and its review by the President that

> [t]he trial, finding, and sentence are the solemn acts of a court organized and conducted under the authority of and according to the prescribed forms of law. It sits to pass upon the most sacred questions of human rights that are ever placed on trial in a court of justice, rights which, in the

> very nature of things, can neither be exposed to danger, nor subjected to the uncontrolled will of any man, but which must be adjudged according to law. And the act of the officer who reviews the proceedings of the court, whether he be the commander of the fleet or the president, and without whose approval the sentence cannot be executed, is as much a part of this judgment, according to law, as is the trial or the sentence. When the president, then, performs this duty of approving the sentence of a court-martial dismissing an officer, his act has all the solemnity and significance of the judgment of a court of law.

Runkle illustrates that, although military law may have defined the extent of due process afforded the servicemember, whatever principles of law Congress specified must be scrupulously adhered to.

Similarly in *Rostker v. Goldberg*, 453 U.S. 57 (1981), the Court refused to particularize the degree of deference due to a law passed by Congress dealing with military affairs and national security, but clearly accorded such laws substantial deference:

> None of this is to say that Congress is free to disregard, the Constitution when it acts in the area of military affairs. In that area, as in any other, Congress remains subject to the limitations of the Due Process Clause [citations omitted], but the tests and limitations to be applied may differ because of the military context. We, of course, do not abdicate our ultimate responsibility to decide the

constitutional question, but simply recognize that the Constitution requires such deference to congressional choice [citations omitted]. In deciding the question before us we must be particularly careful not to substitute our judgment of what is desirable for that of Congress, or our own evaluation of evidence for a reasonable evaluation by the Legislative Branch.

B. EQUAL PROTECTION RIGHTS

In weighing the equal protection interests of members of the armed services, the court looks at the determination of Congress expressed in legislation just as it does in due process inquiries. *Rostker v. Goldberg*, 453 U.S. 57 (1981) (equal protection challenge to male only draft registration) and *Schlesinger v. Ballard*, 419 U.S. 498 (1975) (equal protection challenge to statute granting women naval officers a longer period of commissioned service before mandatory discharge for failing to be promoted).

The Supreme Court, in *Frontiero v. Richardson*, 411 U.S. 677 (1973), considered an equal protection challenge to a law that provided that spouses of male members of the uniformed services are dependents for purposes of obtaining increased quarters allowances and medical and dental benefits, but that spouses of female members are not dependents unless they are in fact dependent for over one-half of their support. The Court held that the different treatment of spouses of men and women violated equal protection. A plurality of the court applied "strict scrutiny," requiring that the classification be narrowly tailored to meet a compelling governmental interest. Four other members of the Court reached the same conclusions under less searching "middle tier" scrutiny, whereby the classification must be closely related to fulfilling an important governmental interest. A major component of Justice Rehnquist's lone dissent was his view that the courts should defer to Congress' policy choices in the area of military rules and regulations.

Indeed, other cases do show more deference than *Frontiero* to Congressional military policy. For example, in *Schlesinger v. Ballard*, 419 U.S. 498 (1975), the Court rejected a male officer's attack on sex-based distinctions in the Navy's promotion system that granted female officers longer to achieve promotion before facing mandatory discharge:

> [T]he different treatment of men and women naval officers under [the statute challenged] reflects, not archaic and overbroad generalizations, but instead, the demonstrable fact that male and female line officers in the Navy are not similarly situated with respect to opportunities for professional service [because of the effects of the combat restriction on women.]

One view is that the law in *Frontiero* rested on "archaic and overbroad" generalizations while that in *Schlesinger* rested on distinctions based on real differences, thus satisfying the applicable equal protection standard for reviewing gender-based discrimination. *Craig v. Boren,* 429 U.S. 190 (1976).

Another interpretation of *Schlesinger* is that it (but not *Frontiero*) is consistent with the line of cases represented by *Parker v. Levy*, 417 U.S. 733 (1974), *Middendorf v. Henry,* 425 U.S. 25 (1976), and *Weiss v. United States*, 510 U.S. 163 (1994). The following excerpt from *Schlesinger* supports this interpretation:

> In both Reed and Frontiero the reason asserted to justify the challenged gender-based classifications was administrative convenience, and that alone. Here, on the contrary, the operation of the statutes in question results in a flow of promotions commensurate with the Navy's current needs and service to motivate qualified commissioned officers to so conduct themselves that they may realistically look forward to higher levels of command. This Court has recognized that "it is the primary business of armies and navies to fight or be ready to fight wars should the occasion arise." [citations omitted] *The responsibility for determining how best our Armed Forces shall attend to that business rests with Congress and with the President [citations omitted]. We cannot say that, in exercising its broad constitutional power here, Congress has violated the Due Process Clause of the Fifth Amendment.* [Emphasis added].

Under this view, *Frontiero* represents a failure by the courts appropriately to defer to congressional judgments regarding governance of military society.

Whether and to what extent the *Parker-Middendorf-Weiss* standard will guide future court appraisals of the constitutionality of regulations of the armed services remains to be seen.

C. FIRST AMENDMENT RIGHTS

The First Amendment provides:

> "Congress shall make no law respecting an establishment of religion, or prohibiting the free exercise thereof; or abridging the freedom of speech, or of the press; or the right of the people peaceably to assemble, and to petition the Government for a redress of grievances."

While First Amendment rights are not absolute with respect to anyone, the First Amendment rights of members of the armed services are more limited than are those of civilians. The legal basis for this distinction is the Constitution: both the First Amendment and the authority to regulate the armed services are granted by the Constitution. Some balance must be struck between the freedoms provided by the First Amendment and the demands of military life and military society. *Welsh v. United States*, 398 U.S. 333 (1970).

1. RELIGION

The issue of freedom to hold religious beliefs rarely arises in the military context. Conscientious objectors who interpose beliefs as a bar to service have been exempt from combatant service during times of conscription. *United States v. Seeger*, 380 U.S. 163 (1965); *Welsh v. United States*, 398 U.S. 333

(1970); and *Gillette v. United States*, 401 U.S. 437 (1971).

Transition to an all-volunteer force has reduced, but not eliminated, the incidence of conscientious objector claims. More frequent deployments abroad, heavier post-Vietnam, reliance on reserve components, family commitments and a desire to escape from service following extensive training at government expense have equated in-service conscientious objector claims with those raised by draftees in earlier years. E.g., *Lipton v. Peters*, 240 F.3d 1074 (W.D. Tex. 1999) (affirming dismissal of habeas corpus petition; review of the record reveals that there is a basis in fact supporting the Secretary's determination that Lipton's professed beliefs were not sincere).

To qualify for discharge from military service as a conscientious objector, an applicant must establish 1) that he or she is opposed to war in any form, *Gillette v. United States*, 401 U.S. 437 (1971); 2) that his or her objection is grounded in deeply held moral, ethical, or religious beliefs, *Welsh v. United States*, 398 U.S. 333 (1970); and 3) his or her convictions are sincere, *Witmer v. United States*, 348 U.S. 375 (1955). Court review of the denial of a servicemember's application for conscientious-objector discharge is extremely narrow. *DeWalt v. Commanding Officer, Fort Benning, Ga.*, 476 F.2d 440, 442 (5th Cir.1973) (review of the denial decision is one of the narrowest known to the law; the court's task is not to impose its own views of human nature upon the armed service's conclusion, but to determine whether that conclusion is supported by fact). A denial must be sustained if this court can discern any basis in fact for it. *Silverthorne v. Laird*, 460 F2d 1175, 1179 (5th Cir.1972).

Following the Supreme Court's decision in *Employment Div., Dept. of Human Resources of Oregon v. Smith*, 494 U.S. 872 (1990), Congress enacted the Religious Freedom Restoration Act of 1993 (RFRA), 42 U.S.C.A. § 2000bb. RFRA's stated purposes are "(1) to restore the compelling interest test as set forth in [*Sherbert v. Verner*, 374 U.S. 389 (1963)] and to guarantee its application in all cases where the free exercise of religion is substantially burdened; and (2) to provide a claim or defense to persons whose religious exercise is substantially burdened by government." Government burdens are prohibited unless the government can demonstrate that the burden "(1) is in furtherance of a compelling governmental interest; and (2) is the least restrictive means of furthering that . . . interest." By its terms, it applies to any "branch, department, agency, instrumentality, and official (or other person acting under color of law) of the United States."

Although RFRA was held beyond the legislative power of Congress to regulate activities by States in *City of Boerne v. Flores*, 521 U.S. 507 (1997), its application to the federal government has been upheld. *In re Young*, 141 F.3d 854 (8th Cir.1998) (to the extent it was constitutional as applied to federal law, portion of Religious Freedom Restoration Act (RFRA) applicable to federal government was fully severable from portion applicable to states). Issues with respect to in-service conscientious objectors arise, for example, as to whether the government's interest is sufficiently compelling to allow the religious burdening of conscientious objectors and whether the accommodations by the service to the conscientious objector represent the least restrictive means of furthering that interest as compared with discharge. In *United States v. Webster*, 65 M.J. 936 (A. Ct. Crim. App. 2008), the court reviewed the court-martial conviction of an accused convicted of missing movement by design, Article 87, UCMJ, 10 U.S.C. § 887, and disobeying a superior commissioned officer, Article 90, UCMJ, 10 U.S.C. § 890, by refusing to deploy to Iraq in support of Operation Iraqi Freedom because of conflict with his Muslim religion. An opinion by Senior Judge Schenck concluded that Webster's rights under RFRA were not violated. The Army had a "compelling interest in requiring soldiers to deploy with their units" and "furthered its compelling interest in the least restrictive manner possible." (at 947) The accommodations offered by the Army in Webster's case are instructive:

> Although the Army required appellant to deploy with his unit, the Army made numerous allowances for him. The Army afforded him the opportunity to request relief as a conscientious objector. See AR 600-43 [Army Regulation 600-43 "Conscientious Objection" (21 August 2006),] The Army gave him the right to request reasonable accommodation of his religious practices. See AR 600-20, para 5-6. [Army Regulation 600-20 "Army Command Policy" (13

> May 2002)] Finally, although apparently not required to do so by any regulation, appellant's commander generously allowed appellant to deploy with his unit in a non-combatant role. We conclude that the First Amendment does not require anything more. . . .

(at 947–48).

The need for good order and discipline can outweigh an individual's interests in pursuing particular religious practices. Thus, religious practice cannot be raised as a defense to a refusal to obey a lawful order. "[C]onflict with religious scruples . . . is 'insufficient as a defense' to a charge of disobedience." *United States v. Wilson*, 41 C.M.R. 100, 101 (C.M.A.1969). For example, a soldier can be ordered to cook on his Sabbath. *United States v. Burry*, 36 C.M.R. 829 (C.G.C.M.R. 1966); may be required to salute despite his religious objections, *United States v. Cupp*, 24 C.M.R. 565 (A.F.B.R.1957). Similarly, members of the armed forces can be precluded from religious practices that conflict with military regulation of such things as uniform standards. *Goldman v. Weinberger*, 475 U.S. 503 (1986) (Air Force regulation banning the wearing of headgear indoors upheld when individual's religious belief required wearing a yarmulke). After the *Goldman* decision, Congress enacted a statute providing for the wearing of religious apparel while in uniform unless "the wearing of the item would interfere with the performance [of] military duties [or] the item of apparel is not neat and conservative." 10 U.S.C. § 774.

Not all military considerations, however, will override individual objections to regulations of religion. In *Anderson v. Laird*, 466 F.2d 283 (D.C.Cir. 1972), *cert. denied*, sub nom. *Laird v. Anderson*, 409 U.S. 1076 (1972) (federal appeals court invalidated the compulsory chapel attendance policies of the military academies at West Point, Annapolis and Colorado Springs as violative of the First Amendment's Establishment Clause).

2. SPEECH

In the civilian realm, the First Amendment protects speech, with some exceptions, unless it is "directed to inciting or producing imminent lawless action and is likely to incite or produce such action." *Brandenburg v. Ohio*, 395 U.S. 444 (1969) (violent, racist speech is protected so long as it is unlikely to produce a violent outcome). The test in the military is less robust. "[I]n the military context, . . . dangerous speech is that speech that 'interferes with or prevents the orderly accomplishment of the mission or presents a clear danger to loyalty, discipline, mission, or morale of the troops.' " *United States v. Wilcox*, 66 M.J. 442, 448 (C.A.A.F. 2008) quoting *United States v. Brown*, 45 M.J. 389, 395 (C.A.A.F. 1996).

The rationale for a more limited right of free speech in the military was aptly identified early on: "An army is not a deliberative body. It is the executive arm. Its law is that of obedience. No question can be left open as to the right to command in the officer, or the duty of obedience in the soldier." *In re Grimley*, 137 U.S. 147 (1890).

Speech-related military prosecutions under Article 134, UCMJ, 10 U.S.C. § 934, were fully examined in *United States v. Wilcox*, 66 M.J. 442 (C.A.A.F. 2008). There the court emphasized that the prosecution must demonstrate not only that the speech presented the dangers to mission, loyalty, discipline or morale as required by the *Brown* case, but also that the speech was prejudicial to good order and discipline. In that case, the accused was charged *inter alia* with wrongfully advocating anti-government and disloyal sentiments while identifying himself as a 'U.S. Army Paratrooper' in an America Online profile, and advocating racial intolerance by counseling and advising individuals on racist views. Measured by "civilian world" standards prescribed by the *Brandenburg* decision, Wilcox's speech is not criminal. To be criminal under military law, an additional element of criminality drawn from Article 134 must be proved by the prosecution. Implicit in this analysis is the degree to which constitutional First Amendment protection avails the servicemember: "No one disputes that servicemembers enjoy some measure of the right to free speech granted by the First Amendment." (69 M.J. 442, 447 citing inter alia *Parker v. Levy*). However reprehensible the court might otherwise view the accused's speech, "condemnation and conviction are drastically different when the First Amendment is involved, and our disagreement with his statements cannot substitute for the Government's failure to introduce evidence legally sufficient to meet the element of either service discrediting behavior or prejudice to good order and discipline necessary for a conviction under Article 134, UCMJ." (69 M.J. 442, 451).

As the *Wilcox court* explained:

> *Parker v. Levy* [417 U.S. 733 (1974)] reiterated the point that differences between the military community and the civilian community result in military law that "regulate[s] aspects of the conduct of members of the military which in the civilian sphere are left unregulated." [citation omitted] But the Supreme Court upheld Article 134, UCMJ, against constitutional attack for vagueness and overbreadth *in light of* the narrowing construction developed in military law through the precedents of this Court and limitations within the *Manual for Courts-Martial* (*MCM*) itself. [citation omitted] As such, a limited Article 134, UCMJ, does not make every "irregular or improper act" a court-martial offense *and* does not reach conduct that is only indirectly or remotely prejudicial to good order and discipline. *MCM* pt. IV, para. 60.c. (2)(a); *see also* William Winthrop, *Military Law and Precedents* 723–24 (2d ed.1920 reprint) (commenting on Article 62 of the American Articles of War, the predecessor to Article 134, UCMJ, and stating that to be punishable, acts prejudicial to good order and discipline "must have been committed under such circumstances as to have directly offended against the government and discipline of the military

state"). If it were otherwise, the forces of narrowing interpretation that saved Article 134, UCMJ, from constitutional challenge in *Parker v. Levy* would fail.

If, however, the government meets its burden by demonstrating that accused's speech was unprotected, e.g., "Indecent language," which is "grossly offensive to modesty, decency, or propriety, or shocks the moral sense, because of its vulgar, filthy, or disgusting nature, or its tendency to incite lustful thought." [*Manual for Courts-Martial, United States (MCM)*, Part IV, ¶ 89.c (2008 ed.)] and service discrediting under Article 134, then the accused's conviction will be upheld. *United States v. Garrigan*, 2013 WL 1129284 (A.F.Ct.Crim.App.2013) (*Wilcox* distinguished).

Other speech-related activities are analyzed in much the same way. For example, on-post petitioning seeking signatures. Servicemembers' rights to circulate petitions can be more narrowly circumscribed than can those of civilians. E.g., *Brown v. Glines*, 444 U.S. 348 (1980) (contesting Air Force regulation regarding circulation of a petition complaining about Air Force grooming standards); *Carlson v. Schlesinger*, 511 F.2d 1327 (D.C.Cir.1975) (anti-war petitions circulated on-post without prior approval as required by regulation).

a. Contemptuous Words

Article 88, UCMJ, 10 U.S.C. § 888 has a direct and obvious effect on servicemember speech: "Any commissioned officer who uses contemptuous words against the President, the Vice President, Congress, the Secretary of Defense, the Secretary of a military department, the Secretary of Homeland Security, or the Governor or legislature of any State, Commonwealth, or possession in which he is on duty or present shall be punished as a court-martial may direct." Several limitations apply to Article 88, however. A purpose of Article 88 is apparently to prevent a threat to civilian control of the military by stifling criticism of the government by the officer corps. By its terms, since the 1950 revision of the UCMJ, Article 88 applies only to commissioned officers (previously officers in the sea services were prosecuted for this offense as conduct unbecoming or under the general article). The textual limitation of Article 88 to commissioned officers necessarily excludes warrant officers, enlisted personnel, cadets, and midshipmen of the military academies who share with civilians the right to criticize the government and its leadership. Retirees subject to the UCMJ are unlikely to be prosecuted for offenses of this sort; they present none of the evils against which Article 88 is directed. The prohibition against disrespectful criticism draws no distinction between contemptuous language directed against an official in either his or her official capacity or personal capacity. Under the Article, the truth or falsity of the statement is irrelevant.

Four exceptions apply to charges under Article 88. First, ordinary or even emphatic political discussion is immune from sanction so long as it is not personally contemptuous. Second, private conversations are immune from prosecution. To constitute a violation of Article 88, the contemptuous speech must become publicly known. Third, Congress has by statute (10 U.S.C. § 1034) protected the right of all military personnel to communicate with members of Congress. Thus, otherwise contemptuous language under Article 88 could not be prosecuted since retaliation against servicemembers (including in this instance commissioned officers) who avail themselves of this statutory right. E.g., *United States v. Schmidt*, 36 C.M.R. 213 (C.M.A.1966) (accused wrote to his Senator complaining of poorly prepared food and extremely crowded living conditions existing in parts of Fort Riley, Kansas). Complaints pursuant to Article 138 enjoy an exemption similar to communications under 10 U.S.C. § 1034. Fourth, information submitted as part of legal proceedings is privileged and cannot be prosecuted as contemptuous under Article 88. For example, even a complaint about the President, the Commander in Chief, alleging attorney misconduct submitted as part of legal proceedings is protected. E.g., *Hogue v. Neal*, 12 S.W.3d 186 (E.D. Ark. 2000) (accusing the President of attorney misconduct in in the case of Paula Jones. *Jones v. Clinton*, 57 F.Supp.2d 719 (E.D.Ark.1999)).

b. Disloyal Statements

Articles 133 (conduct unbecoming) and 134 (service-discrediting conduct) UCMJ, 10 U.S.C. §§ 933 and 934 are the usual bases for prosecution of disloyal statements. To be prosecuted under Article 134, the statement must be directed to the United States as a political entity, and not to a department or other agency that forms part of its administrative operation. A statement against the President, a branch of the service, or a national policy may not be prosecuted under Article 134, although it may be prosecuted under Article 88, as discussed above. Case law indicates that the statement must be made publicly and with the intent to promote disloyalty toward the United States. *United States v. Gray*, 42 C.M.R. 255 (C.M.A. 1970); *United States v. Priest*, 45 C.M.R. 338 (C.M.A.1972). Despite the inherent ambiguities concerning what constitute disloyal statements, both Articles 133 and 134 have been upheld against allegations of unconstitutional vagueness and overbreadth. *Parker v. Levy*, 417 U.S. 733 (1974).

c. Political Participation

The subject of political participation is sensitive because of America's tradition of subordination of the military to civilian control and a desire to exclude the military from interference with the functioning of our democratic society. The utilization of Union soldiers to protect voting by Freedmen in southern elections during Reconstruction was a source of friction after the Civil War. It is clear, however, that members of the armed services have a right to vote and participate in the election of the government. *Carrington v. Rash*, 380 U.S. 89 (1965) and enjoy statutory protections of their right to vote.

Voting by servicemembers is regulated by the Federal Voting Assistance Program and Department of Defense policy in compliance with the Uniformed and Overseas Citizens Absentee Voting Act. 52

U.S.C. § 20301. That policy requires disseminating information about registration and voting procedures and materials pertaining to scheduled elections, including dates, offices, constitutional amendments, and other ballot proposals. Furthermore, in recognition that the right of U.S. citizens to vote is a fundamental right that is afforded protection by the U.S. Constitution, every eligible voter shall (1) Be given an opportunity to register and vote in any election for which he or she is eligible; and (2) Be able to vote in person or by absentee. All persons assisting in the voting process shall take all necessary steps to prevent discrimination, fraud, intimidation or coercion, and unfair registration and voting assistance procedures. This includes, but is not limited to, preventing actions such as using military authority to influence the vote of any other member of the uniformed services or to require any member to march to any polling place or place of voting. 32 C.F.R. § 233.4.

d. Symbolic Expression

Members of the armed services can be disciplined for participating in parades and demonstrations as a means of protest. *Cortright v. Resor*, 447 F.2d 245 (2d Cir.1971). Moreover, servicemembers can be required to participate in parades sponsored by organizations supporting political viewpoints with which they disagree so long as the parade was not coextensive with or held on the same day as the appearance or any speech before the convention of any candidate of any party for either the presidency or the vice presidency. *Jones v. United States Secretary of Defense*, 346 F.Supp. 97 (D.Minn.1972).

3. PUBLICATIONS

a. Publications by Servicemembers

Blogs present problems requiring treatment beyond the scope of the Nutshell. For a detailed analysis of the first amendment issues regarding blogging, see Major Frederick D. Thaden, "Blogs v. Freedom of Speech: A Commander's Primer Regarding First Amendment Rights As They Apply to the Blogosphere," 33 No. 2 The Reporter 19 (June 2006).

The services may restrict writing or speaking in an individual capacity when the subject involves military matters or foreign policy. For example, the Army requires submission to appropriate headquarters of materials, including fiction, which relate to military matters. E.g., AR 360-5, Army Public Affairs, Public Information. Submitted material will be reviewed to ensure that it contains no classified information and statements of policy will be reviewed for accuracy and propriety. Under the regulations, fiction is subjected to a security clearance only. All other public writings and speeches will be reviewed for conformity with Department of Defense and other government policies, and will be subjected to "constructive suggestions" on matters of accuracy and propriety. Prior review was upheld in *United States v. Voorhees*, 16 C.M.R. 83 (C.M.A. 1954). Voorhees, an Army officer, had written and published material relating to his experiences during the Korean War, including his description of a major breach of military security by the Supreme Commander of the United Nations forces, General Douglas MacArthur. The material was published without the clearance required by Army regulations, and this led to Voorhees' court-martial. Although the Court of Military Appeals upheld the regulations, the three opinions from the court are so fragmented on the First Amendment issue that the case is of little precedential value.

b. On-Base Distribution

The sale, distribution and display of publications on a military installation are subject to restraints imposed by the installation's commanding officer. *Dash v. Commanding General*, 307 F.Supp. 849 (D.S.C. 1969), aff'd., 429 F.2d 427 (4th Cir.1970), *cert. denied*, 401 U.S. 981 (1971). To impose a restriction, the commander must have cogent reasons supported by evidence for the restriction. The commander may not impose a restriction merely because he or she disagrees with a publication's content, finds it personally objectionable, or because it is critical of government policies or officials. Reasons could include interfering with the loyalty, discipline, or morale of troops, or the disruption of training or the performance of any military mission.

Congress has authorized restrictions on the sale or rental of "sexually explicit material" in commissaries and post exchanges (PXs) including all facilities operated by the Army and Air Force Exchange

Service, the Navy Exchange Service Command, the Navy Resale and Services Support Office, Marine Corps exchanges, and ships' stores. "Sexually explicit material" is defined as "an audio recording, a film or video recording, or a periodical with visual depictions, produced in any medium, the dominant theme of which depicts or describes nudity, including sexual or excretory activities or organs, in a lascivious way." 10 U.S.C. § 2459b. Even in a civilian context, obscenity, narrowly defined as "[p]atently offensive representations or descriptions of ultimate sexual acts, normal or perverted, actual or simulated, [or patently] offensive representations or descriptions of masturbation, excretory functions and lewd exhibition of the genitals" is not protected by the First Amendment and may be banned. *Miller v. California*, 413 U.S. 15 (1973). There is a legal distinction between obscenity and pornography, however. Not all pornography is obscene. Some sexually explicit (even lascivious) material is protected by the First Amendment. E.g., *Jenkins v. Georgia*, 418 U.S. 153 (1974) (nudity in a film); *Erznoznik v. Jacksonville* (1975) (nude film on outdoor move screen); *Southeastern Promotions, Ltd. v. Conrad*, 420 U.S. 546 (1975) (live musical "Hair" with nude actors); and sexually graphic sound recording by 2 Live Crew, "As Nasty As They Wanna Be." *Luke Records, Inc. v. Navarro*, 960 F.2d 134 (11th Cir.1992).

Regulation under 10 U.S.C. § 2495b has been upheld against First Amendment challenges confirming the authority of the Defense Department to restrict the sale and rental of sexually explicit materials in on-post media outlets. *PMG Intern. Div. L.L.C. v. Rumsfeld*, 303 F.3d 1163 (9th Cir.2002); *General Media Communications, Inc. v. Cohen*, 131 F.3d 273 (2d Cir.1997).

c. On-Base Civilian Activity

Civilians are subject to restrictions to protect the order, discipline and military readiness of the installation. *Ethredge v. Hail*, 56 F.3d 1324 (11th Cir. 1995) (bumper sticker on civilian base employee's truck castigating Presidents Reagan and Bush violated a base administrative order barring "bumper stickers or other similar paraphernalia" that "embarrass or disparage" the Commander in Chief).

The federal Supreme Court has held that in instances where the military has abandoned any interest in regulating speech activities, for example by opening the door to on-post leafleting, then the power to regulate is lost. *Flower v. United States*, 407 U.S. 197 (1972). However, where the installation had never abandoned its special interest in regulating political activities, speakers and leafleting could be barred by regulation. *Greer v. Spock*, 424 U.S. 828 (1976). Merely inviting the general public to enter a facility, for example to an annual "post open house," will not, however, transform the post into a public forum under *United States v. Albertini*. 472 U.S. 675 (1985) (reentry onto a military base after having received a bar letter from the commanding officer upheld).

d. Servicemember Possession of Publications

Generally, a member of the armed services may possess any form of media that is not otherwise illegal. *United States v. Campbell*, 66 M.J. 578 (N.M. Ct. Crim. App. 2008) (conviction for storing sexually explicit materials on a government computer in violation of Articles 92 and 134 containing images of child pornography in violation of 18 U.S.C.A. § 2252A).

4. ASSEMBLY

a. Demonstrations by Servicemembers

On-base demonstrations and meetings conducted by servicemembers are subject to the same prior restriction as distribution of publications. *Dash v. Commanding General*, 307 F.Supp. 849 (D.S.C. 1969), aff'd., 429 F.2d 427 (4th Cir.1970), *cert. denied*, 401 U.S. 981 (1971). Off-base meetings or demonstrations by members of the armed services are subject to restriction when any of the following factors are present: (1) the servicemember is in uniform; (2) the servicemember is on duty; (3) the demonstration takes place in a foreign country; (4) the activity constitutes a breach of law and order; or (5) violence is likely to result. AR 600-20. These provisions of Army regulations are typical of the policies of other military departments. For example, the court-martial of a member of the Air Force for participating in a demonstration in London was upheld. *Culver v. Secretary of Air Force*, 559 F.2d 622 (D.C.Cir.1977).

Just as the speech of servicemembers can by limited by the demands of good order and discipline, so can activities such as union organizing that are ordinarily protected in the civilian realm. For example, union organizing activities by servicemembers is forbidden by statute, 10 U.S.C.A. § 976, and can be prosecuted as a violation of the UCMJ. *United States v. Brown,* 45 M.J. 389 (C.A.A.F. 1996).

b. Demonstrations by Civilians

Civilians are subject to restriction with respect to demonstrating on post. They may be excluded if they pose a threat to the military mission of the post. *Greer v. Spock*, 424 U.S. 828 (1976). The threat must be real, and exceed the interest of the civilian in exercising constitutionally protected First Amendment rights. For example, in *Kiiskila v. Nichols*, 433 F.2d 745 (7th Cir.1970), the commanding officer ordered a civilian employee of the credit union permanently excluded from the base on the ground that she had distributed anti-war literature near the base and had, in an on-base conversation, given an officer a ticket to an anti-war rally for which she was the chairperson. The Seventh Circuit overturned the commander's order on First Amendment grounds, finding that the military had failed to produce evidence that military discipline was actually affected either by the plaintiff's presence on the installation or by her extension of an invitation to participate in off-base activities. "A citizen's right to engage in protected expression or debate is substantially unaffected by the fact that he is also an employee of the government and, as a general rule, he cannot be deprived of his employment merely because he exercises those rights. [And to] protect society's interest in uninhibited and robust debate the first amendment demands that government be prohibited from inhibiting or suppressing speech by indirection through discharge of a government employee when the same objective could not constitutionally be achieved by criminal sanctions or other direct means." (at 749)

5. COMMUNICATIONS WITH CONGRESS

Congress has provided that "no person may restrict a member of the armed forces in communicating with a Member of Congress or an Inspector General[,]" unless the communication is unlawful. 10 U.S.C. § 1034. That statute, directed specifically to members of the armed forces, reflects the First Amendment right to petition the Government for a redress of grievance. There is no doubt that the statute protects from military scrutiny and restriction all individual letters of servicemembers to members of Congress. As discussed above, however, the concerted action of circulation of a petition on base for the purpose of gathering the signatures of others presents other issues. The servicemember's right under § 1034 is to correspond directly with his or her elected representative without going through official channels.

6. ASSOCIATION

The First Amendment protection of freedom of association arose indirectly in *Stapp v. Resor*, 314 F.Supp. 475 (S.D.N.Y.1970). The plaintiff was discharged from the Army for security reasons because he had maintained a personal association with a member of the Communist Party. The plaintiff challenged the discharge on grounds that it violated his First Amendment rights. The district court declared the discharge void because it was based on mere associations and political beliefs wholly removed from the plaintiff's military duties. The associates and political beliefs of a member of the armed services are not immune from scrutiny, but adverse actions must be based on a connection between the associations and the servicemember's military duties and constitute violations of the UCMJ.

D. OTHER RIGHTS OF SERVICEMEMBERS

1. PRIVACY

Civilians enjoy a rather robust right of privacy that has been developed through a series of Supreme Court decisions. These decisions are based on values that cannot be traced directly to constitutional text, history or structure but are a product of "substantive due process" based on an interpretations of the right to "liberty" in the Fifth or Fourteenth Amendments or "substantive equal protection" in the Fourteenth Amendment. Many of these cases deal with rights related to such interests as the family, sex, procreation and abortion. For example, *Meyer v. Nebraska*, 262 U.S. 390 (1923) recognized "liberty" interests in "the right of the individual to contract, to engage in any of the common occupations of life, to acquire useful knowledge, to marry, establish a home and bring up children, to worship God according to the dictates of his own conscience. . . ." Subsequent cases acknowledged "the liberty of parents and guardians to direct the upbringing and education" of their children, *Pierce v. Society of Sisters*, 268 U.S. 510 (1925) and *Troxel v. Granville*, 530 U.S. 57 (2000); as well as the right to marry, *Loving v. Virginia*, 388 U.S. 1 (1967) and *Zablocki v. Redhail*, 434 U.S. 374 (1978); to have consensual sex with another person, *Lawrence v. Texas*, 539 U.S. 558 (2003) (right of persons of the same sex to engage in certain intimate sexual conduct) to procreate, *Skinner v. Oklahoma*, 316 U.S. 535 (1942), to use contraceptives, *Griswold v. Connecticut*, 381 U.S. 479 (1965); to have access to contraceptives even if unmarried, *Eisenstadt v. Baird*, 405 U.S. 438 (1972), or a minor, *Carey v. Populations Services International*, 431 U.S. 678 (1977) see also *Tummino v. Hamburg*, 936 F.Supp.2d 198 (E.D.N.Y.2013) (ordering availability of emergency contraception without age restriction); to have an early abortion, *Roe v. Wade*, 410 U.S. 113 (1973) and an abortion if necessary at any point to save a pregnant woman's life, *Planned Parenthood of Southeastern Pennsylvania v. Casey*, 505 U.S. 833 (1992) and *Ayotte v. Planned Parenthood of Northern New England*, 546 U.S. 320 (2006), and to live together as an extended family, *Moore v. East Cleveland*, 431

U.S. 494 (1977). Cases such as these have created a constitutional preference for liberty that favors individual decision making over community preferences collectively expressed through governmental regulation. There is little doubt that as a general matter, servicemembers enjoy most if not all of these rights just as civilian members of American society do.

This libertarian, privacy culture, is in many respects at odds with military culture. The Supreme Court has cautioned that, "The fundamental necessity for obedience, and the consequent necessity for imposition of discipline, may render permissible within the military that which would be constitutionally impermissible outside of it." *Parker v. Levy*, 417 U.S. 733 (1974). Lower courts, both civilian and military, have echoed similar views. *Committee for GI Rights v. Callaway*, 518 F.2d 466 (D.C. Cir.1975) ("The soldier cannot reasonably expect the Army barracks to be a sanctuary like his civilian home."). Military culture subordinates the interests of the individual soldier, sailor, marine or airman to those of the mission and the units that will carry it out. Base and installation commanders permissibly promulgate numerous regulations that foster such values as orderliness, civility, and uniformity with the objective of fostering the overall fitness of a unit to perform its military mission that in turn result in a communal environment vastly different from that in the civilian world.

The court's description of the differences between a civilian and military home and the respective degree of privacy they afford is reflected in *United States v. McCarthy*, 38 M.J. 398 (C.M.A.1993) (warrantless search upheld):

> While the physical trappings of a modern barracks or military dormitory may be more comfortable and private than an open bay barracks, the need for discipline and readiness has not changed. . . . A soldier may lawfully be ordered to move from private family quarters into the barracks, for reasons related to military discipline or military readiness [or ordered to stay away from on-base family quarters]. . . . While a civilian may retreat into the home and refuse the entreaties of the police to come out, a soldier may lawfully be ordered to come out of his or her quarters [or ordered to leave an off-base residence and report for duty]. In short, the threshold of a barracks/dormitory room does not provide the same sanctuary as the threshold of a private home.

(at 403).

Personal choice and autonomy is also limited. Again, as *McCarthy* notes, "[The servicemember] was assigned his room; he did not choose it. [He] was assigned his roommate; he did not choose him. [He] could not cook in his room, have overnight guests, or have unaccompanied underage guests. [And] he was subject to inspection to a degree not contemplated in private homes [in that] the CQ had a key to the room and was authorized to enter the room on official business.]" (at 403).

Similarly, the military can prescribe grooming standards that regulate such matters as hair length and styling and can set different standards for male and female servicemembers. *United States v. Young*, 1 M.J. 433 (C.M.A.1976). Military uniform regulations can be just that—uniform—and individual variations, even for deeply held personal or political reasons, forbidden. *United States v. New*, 55 M.J. 95 (C.A.A.F. 2001) (upheld a conviction for failure to obey a lawful order to wear United Nations (UN) accoutrements on his uniform while deployed as part of the United Nations Preventive Deployment Force (UNPREDEP)).

Differences in military and civilian practice exist even in the area of sexual privacy. For example, a servicemember who has tested positive for HIV infection can lawfully be given a "safe sex" order and required to wear a condom while engaging in sexual relations, even including those with a spouse, although it might interfere with procreation. *United States v. Pritchard*, 45 M.J. 126 (C.A.A.F.1996) (no constitutional issues raised by order requiring accused to wear condoms when having sex with his wife). Compare this holding with the cases of *Skinner* and *Griswold* discussed above.

The lack of choice extends to personal medical decisions. For example, servicemembers may be ordered vaccinated against such agents as anthrax in order to assure mission readiness. *Bates v. Donley*, 935 F.Supp.2d 14 (D.D.C.2013) (rejecting a challenge the decision of the Air Force Board for the Correction of Military Records (AFBCMR), which denied his request to correct or remove disciplinary records from his file, i.e., an Article 15 and an administrative discharge for refusing an order to take an anthrax vaccine); *Mazares v. Department of Navy*, 302 F.3d 1382 (Fed Cir.2002) (civilian seamen employed aboard a Navy vessel removed from the ship for refusing an order to take an anthrax vaccine).

This relatively settled law on compulsory vaccination of servicemembers has recently been subjected to challenge. In August 2021, the Department of Defense (DoD) issued a vaccine mandate directing the vaccination of all DoD servicemembers against COVID-19. The Department of the Navy implemented that mandate by requiring all of its active-duty servicemembers to be fully vaccinated before November 28, 2021, or face disciplinary action. Navy servicemembers who objected to the Navy's action on religious grounds under the First Amendment and RFRA sought to enjoin enforcement of the mandate. A federal district court granted the plaintiffs a preliminary injunction. *U.S. Navy Seals 1-26 v. Biden,* ___ F. Supp. 3d (ND Tex. 2022). And the Supreme Court granted a partial stay in the case. sub nom. *Austin v. U.S. Navy Seals,* ___ U.S. ___, 142 S.Ct. 1301 (2022). COVID-19 litigation like this may invite reconsideration of such issues as the deference owed by the judiciary to the executive branch and the military in the regulation of the armed services, and the authority of the military to issue vaccination orders and the rights of servicemembers to refuse them on religious grounds.

2. RESIDENCY AND TAX SITUS

Members of the armed forces are immunized to a certain extent from invidious treatment by states because of their status. Because they are assigned involuntarily by orders to where they will work and live the law protects their choices as to state residency and protects them against taxation of their income by states of which they are not a resident. For example, a member of the armed services is presumed to retain "the domicile which he had at the time of enlistment" unless there is "clear and unequivocal" evidence of a change of domicile. *Deckers v. Kenneth W. Rose, Inc.*, 592 F.Supp. 25 (M.D.Fla.1984) (denial of diversity jurisdiction in a wrongful death action). The Servicemembers Civil Relief Act (SCRA), 50 U.S.C. § 4001 expressly preserves the original, pre-enlistment residence of a servicemember for property tax and income tax purposes. *Woodroffe v. Park Forest,* 107 F.Supp. 906 (N.D.Ill.1952) (decided under SSCRA). See Lieutenant Colin A. Kisor, "Who's Defending the Defenders?: Rebuilding the Financial Protections of the Soldiers' and Sailors' Civil Relief Act," 48 Naval L. Rev. 161 (2001).

A member of the armed forces who is stationed in a state other than his or her state of residence may change residence to a new state by undertaking clear and unequivocal acts such as registering to vote, registering a motor vehicle, securing a driver's license and otherwise establishing a nexus with the new state that indicates an intention to change state citizenship.

3. SERVICEMEMBERS CIVIL RELIEF ACT

The Servicemembers Civil Relief Act (SCRA), 50 U.S.C. §§ 3901 et seq., was enacted at the end of 2003 to recodify and modernize the law formerly known as the Soldiers' and Sailors' Civil Relief Act (SSCRA) of 1940. The purpose of the SCRA like its predecessor the SSCRA is to protect members of the armed services from legal or financial disadvantage on account of their being ordered to active duty military service. 50 U.S.C. § 3902. (The purpose of the SCRA is "to provide for, strengthen and expedite the national defense through protection extended by [the SCRA] to servicemembers of the United States to enable such persons to devote their entire energy to the defense needs of the Nation; and to provide for the temporary suspension of the judicial and administrative proceedings and transactions that may adversely affect the civil rights of servicemembers during their military service.")

The constitutionality of the SSCRA was upheld in *Dameron v. Brodhead*, 345 U.S. 322 (1953) (taxable domicile of servicemen should not be changed by military assignments, interpreting the SSCRA). Courts have repeatedly held that the SCRA—like its predecessors including the SSCRA—" 'must be read with an eye friendly to those who dropped their affairs to answer their country's call.' " *LeMaistre v. Leffers*, 333 U.S. 1 (1948).

The SCRA applies to servicemembers in the Army, Navy, Air Force, Marine Corps and Coast Guard as well as the commissioned corps of the National Oceanic and Atmospheric Administration (NOAA) and the commissioned corps of the Public Health Service (PHS as defined in 10 U.S.C. § 101(d)(1). These servicemembers are covered by the SCRA when they are on "active duty" or "active service" in the case of those serving in the NOAA and PHS as defined in 10 U.S.C. § 101(d)(1). Servicemembers are also protected by the SCRA in any period "during which [they] are absent from duty on account of sickness, wounds, leave, or other lawful cause." 50 U.S.C. § 3911. Members of the armed forces reserves, however, are covered by the SCRA only when they are on active duty as opposed to reserve duty. Members of the National Guard and Air National Guard are covered when they are called into federal service.

The protections of the SCRA also extend to military dependents. This includes the servicemember's spouse. 50 U.S.C. § 3911(4)(A) and child as further defined in 38 U.S.C. § 101(4)(A); 50 U.S.C. § 3911(4)(B). And also includes others, such as an elderly parent, for whom the servicemember provided more than one-half of that individual's support for 180 days immediately preceding application for relief under the SCRA. 50 U.S.C. § 3911(4)(C).

The SCRA does not cover members of the National Guard or Air National Guard when they are not performing federal service or members of the reserves who are not on active duty. It doesn't cover those incarcerated in military prisons, *Reed v. Albaaj*, 723 N.W.2d 50 (Ct. of App. 2006) (held in a case of first impression, husband, who was incarcerated in out-of-state military prison, was not entitled to protection of the SCRA in action for divorce and custody of the children). Nor does it cover retired members of the military. *Jax Navy Federal Credit Union v. Fahrenbruch*, 429 So.2d 1330 (Fla. App. 1983) (judgment debtor was not a serviceman but only a former or retired serviceman; decided under SSCRA). And it does not cover civilian employees of a defense contractor. *In re Gaddy*, 2004 WL 2044107 (unpublished decision) ("[The SCRA] clearly does not apply to someone who is simply a civilian employee of a private contractor doing work for the uniformed services of the United States.").

Although it is possible for servicemembers to waive the protections of the SCRA, courts strictly construe such waivers. A waiver of rights under the SCRA must be 1) in writing, 2) in a document that is separate from that creating the obligation or liability affected by the waiver, 3) specifically identifying the separate document to which the waiver applies, 4) executed during or after military service, and 5) is printed on a form in at least 12 point type. Waivers of SCRA protections are required for modification, termination, or cancellation of a contract, lease, or bailment; or of an obligation secured by a mortgage, trust, deed, lien, or other security in the nature of a mortgage as well as for the repossession, retention, foreclosure, sale, forfeiture, or taking possession of property that is security for any obligation; or was purchased or received under a contract, lease, or bailment. 50 U.S.C. § 3918.

The SCRA provides procedural as well as substantive protections for servicemembers. A major protection is that against default in "any civil action or proceeding, including any child custody proceeding, in which the defendant does not make an appearance." 50 U.S.C. § 3931(a). In many ways this is the core of the SCRA and the SSCRA that preceded it. The intent of the law was to protect servicemembers from the distractions of litigation or other legal proceedings that could compromise their dedication to their important role in protecting the Nation.

The SCRA imposes on the *plaintiff* seeking a default judgment against a putative servicemember to submit an affidavit stating whether or not the defendant is in military service and showing necessary facts to support the affidavit; or if the plaintiff is unable to determine whether or not the defendant is in military service, stating that the plaintiff is unable to determine whether or not the defendant is in military service. 50 U.S.C. § 3931(b). Note that the requirement is to file the nonmilitary affidavit before seeking a default judgment, and not, for example, before merely commencing a lawsuit. *Willhoit v. Suntrust Mortgage, Inc.*, 2013 WL 1111823 (N.D. Ill. 2013) (Westlaw citation only available).

The plaintiff must make a reasonable effort to verify the defendant's status and the affidavit must show the necessary facts to support the affidavit. *In re Templehoff*, 339 B.R. 49 (Bankr. S.D.N.Y. 2005) (Chapter 7 bankruptcy action; decided under the

SSCRA). The filing of the required affidavit is not jurisdictional, and a resulting default judgment is not void but merely voidable upon application of the serviceman. *United States v. Hampshire*, 892 F. Supp. 1327, 1332 (D.Kan. 1995) ("A judgment rendered in violation of the Act is merely voidable, rather than void, and does not violate due process.") In the event a plaintiff is unable to ascertain a defendant's military status after exercising due diligence, the court may require the plaintiff to post a bond indemnifying the defendant in the event he or she is an active duty servicemember covered by the SCRA. 50 U.S.C. § 3931(b)(3) ("If the defendant is later found to be in military service, the bond shall be available to indemnify the defendant against any loss or damage the defendant may suffer by reason of any judgment for the plaintiff against the defendant, should the judgment be set aside in whole or in part.").

If it is determined that the defendant is in military service, the court is required to grant a stay of proceedings for a minimum period of 90 days either upon application of counsel, or on the court's own motion, should it be determined that there may be a defense to the action and a defense cannot be presented without the presence of the defendant; or after due diligence, counsel has been unable to contact the defendant or otherwise determine if a meritorious defense exists. 50 U.S.C. § 3931(d). In order to secure a stay any civil action or proceeding, including any child custody proceeding, the servicemember must make application and include two letters: 1) a letter or other communication setting forth facts stating the manner in which current military duty requirements materially affect the servicemember's ability to appear and stating a date when the servicemember will be available to appear; and 2) a letter or other communication from the servicemember's commanding officer stating that the servicemember's current military duty prevents appearance and that military leave is not authorized for the servicemember at the time of the letter. The application may be made at any stage before final judgment in a civil action or proceeding in which a servicemember is a party. The court, either on its own motion, or upon application by the servicemember, shall then stay the action for a period of not less than 90 days. 50 U.S.C. § 3932(b)(1). An application for a stay under this section does not constitute an appearance for jurisdictional purposes nor does it constitute a waiver of any substantive or procedural defense (including a defense relating to lack of personal jurisdiction). 50 U.S.C. § 3932(c). The statutory requirement that the servicemember demonstrate that current military duty requirements "materially affect the servicemember's ability to appear" impose a pleading responsibility on the servicemember. 50 U.S.C. § 3932(b)(2)(A). Courts have held that the SCRA's pleading requirement must be met by that must be met by competent factual evidence. *Hibbard v. Hibbard*, 431 N.W.2d 637 (Neb. 1988) (a mere showing that the defendant is in the military service is insufficient). Such things as overseas deployment, mandatory training and denial of leave should meet the test of factual evidence.

The SCRA provides in certain circumstances for the tolling of the statute of limitations. For example, in *Mason v. Texaco*, 862 F.2d 242 (10th Cir.1988), the court held in the case of a Coast Guard member, that the Kansas statute of limitations was tolled by the plaintiff's military service in a products liability action claiming personal injury and wrongful death under Kansas law. Tolling applies whether the servicemember is a plaintiff or a defendant. *Ray v. Porter*, 464 F.2d 452 (6th Cir.1972) (under the SSCRA, the Kentucky statute of limitations was tolled during period of defendant owner's military service thereby entitling plaintiff to maintain action against owner under family purpose doctrine). See also, *In re Brandt*, 437 B.R. 294 (Bankr. M.D. Tenn. 2010) ("may not" in § 3936(a) of the SCRA, 50 U.S.C. § 3936(a), mandates the tolling of all state statutes of limitations; the tolling provision is mandatory).

If it is determined that the defendant is a servicemember covered by the SCRA, the court cannot enter a judgment until after appointing counsel to represent the defendant. If the attorney is unable to locate or communicate with his client, the attorney is precluded from taking any actions in the case that would waive any defense of the servicemember or otherwise bind the servicemember. 50 U.S.C. § 3931(b)(2).

In the event a default judgment is entered against a servicemember protected the SCRA, the law provides for reopening it. 50 U.S.C. § 3931(g). To be eligible for opening under the SCRA, the default judgment must have been entered during the servicemember's period of military service (or within 60 days after termination of or release from such military service). The court that entered the default judgment shall, upon application by or on behalf of the servicemember, reopen the judgment for the purpose of allowing the servicemember to defend the action if it appears that the servicemember was materially affected by reason of that military service in making a defense to the action; and the servicemember has a meritorious or legal defense to the action or some part of it. An application to reopen under this provision of the SCRA must be filed not later than 90 days after the date of the termination of or release from military service.

Note that bona fide purchasers are protected under SCRA. If a court vacates, sets aside, or reverses a default judgment against a servicemember under the provisions of the SCRA, that action shall not impair a right or title acquired by a bona fide purchaser for value under the default judgment. 50 U.S.C. § 3931(h). Courts remain vigilant, however, to protect the interests of servicemembers covered by the SCRA. *Bernhardt v. Alden Café*, 374 N.J.Super. 271, 864 A.2d 421 (2005).

The SCRA provides substantive protection with respect to obligations that arose prior to the servicemember's entry into active duty. For example, the law sets the maximum rate of interest on debts incurred before military service at 6 percent per year. Obligations covered by the SCRA include credit cards, automobile financing, mortgages on chattels and real property and student loans. 50 U.S.C. § 3937 and 20 U.S.C. § 1078(d).

Interest on an obligation or liability incurred by a servicemember, or the servicemember and the servicemember's spouse jointly, before the servicemember entered military service cannot bear interest at a rate in excess of 6 percent (Six Percent Rule). Interest is limited during the period of military service and one year thereafter, in the case of an obligation or liability consisting of a mortgage, trust deed, or other security in the nature of a mortgage or during the period of military service, in the case of any other obligation or liability. Interest in excess of 6 percent is forgiven, and the SCRA proscribes acceleration of the principal. 50 U.S.C. § 3937. Because this protection under the SCRA applies only to interest obligations incurred prior to enlistment or activation to federal service, servicemembers and their spouses may wish to open new credit accounts after military service begins in order to segregate those accounts that are entitled to special treatment under the SCRA.

By law, the servicemember has a private right of action against a creditor to enforce the Six Percent Rule. *Gordon v. Pete's Auto Service of Denbigh, Inc.*, 637 F.3d 454 (4th Cir.2011). A 2010 amendment to the SCRA allows the court to "(1) grant any appropriate equitable or declaratory relief with respect to the violation of this chapter; and (2) award all other appropriate relief, including monetary damages to any person aggrieved by the violation;

and (3) may, to vindicate the public interest, assess a civil penalty . . . ." 50 U.S.C. § 4041(b).

A servicemember must strictly comply with the notification requirements of the SCRA in order to avail him or herself of the Six Percent Rule. The servicemember must provide to the creditor written notice and a copy of the military orders calling the servicemember to military service and any orders further extending military service, not later than 180 days after the date of the servicemember's termination or release from military service. 50 U.S.C. § 3937(b)(1). To secure the full benefits of the statute, however, the servicemember should provide written notice as soon as practicable. Upon receipt of the servicemember's notification, the creditor must re-amortize the debt consistent with the requirements of the Six Percent Rule effective from the date the servicemember enters active duty or federal service. 50 U.S.C. § 3937(b). There is a relief provision for creditors of which servicemembers should be aware. In the event that a court determines that the ability of the servicemember to pay interest upon the obligation or liability at a rate in excess of 6 percent per year is not materially affected by reason of the servicemember's military service, i.e., the burden of service is not detrimental to the servicemember's income, then the servicemember may be compelled to pay the rate of interest called for in the documents creating the interest obligation. 50 U.S.C. § 3937(c).

Protections similar to those provided for installment contracts, student loans and credit card debt are similarly available for mortgages and deeds to secure debt. As with other debts, the obligation must have preceded the servicemember's entry onto active duty or federal service and relate to a mortgage, trust deed, or other security in the nature of a mortgage. 50 U.S.C. § 3953. A sale, foreclosure or seizure of property made during the servicemember's time of service or 90 days thereafter is invalid unless done with court approval or based upon a waiver that meets all the tests for a valid waiver under 50 U.S.C. § 3918. The effect of this provision is to invalidate nonjudicial foreclosure in the absence of a valid waiver. 50 U.S.C. § 3953(c).

Stay relief is available in any mortgage foreclosure proceeding upon a showing that the servicemember's military service materially affects his or her ability to comply with the obligation. 50 U.S.C. § 3953(b). the servicemember will be required to produce information regarding pre- and in-service income including pay and allowances sufficient to demonstrate that the servicemember's in-service income not enough to cover mortgage payments.

The SCRA also provides protections for storage liens on the servicemember's belongings, 50 U.S.C. § 3958; lease terminations, 50 U.S.C. § 3955; and eviction and distress, 50 U.S.C. § 3951. Self-help eviction by a landlord is prohibited. Eviction may only occur as a result of a court order. Otherwise, a landlord may not evict a servicemember, or the dependents of a servicemember, during a period of military service of the servicemember, from premises that are occupied or intended to be occupied primarily as a residence and for which the monthly rent does not exceed $2,400, as adjusted or subject such premises to a distress during the period of military service. 50 U.S.C. § 3951. Housing price adjustment is determined according to 50 U.S.C. § 3951(a)(2) and (3). Dependency under the statute is determinable empirically. *Balconi v. Dvascas*, 133 Misc.2d 685, 507 N.Y.S.2d 788 (City Court of Rochester, 1986) (despite her divorce, ex-spouse and her seven-year-old daughter are financially dependent upon her ex-husband and are, thus, entitled to protection as qualified dependents under the SSCRA).

Stays with respect to eviction or distress are governed by 50 U.S.C. § 3951(b). Since under 50 U.S.C. § 3951(e), 50 U.S.C. § 3932 is inapplicable to eviction under this section, the § 3951 stay procedure is the only one available. Also, a court may require some rent allotment from the servicemember's pay as provided for in 50 U.S.C. § 3951(d) which affords a landlord some measure of relief under the SCRA. Landlord's should, however, proceed with caution since criminal penalties are available for violation of this section as they are for other provisions of the SCRA. *United States v. McLeod*, 2008 WL 114789 (W.D.Mich.2008) (misdemeanor criminal conviction for unlawful eviction of dependents of a servicemember without a court order).

The SCRA provides for termination of both residential and motor vehicle leases. Residential leases are cancellable when a servicemember lessee is transferred pursuant to military orders and can no longer use the leased premises. Motor vehicle lease obligations are eligible for release when a servicemember is transferred overseas and will not be able to use the motor vehicle. Termination of a servicemember's obligation under a lease may be sought upon entry into active duty or federal service, or transfer pursuant to orders. It releases both the servicemember and the servicemember's dependents. 50 U.S.C. § 3955.

To be eligible to terminate a lease of premises, a servicemember must receive military orders for a permanent change of station (PCS) or deployment in excess of 90 days. 50 U.S.C. § 3955. The types of leased premises covered by the SCRA are quite extensive and include premises occupied, or intended to be occupied, by a servicemember or a servicemember's dependents for a residential, professional, business, agricultural, or similar purposes. One of the principal differences in the approach of § 3955 and other provisions of the SCRA is that the lease termination provisions are available to a servicemember for leases entered into both *before and after* entering service while provisions such as the Six Percent Rule apply only to debts incurred *prior to* beginning active duty or federal service.

Motor vehicle lease termination is available with respect to leased vehicles used or intended for use by the servicemember or the servicemember's dependents for personal or business transportation. Like the provision for premises lease termination, the SCRA allows termination of leases entered into prior to entry into active duty or federal service or during active duty or federal service. In order to be eligible to terminate a motor vehicle lease, a servicemember must be called to active duty or be deployed for 180 days or more resulting in a permanent change of station (PCS) or deployment from a location within the continental United States to a location outside the continental United States or from a location in a State outside the continental United States to a location outside that State. 50 U.S.C. § 3955(b)(2). To terminate a motor vehicle lease, a servicemember must deliver to the lessor or the lessor's grantee, or an agent of either of them, a written notice of termination and a copy of the servicemember's military orders. The vehicle must be surrendered within 15 days after the date of delivery of the written notice. The notice may be delivered by hand, by private business carrier, or by mailing the notice. 50 U.S.C. § 3955(c).

Termination with respect to leased premises is effective 30 days after the first date on which the next rental payment is due after delivery of the written notice of termination. Termination with respect to motor vehicle leases is effective after written notice is provided and the motor vehicle has been returned to the lessor or the lessor's authorized agent. 50 U.S.C. § 3955(b)(2).

The SCRA provides for the proration of rents or lease payments due a landlord. Rent paid in advance must be returned within 30 days of the effective date of lease termination. In the case of a motor vehicle lease, the SCRA prohibits the imposition of an early termination charge, but makes provision for reasonable charges for such things as excess wear, use and mileage. 50 U.S.C. § 3955(e)–(f).

In the event a lease termination works a hardship on a landlord, he or she may seek relief in court. The servicemember's obligation under the lease "may be modified as justice and equity require." 50 U.S.C. § 3955(g).

The remedies provided for under the SCRA are not exclusive, and applicable state law may also provide additional remedies. A servicemember should contact an attorney with questions about specific legal matters. More importantly, the SCRA expressly provides a private right of action to enforce its provisions allowing for (1) appropriate equitable or declaratory relief with respect to the violation, (2) recovery all other appropriate relief, including monetary damages, and (3) the right to represent a class or be a member of a class in a class action notwithstanding any previous contrary agreement. It also provides for recovery of costs and attorney fees. 50 U.S.C. § 4042. Servicemembers, and their spouses and dependents who suspect that they are being victimized with respect to rights protected by the SCRA should contact an attorney. In the event of a successful claim, the defendant will pay the plaintiff's attorney's fees and costs.

In addition to the protections discussed above, the SCRA protects against insurer abuses with respect to individual contracts for whole, endowment, universal, or term life insurance (other than group term life insurance coverage), including any benefit in the nature of such insurance arising out of membership in any fraternal or beneficial association. The SCRA prohibits decreasing the amount of coverage or requiring the payment of an additional amount as premiums if the insured engages in military service (except increases in premiums in individual term insurance based upon age); or limiting or restricting coverage for any activity required by military service. 50 U.S.C. § 3971. Coverage under a policy within the protection of the SCRA shall not lapse or otherwise terminate or be forfeited for the nonpayment of a premium, or interest or indebtedness on a premium. 50 U.S.C. § 3974.

The SCRA protects against the loss or acquisition of a residence or domicile for purposes of taxation with respect to the person, personal property, or income of the servicemember by reason of being absent or present in any tax jurisdiction of the United States solely in compliance with military orders. This protection extends as well to the servicemember's spouse. 50 U.S.C. § 4001. A servicemember's and spouse's compensation and personal property is taxable only by the State of his or her tax residence although property used for trade or business in a State other than the tax residence is taxable.

The applicability of the SCRA to servicemember bankruptcy is a more technical problem beyond the scope of this Nutshell. Those affected by servicemember bankruptcy should consult with a qualified professional.

E. COMPENSATING SERVICEMEMBER INJURY AND DEATH

Injury and death afflict servicemembers and civilians alike. The law, however, provides far different routes for servicemembers and civilians to deal with these human conditions. Civilians seek compensation for injury and death caused by largely through tort law and insurance mechanisms, supplemented by such public programs as Social Security Disability Insurance. For injuries caused by the government, recovery can be sought through the Federal Tort Claims Act. Servicemembers are often precluded from tort remedies against the government which they serve. They are, however, provided with comprehensive medical treatment while in the military and thereafter are provided access to veterans' benefits, which are administered by the Department of Veterans' Affairs.

1. TORT CLAIMS OF SERVICEMEMBERS

The United States government, as sovereign, may not be sued without its consent. *United States v. Lee*, 106 U.S. 196 (1882). The sovereign immunity it enjoys exempts it from liability for the acts of its agents and employees. Through the Federal Tort Claims Act the federal government has waived its immunity from suit "for injury or loss of property, or personal injury or death caused by the negligent or wrongful act or omission of any employee of the Government while acting within the scope of his office or employment." 28 U.S.C. § 1346(b).

a. The Federal Tort Claims Act

The Federal Tort Claims Act (FTCA), 28 U.S.C. §§ 1346(b) (federal court jurisdiction), and 2671–2680, waives the United States' immunity for common law torts and is the exclusive remedy for torts committed by a federal official. As such, the FTCA creates absolute immunity for federal employees, and makes the United States the sole defendant. Plaintiffs who qualify for recovery under the FTCA are allowed 1) monetary recovery; 2) for damage to or loss of property, personal injury, and death; 3) caused by the negligent or wrongful act or omission; 4) of a United States employee; 5) while acting within the scope of the person's office or employment; 6) under circumstances where the United States, if a private person, would be liable to the claimant; and 7) under the law of the place where the act or omission occurred.

There are several exceptions to liability listed in the Act, two of which bear on liability for damage or personal injury arising out of military actions: 1) the "combat activities" exception; 2) the "discretionary function" exception, and 3) the "foreign country" exception.

The "combatant activities" exception, provides that the FTCA's waiver of sovereign immunity shall not apply to "[a]ny claim arising out of the combatant activities of the military or naval forces, or the Coast Guard, during time of war." 28 U.S.C.A. § 2680(j). This exception covers actions in both declared and undeclared wars. *Koohi v. United States*, 976 F.2d 1328 (9th Cir.1992) (extending the combatant activity exception to bar the claims against the private contractors).

A distinction respecting the "combat activities" exception was suggested in the case of *McMahon v. General Dynamics Corp.*, 933 F.Supp.2d 682 (D.N.J. 2013). *McMahon* involved injuries arising out of the test firing of an M2 .50 caliber Browning machine gun, Heavy Barrel ("M2") at Forward Operating Base Kunduz, Afghanistan, on July 4, 2010. McMahon was then a soldier on active duty in the United States Army. When he fired the M2, a shell casing pierced his right calf, causing physical and neuropsychological injuries. McMahon maintains that the M2 malfunctioned and that General Dynamics, as the manufacturer of the gun, is liable under theories of manufacturing defect and failure to warn. General Dynamics raised the "combat activities" exception based on the place and circumstances of the injuries. *McMahon* analyzed three rationales prominent in *Koohi*—promotion of caution, just compensation, and civil punishment—that justified extending the "combat activities" exception to a manufacturer and concluded they were inapposite to McMahon's facts. With respect to the danger of fostering timidity in combat, manufacturer like General Dynamics should not act in a spirit of bold improvisation, but should follow specifications scrupulously and exercise the highest level of care in the manufacturing process; with respect to matters of just compensation for wartime injury and the possibility of unjust enrichment distinguishing between victims, typically citizens and soldiers of hostile countries, the judge saw that the principle would bar justice for members of our own military who are injured by the actions of U.S. civilians; and finally, the regarding punishment aspect of tort litigation:

> [when] a U.S. serviceman asserts that a manufacturing defect at the defendant's U.S. plant resulted in the production of a defective gun that injured him [,s]uch a claim does not implicate government design specifications, battlefield operations, political questions or secret technology. Such a claim is the ordinary stuff of civil, and civilian, tort law. Here, as elsewhere, tort law has a role to play in ensuring redress for injuries, spreading the cost of accidents, and—most of all—enforcing the highest standards of care in the manufacture of the equipment upon which our servicemen and servicewomen rely.

The "foreign country" exception bars "any claim arising in a foreign country." 28 U.S.C.A. § 2680(k). Claims arising on military facilities outside the United States are barred. *Bird v. United States*, 923 F.Supp. 338 (D.Conn.1996) (Guantanamo Bay, Cuba, is a "foreign country" even though the United States exercises "complete jurisdiction and control" under the terms of its lease); *Cobb v. United States*, 191 F.2d 604 (9th Cir.1951) (Okinawa a "foreign country" where United States has de facto sovereignty over island); *Smith v. United States*, 499 U.S. 160 (1993) (Antarctica is a "foreign country" although it lacks a recognized government). United States embassies in foreign countries also fall within this exception. See *Meredith v. United States*, 330 F.2d 9 (9th Cir.1964).

The "discretionary function" exception to the FTCA excludes claims arising from discretionary acts or omissions of government employees, whether or not discretion was abused. 28 U.S.C.A. § 2680(a). The "discretionary function" exception embodies a Congressional policy to "prevent judicial 'second-guessing' of legislative and administrative decisions grounded in social, economic, and political policy through the medium of an action in tort." *United States v. S.A. Empresa de Viacao Acrea Rio Grandense*, 467 U.S. 797 (1984). As an example, the decision to admit a military dependent into a military hospital is discretionary, but the rendering of negligent treatment is not. Similarly, a chief chemical officer's decision, made at the planning level, to use a particular strain of bacterium in a simulated biological warfare attack on San Francisco was a discretionary function. *Nevin v. United States*, 696 F.2d 1229 (9th Cir.1983).

In *Westfall v. Erwin*, 484 U.S. 292 (1988), the Supreme Court ruled that a discretionary act is one which requires personal judgment, deliberation, and decision on the part of the employee. Discretionary acts usually occur at the planning rather than the operational stage of an activity; once discretion has been exercised and the decision made, the activity must be carried out with reasonable care. *Westfall* created a distinction between employees' actions in their "operational" as opposed to their "discretionary capacities" and thereby exposed federal employees to liability where they had previously enjoyed immunity. So, Congress passed the Federal Employees Liability Reform and Tort Compensation Act of 1988 (FELRTCA) which superseded that aspect of *Westfall* and created absolute tort immunity for acts of Federal employees within the course and scope of their employment. 28 U.S.C.A. § 2679(d)(1).

Under the FTCA, the federal government is liable in tort "under circumstances where the United States, if a private person, would be liable to the claimant in accordance with the law of the place where the act or omission occurred." 28 U.S.C. § 1346(b). The phrase "the law of the place" was held in *Richards v. United States*, 369 U.S. 1 (1962) to refer to the "whole law" of the place where the defendant acted, i.e., the substantive law of the state as well as its choice-of-law rule. The federal government can assert any defenses that would be available to a private person under the law of the state where the injury occurred. These defenses include contributory negligence, assumption of risk, comparative negligence, and release.

b. Ineligible Claimants: The *Feres* Doctrine

Note that former servicemembers may bring claims under the FTCA for injuries suffered after their discharge from the service. *Brown v. United States*, 451 F.3d 411 (6th Cir.2006) (claims related to allegedly negligent medical examination of serviceman which occurred three years after his release from active duty were not barred by *Feres* doctrine). Veterans and former servicemembers ineligible for veterans' benefits suffer no disability in seeking recovery for post-discharge injury because of their prior service.

The eligibility of servicemembers to sue under the FTCA is governed by case law. For example, servicemen who were passengers in a car struck by a U.S. Army truck were allowed to recover under the FTCA because 1) the facts of the case did not meet any of the FTCA exceptions; and 2) the claims of the plaintiffs, who were off duty and off post when the incident occurred, had no significant relationship to military service. The fact that the claimants, because of their military status, received government benefits following the injuries did not bar the claim; the Court held such benefits were simply to be deducted from the final judgment. *Brooks v. United States*, 337 U.S. 49 (1949). Accord, *Elliott By and Through Elliott v. United States*, 877 F.Supp. 1569 (M.D.Ga.1992), aff'd. by an equally divided en banc court, 37 F.3d 617 (11th Cir.1994) (for an injury to be deemed as "incident to service," that injury must be sustained "while performing duties under orders"; at time of injury plaintiff was ordinary leave status; FTCA recovery allowed).

Members of the armed services whose injuries are incident to their military service cannot recover under the FTCA. *Feres v. United States*, 340 U.S. 135 (1950). The *Feres* doctrine or "incident to service rule" is based primarily on the "peculiar and special relationship of the soldier to his superiors, the effects of the maintenance of such suits on discipline, and the extreme results that might obtain if suits under the Tort Claims Act were allowed for negligent orders given or negligent acts committed in the course of military duty." *United States v. Brown*, 348 U.S. 110, 112 (1954).

Although the underlying prohibition of FTCA suits by servicemembers is based upon discipline and command concerns, the *Feres* doctrine has been dramatically expanded to cover nearly any tort committed while an armed servicemember is on active duty, on a military base, or engaged in a military mission. *Stencel Aero Engineering Corp. v. United States*, 431 U.S. 666, 674 (1977) ("the right of a third party to recover in an indemnity action against the United States . . . , must be held limited by the rationale of *Feres* where the injured party is a serviceman").

This expansion has not gone unquestioned:

> Although [the Ninth] circuit has accepted *Feres,* albeit grudgingly, as "an ineradicable feature of our legal landscape," [citation omitted], we have also recognized that "even *Feres* concatenations must come to an end." *Id.* Intentional tortious and unconstitutional acts directed by one servicemember against another which further no conceivable military purpose and are not perpetrated during the course of a military activity surely are past the reach of *Feres*. The Tenth Circuit in *Durant v. Neneman* has expressed it well:
>
> [O]ur evolving jurisprudence has created a zone of protection for military actors, immunizing

actions and decisions which involved military authority from scrutiny by civilian courts. It is our conclusion, however, that this zone was never intended to protect the personal acts of an individual when those acts in no way implicate the function or authority of the military.

* * * * * *

When a soldier commits an act that would, in civilian life, make him liable to another, he should not be allowed to escape responsibility for his act *just because those involved were wearing military uniforms at the time of the act.* When military personnel are engaged in distinctly nonmilitary acts, they are acting, in effect, as civilians and should be subject to civil authority.

Durant v. Neneman, 884 F.2d 1350, 1353, 1354 (10th Cir.1989) (original emphasis).

Lutz v. Secretary of the Air Force, 944 F.2d 1477, 1487 (9th Cir.1991).

The *Feres* doctrine has been criticized. *In* his dissent in *Costco v. United States*, 248 F.3d 863, 869 (9th Cir.2001), Circuit Judge Warren J. Ferguson lays out his case against the constitutionality of the *Feres* doctrine as a violation of the equal protection rights of military service men and women and also a violation of the constitutional doctrine of separation of powers. Recently, Justice Thomas attacked *Feres* as wrongly decided and called on the Court to correct its error in his dissent from a denial of *certiorari* in a case alleging plaintiff's rape by a fellow cadet while she was a student at the U.S. Military Academy at

West Point. *Jane Doe v. United States*, 141 U.S. 1498 (2021).

The *Feres* doctrine persists as an important limitation on lawsuits by servicemembers. For example, concern for discipline and command cannot be avoided by characterizing it as a "straightforward personnel decision." *United States v. Shearer*, 473 U.S. 52 (1985), and a claim is barred even if the person responsible for the alleged negligence is a civilian employee of the FAA whose activities would not implicate military discipline. *United States v. Johnson*, 481 U.S. 681 (1987). The *Feres* doctrine even bars claims of a servicemember arising while he or she is on leave. *Lampitt v. United States*, 585 F.Supp. 151 (E.D.Mo.1984) (convalescent leave).

The *Feres* doctrine bars non-FTCA claims by servicemembers against the federal government. For example, civilian victims of constitutional torts can sue the United States for their injuries under an implied cause of action for damages against federal officials. Such a suit is comparable to a civil rights action against a State under 42 U.S.C. § 1983. *Bivens v. Six Unknown Named Federal Narcotics Agents*, 403 U.S. 388 (1971). In a case involving five black sailors who brought suit under *Bivens* against their commanding officers alleging racial discrimination, the Supreme Court ruled that allowing members of the armed services to challenge their supervisors would undermine military discipline and applied the *Feres* doctrine. *Chappell v. Wallace*, 462 U.S. 296 (1983). Compare a similar case rejecting the *Feres* doctrine defense because of an absence of military purpose. *Brown v. United States*, 739 F.2d 362 (8th Cir.1984) (permitting a black National Guardsman who had been the victim of a mock lynching at an on-base drinking party who later attempted suicide and suffered severe injury as a result to sue military perpetrators), *cert. denied*, 473 U.S. 904 (1985). "The extreme nature of the alleged conduct and its total antipathy to any conceivable military purpose sets this apart from our earlier decisions." (at 367).

The *Feres* doctrine generally extends to "suits between individual members of the military, recognizing an 'intramilitary immunity' from suits based on injuries sustained incident to service." *Lutz v. Secretary of the Air Force*, 944 F.2d 1477 (9th Cir.1991) (individual acts by sergeants who broke into an Air Force Major's office, took personal papers and disseminated them to other military personnel with the intent to injure her reputation and career were not "incident to military service" and thus not protected by the *Feres* doctrine although military superiors and the federal government were protected).

Numerous lower courts have held that the *Feres* doctrine protects state as well as federal officials from suit by members of the National Guard. "It is beyond question that the Feres doctrine generally applies to claims brought by National Guard members." *Bowen v. Oistead*, 125 F.3d 800 (9th Cir.1997) (*Feres* doctrine bars suit against the Alaska National Guard, certain of its members, the United States, and certain commissioned officers of the United States Air Force); *Stauber v. Cline*, 837 F.2d

395 (9th Cir.1988) (Feres applied to a Guardsman's claims against individual members of the Alaska National Guard, the Alaska Adjutant General, the Alaska Department of Military and Veterans Affairs, and the State of Alaska itself); *Uhl v. Swanstrom*, 79 F.3d 751 (8th Cir.1996) (applying *Feres* bar to suit by National Guardsman against his commanding state officer, the Adjutant General of the Iowa Air National Guard, and the Iowa Air National Guard). Other courts have rejected the *Feres* doctrine in cases based on state law. *Trankel v. State Dept. of Military Affairs*, 282 Mont. 348 (1997) (*Feres* doctrine defense rejected recovery allowed under Montana State Tort Claims Act).

In addition to the *Feres* doctrine which forecloses suits by members of the armed forces under a number of FTCA and non-FTCA causes of action, servicemembers are precluded from recovery under other laws as well. For example, servicemembers are specifically excluded from Title VII coverage. *Hodge v. Dalton*, 107 F.3d 705 (9th Cir.1997). The decision in *Hodge* holding that servicemembers are not covered by Title VII rests on two bases. The first basis is statutory. Although Title VII provides for freedom from any discrimination based on race, color, religion, sex, or national origin for certain employees, enforcement is limited. Because of sovereign immunity, the United States is not an employer amenable to suit under the general provisions of Title VII. Waiver of sovereign immunity in suits involving federal employment is governed by 42 U.S.C. § 2000e–16, and Congress delegated implementation and enforcement powers under Title VII to the

EEOC. In its regulations, the EEOC has interpreted Title VII as inapplicable to complaints of discrimination by active-duty servicemembers. 29 C.F.R. § 1614.103. The second basis comes from *Feres*. "The doctrine of intramilitary immunity, or "the *Feres* doctrine," lends further support to the conclusion that Hodge is not covered by § 2000e–16." *Hodge v. Dalton*, 107 F.3d 705, 710 (9th Cir.1997) (citations omitted). The judicial doctrine of intra-military immunity is affirmed in *Zuress v. Donley*, 606 F.3d 1249 (9th Cir.2010).

The False Claims Act (FCA), 31 U.S.C.A. § 3730 provides a civil action for false or fraudulent claims against the federal government that can be brought by private individual (known as the qui tam relator) in the name of the government. Servicemembers are precluded from bringing qui tam actions by the FCA's statutory intramilitary bar: "No court shall have jurisdiction over an action brought by a former or present member of the armed forces . . . against a member of the armed forces arising out of such person's service in the armed forces." 31 U.S.C. § 3730(e)(1). *United States ex rel. Conover v. Anthony*, 781 F.Supp.2d 257 (D.Md.2011) (dismissing qui tam action under FCA alleging that present and former fighter pilots of state air national guard submitted false claims for payment to United States for training missions which they did not complete).

Although servicemembers' claims under such laws as the FTCA, Title VII, and the FCA, are foreclosed as discussed above, veterans may sue for such things as malpractice in VA hospitals under the FTCA. The subject of veterans' rights is beyond the scope of the Nutshell.

Subsequent to the end of the Second World War, the United States embarked on a series of experiments designed to study the effects on American soldiers of modern warfare techniques such as nuclear and biological weapons. This intentional use of military personnel as guinea pigs raised constitutional questions as well as issues about the scope of the *Feres* doctrine. Generally, in light of alternative remedies under the Veterans' Benefits Act, 38 U.S.C. § 301 et seq., and the effect of such suits on military effectiveness under *Feres*, courts generally have held that veterans exposed to such agents are ineligible for recovery under the FTCA and avoided the *Feres* doctrine problem. *Jaffee v. United States*, 663 F.2d 1226 (3d Cir.1981) (recovery denied for soldiers exposed to radiation test of nuclear device; alternative remedy under Veterans' Benefits Act); *Laswell v. Brown*, 683 F.2d 261 (8th Cir.1982) (recovery denied for soldier ordered to attend three atmospheric test explosions in the Eniwetok Atolls where he was exposed to low-level ionizing radiation); *Gaspard v. United States*, 713 F.2d 1097 (5th Cir.1983) (claims of serious disabilities incurred as a result of orders to participate in atmospheric atomic weapons tests precluded). See also *United States v. Stanley*, 483 U.S. 669 (1987) (serviceman denied recovery for secret administration of LSD by the government in chemical warfare tests).

c. Personal Liability of the Employee

Recovery of a judgment under the FTCA completely bars further action against the employee responsible for the injury. However, where a suit against the United States is not available, the employee may be subject to personal liability. To counter this apparent imposition of liability on government agents when the government itself would not be liable, certain employees have been given separate statutory immunity. Two important areas in which such immunity has been granted relate to malpractice claims against military-affiliated doctors, dentists, nurses and other medical professionals and claims against government contractors.

i. Malpractice

Military medical personnel are immune from individual liability because the Military Malpractice Act of 1976, 10 U.S.C. § 1089, makes the FTCA the sole basis for malpractice suits. When plaintiffs turn to the FTCA, however, they generally find that *Feres* precludes malpractice claims where the injuries sustained are from service-related activities, or "incident to service." In *Hayes v. United States*, 44 F.3d 377 (5th Cir.1995), for example, a servicemember suffered complications when he underwent an elective hernia operation for a non work-related injury. Despite the fact that the injury was not service-related, the court ruled that the tort—malpractice by a military doctor—was service related and barred by *Feres*. The "incident to service test" focus, the court held, is not on where the treatment was rendered or by whom, but rather on the servicemember's military status in relation to the treatment.

The Supreme Court in *United States v. Smith*, 499 U.S. 160 (1991), considered the impact of the Military Malpractice Act on the FTCA foreign tort exception barring recovery for injury occurring overseas. The Court affirmed the FTCA exception despite the fact that this would leave some plaintiffs without redress. Under the facts of the case the tortfeasor was immunized from liability under the Federal Employees Liability Reform and Tort Compensation Act which made the FTCA the exclusive remedy for malpractice, and suit was barred by the FTCA because the injury occurred overseas. This result would be more troubling from a policy perspective were it not for the fact that veterans and servicemembers are accorded extensive medical benefits which serve as part of a compensation system, making tort remedies less necessary than in a civilian context.

ii. Government Contractor Immunity

One of the most interesting expansions of immunity under the *Feres* doctrine occurred in *Boyle v. United Technologies Corporation*, 487 U.S. 500 (1988). There, the father of a drowned serviceman claimed that the death could have been avoided if not for a defectively designed emergency escape system in a military helicopter. Lacking any legislation specifically immunizing government contractors, the plaintiff argued that there was no basis for judicial recognition of the government contractor defense. Writing for a majority, Justice Scalia recognized (1) that government contracting was an area involving "uniquely federal interests" so that (2) where a significant conflict exists between the application of state law and a federal policy or interest, the federal policy may override state law. The effect of *Boyle* is to allow a government contractor to assert sovereign immunity as an affirmative federal preemption defense.

The case of *McMahon v. General Dynamics Corp.*, 933 F.Supp.2d 682 (D.N.J.2013) discussed above also rejected the application of the government contractor defense of *Boyle*. Noting the rationale of the government contractor defense rested on a discretionary design rationale. The *Boyle* defense protects a private government contractor from liability "when (1) the United States approved reasonably precise specifications; (2) the equipment conformed to those specifications; and (3) the supplier warned the United States about the dangers in the use of the equipment that were known to the supplier but not to the United States." *Boyle v. United Technologies Corporation*, 487 U.S. 500, 511. However, in *McMahon* plaintiff sought recovery on theories of manufacturing defect and failure to warn; the discretionary function exception does not apply to a mistake or defect in manufacturing. Such a process error is not a governmental, discretionary decision.

d. Benefit Offsets

When a claimant receives injury-related government benefits in addition to a FTCA judgment or award, the FTCA award is reduced by the amount of the benefit payments. The theory is that both compensations come from the same general revenues. But if the benefit payments are paid from a special fund supplied in part by the beneficiary, such as insurance, the FTCA award is not reduced by that amount.

F. ADMINISTRATIVE CLAIM REMEDIES

1. MILITARY PERSONNEL AND CIVILIAN EMPLOYEES CLAIMS ACT

The Military Personnel and Civilian Employees Claims Act, 31 U.S.C. § 3721, provides military personnel and civilian employees of the military an administrative remedy for damages inflicted on them by others. As noted above, servicemembers are generally precluded from recovery under the FTCA by the *Feres* doctrine. Instead, the Military Personnel and Civilian Employees Claims Act provides the exclusive remedy for servicemembers in such cases. *Barr v. Brezina Const. Co.*, 464 F.2d 1141 (10th Cir. 1972), *cert. denied*, 409 US. 1125 (1973). It covers damage to or loss of property, but not personal injury or death, which arises during activities incident to the service of the claimant. The claim may arise either in the United States or in a foreign country. There is no requirement of proof of negligence or wrongdoing. Rather, the claim must simply be "substantiated" and a determination made that possession of the property was "reasonable or useful under the circumstances." The government does not have to be responsible for the loss in any way. The Act excludes, however, any loss caused wholly or in part by the negligence of the claimant.

The claim is limited to $40,000 damages, and there is no provision for submission of greater amounts to Congress. Settlement of a claim is final and conclusive; there is no provision for appeal. Attorney's fees are limited to 10% of the award. The statute of limitations is two years from the date of accrual of the claim. If it accrues during time of war, or such conflict intervenes, the claim may be submitted two years after the activity ceases if good cause is shown. The claim must be submitted to the head of the organization to which the claimant is attached.

2. COMPLAINTS UNDER ARTICLE 138

Military policy and regulations ensure that all military personnel may present complaints either orally or in writing through the command structure without fear of reprisal or disciplinary action. Article 138, UCMJ, 10 U.S.C. § 938 provides that any member of the armed forces who is refused redress by his commanding officer may complain to any superior officer, who will then forward the complaint to the officer exercising general court-martial jurisdiction over the complainant's commanding officer.

The complaint procedure under Article 138 is an important mechanism for the resolution of grievances within the military:

> The right to seek redress of wrongs is an integral part of the complex of rights granted by the Congress to those subject to military law. Those to whom an application for relief under [Article 138] is submitted may not lightly regard the right it confers, nor dispose of such application in a perfunctory manner. Its provisions should not be construed by those charged with the administration of military justice, at any level, in a manner calculated to lead anyone to believe that the right of redress of wrongs is of minor importance and one which may be disregarded entirely or perfunctorily complied with.

Tuttle v. Commanding Officer, 45 C.M.R. 3, 4 (C.M.A. 1972).

Exhaustion of remedies is required before resort to the Article 138 complaint procedure. For example, military regulations provide for appeals of unfavorable efficiency reports, appeals of administrative reductions in grade, appeals from findings of pecuniary liability under Article 139 and appeals from administrative reprimands. These appellate routes must be pursued before an Article 138 complaint will be acted upon.

In addition, military administrative regulations also provide for complaints, grievances and requests for assistance from the Inspector General (IG) and his office. The IG investigates complaints and, if the complaint is justified, recommends corrective action. As with Article 138, available appellate remedies must be exhausted before the IG can act. One significant way in which the IG complaint procedure differs from the Article 138 procedure is that Article 138 is limited to complaints by members of the armed services, while the IG complaint procedure may be utilized by anyone, thus affording an avenue of redress to a servicemember's family or friends.

G. EMPLOYMENT AND REEMPLOYMENT RIGHTS

The Uniformed Services Employment and Reemployment Rights Act (USERRA) (38 U.S.C.A. § 4301 et seq.) protects the reemployment rights as well as rights respecting health insurance, pension benefits and fringe benefits following service in the armed forces. The stated purpose of USERRA is "to prohibit discrimination against person because of their service in the uniformed services." 38 U.S.C. § 4301. The antidiscrimination reach of USERRA is quite broad. It requires that all employers, regardless of size, reemploy former employees (both full-and part-time) returning from five years or less of military service. The law protects both deployed servicemembers as well as reservists whose employment is interrupted by the demands of temporary duty or training.

In the words of the statute, USERRA forbids an employer to deny "employment, reemployment, retention in employment, promotion, or any benefit of employment" based on a person's "membership" in or "obligation to perform service in a uniformed service." 38 U.S.C. § 4311(a). The employer is liable under USERRA "if the person's membership . . . is a motivating factor in the employer's action." 38 U.S.C. § 4311(c).

Federal district courts have jurisdiction over USERRA claims. 28 U.S.C. § 1331 and 38 U.S.C. § 4323(b)(3), unless the USERRA claim is subject to arbitration. Venue in USERRA cases is controlled by 38 U.S.C. § 4323(c)(2) (In actions against a private employer, "the action may proceed in the United States district court for any district in which the private employer of the person maintains a place of business.")

1. REEMPLOYMENT RIGHTS UNDER USERRA

In order for a servicemember's rights to be protected under USERRA, his or her absence must be "necessitated by reason of service in the uniformed services." 38 U.S.C. § 4312(a). The servicemember must give advance verbal or written notice to the employer unless giving such notice is "precluded by military necessity" or, under all of the relevant circumstances is "otherwise impossible or unreasonable." Obviously, the best practice is to give written notice together with a copy of one's military orders and retain copies in order to document compliance with the statute. 38 U.S.C. § 4312.

USERRA protection is limited to a cumulative total of all absences to five years. 38 U.S.C. § 4312(a)(2). The five-year total may be exceeded under several circumstances, however. 38 U.S.C. § 4312(c).

An employer is not required to reemploy a servicemember if (1) it would be impossible or unreasonable for the employer to do so, (2) if accommodation, training or effort would impose an undue hardship on the employer, or (3) the servicemember's absence is for a brief, nonrecurrent period and there is no reasonable expectation that such employment will continue indefinitely or for a significant period. 38 U.S.C. § 4312(d).

A returning servicemember is entitled to reemployment in the "position of employment in which they would have been employed" had their continuous employment not been interrupted by military service. 38 U.S.C. § 4313(a)(1)(A). This provision is known as the "escalator position." As explained in Milhauser v. Minco Products, Inc., 701 F.3d 268, 271n. 2 (8thCir.2012): "This term of art imagines the employee on a particular step of an escalator which may move up or down during a military leave. The returning employee does not revert to the same position held upon leaving, but rather is placed in whatever position his or her "step" had moved to during the leave." [citation omitted])." Thus, the reemployed servicemember is entitled to seniority credit both for pre-military service time as well as time spent serving in the military. *Wrigglesworth v. Brumbaugh*, 121 F.Supp.2d 1126 (W.D.Mich. 2001). Once reemployed, a returning servicemember may be involuntarily terminated for "just cause."

2. ANTIDISCRIMINATION PROTECTIONS UNDER USERRA

In addition to reemployment rights protection, USERRA also contains an anti-discrimination provision: "A person who is a member of . . . a uniformed service shall not be denied initial employment, reemployment, retention in employment, promotion, or any benefit of employment by any employer on the basis of that membership." 38 U.S.C. § 4311(a). A "benefit of employment" is broadly defined as "any advantage, profit, privilege, gain, status, account, or interest (other than wages or salary for work performed) that accrues by reason of an employment contract or agreement." 38 U.S.C. § 4303(2). For the purposes of USERRA, a loss of a benefit of employment under § 4311(a) constitutes an adverse employment action, so long as the loss is material. *Grosjean v. FirstEnergy*, 481 F.Supp.2d 878 (N.D.Ohio 2007). An employer engages in a prohibited act if the person's membership . . . in the uniformed services is a motivating factor in the employer's action, unless the employer can prove that the action would have been taken in the absence of such membership." 38 U.S.C. § 4311(c)(1). Note that under USERRA a violation can be established if the individual's military service was a "motivating factor" in the discriminatory action, even if it was not the only factor. *Sheehan v. Dep't of Navy*, 240 F.3d 1009, 1012–13 (Fed.Cir. 2001).

The allocation of respective burdens of proof as between employee and employer is explained in

Maxfield v. Cintas Corp. No. 2, 427 F.3d 544, 551 (8th Cir.2005):

> An employer violates USERRA "when a person's membership in the uniformed services is a *motivating factor* in the employer's action, 'unless the employer can prove that the action would have been taken in the absence of such membership . . . or obligation for service.'" (quoting 38 U.S.C. § 4311(c)(1)). "Unlike the *McDonnell Douglas* framework [utilized in Title VII claims], the procedural framework and evidentiary burdens set out in section 4311 shift the burden of persuasion, as well as production, to the employer." [*Gagnon v. Sprint Corp.*, 284 F.3d 839, 854 (8th Cir.2002) (*Gagnon*), abrogated on other grounds, *Desert Place, Inc. v. Costa*, 539 U.S. 90 (2003).] Under USERRA, an employee must make " 'an initial showing . . . that military status was at least a motivating or substantial factor in the [employer's] action.' " *Gagnon, at 854* (quoting *Sheehan v. Dep't of Navy, 240 F3d 1009, 1014 (Fed.Cir.2001)* (*Sheehan*)). If the employee makes such a showing, " 'the [employer] must prove, by a preponderance of evidence, that the action would have been taken despite the protected status.' " *Gagnon*, at 854 (quoting *Sheehan, 240 F3d at 1014)*.

Under USERRA, courts have the following remedies available: A court may (1) require the employer to comply with the provisions of USERRA, (2) require the employer to compensate the person for any loss of wages or benefits suffered by reason of such employer's failure to comply with USERRA, or (3) require the employer to pay liquidated damages, if the court determines that the employer's failure to comply with the law was willful. In addition, the law expressly provides that a court may use its full equity powers, including temporary or permanent injunctions, temporary restraining orders, and contempt orders, to vindicate fully the rights or benefits of servicemembers. *Groom v. Department of Army*, 82 M.S.P.R. 221 (M.S.P.R. 1999) (holding that USERRA authorized remedies including reinstatement with like status and back pay). See generally, John F. Beasley, Jr. and Marisa Anne Pagnattaro, "Reemployment Rights for Noncareer Members of the Uniformed Services: Federal and State Law Protections," 20 Labor Lawyer 155 (Fall 2004); Elizabeth A. Leyda, Note and Comment, "The War(riors) at Home: Examining USERRA's Veterans' Reemployment Protections When Hostility Follows Soldiers to the Workplace," 28 Ga. St. U. L. Rev. 851 (2012).

3. ARBITRATION

Mandatory binding arbitration of USERRA claims against private, state, or local government employers appears to conflict with USERRA:

> [USERRA] supersedes any State law (including any local law or ordinance), contract, agreement, policy, plan, practice, or other matter that reduces, limits, or eliminates in any manner any right or benefit provided by [USERRA],

including the establishment of additional prerequisites to the exercise of any such right or the receipt of any such benefit.

38 U.S.C. § 4302(b).

However, in *Garrett v. Circuit City Stores, Inc.*, 449 F3d 672 (5th Cir.2006), the U.S. Court of Appeals for the Fifth Circuit held that § 4302(b) does not bar enforcement under the Federal Arbitration Act of individual contracts requiring binding arbitration of USERRA claims. The court concluded that the rights protected by USERRA are substantive, rather than procedural, and that enforcement of employment arbitration agreements does not disserve or impair the rights protected by USERRA. Other circuits have since followed the Fifth Circuit's lead. *Landis v. Pinnacle Eye Care, LLC*, 537 F.3d 559 (6th Cir.2008).

Compelled binding arbitration of USERRA claims conflicts with congressional intent as stated in the House Report, H.R. Rep. No. 103–65 pt. 1, at 20 (1993), *as reprinted in* 1994 U.S.C.C.A.N. 2449, 2453, so it remains possible that Congress will amend USERRA to expressly prohibit mandatory binding arbitration of USERRA claims. In the meantime, servicemembers, particularly reservists, should be cautious in signing arbitration agreements in employment contracts that will cover their potential USERRA claims. This advice applies as well to other federal and state antidiscrimination provisions such as Title VII and the Age Discrimination Act. Should the provisions be nonnegotiable, care should be taken to assure that any costs of arbitration will be borne by the employer. Court costs in a USERRA case are nominal as compared with the cost of arbitration.

There is no statute of limitations on USERRA claims. 38 U.S.C. § 4324(c)(1); e.g., *Hernandez v. Department of Air Force*, 498 F.3d 1328, 1331–32 (Fed.Cir.2007) (decided under § 4324, limit on length of recovery period prescribed in other federal laws inapplicable to USERRA).

States are made subject to the remedies under USERRA, including awards for prejudgment interest. Courts have rejected Tenth Amendment objections to applying USERRA to states. *United States v. Nevada*, 817 F.Supp. 2d 1230, 1247–48 (D.Nev.2011) (USERRA may fairly be construed so as to avoid Tenth Amendment concerns).

Employee benefits constitute a specialized area of the law beyond the scope of this Nutshell. The extent of specific protections and their ascertainment requires the assistance of a legal professional.

INDEX

References are to Pages